W9-AEM-182

Construyendo Puentes (Building Bridges)

Concepts and Models for Service-Learning in **Spanish**

Josef Hellebrandt and Lucía T. Varona, volume editors

Edward Zlotkowski, series editor

A PUBLICATION OF THE

AMERICAN ASSOCIATION
FOR HIGHER EDUCATION

Construyendo Puentes (Building Bridges): Concepts and Models for Service-Learning in Spanish
(AAHE's Series on Service-Learning in the Disciplines)
Josef Hellebrandt and Lucía T. Varona, *volume editors*
Edward Zlotkowski, *series editor*

About This Publication
This volume is part of AAHE's Series on Service-Learning in the Disciplines. For information about additional copies of this publication, or others in the series from other disciplines, contact:

AMERICAN ASSOCIATION FOR HIGHER EDUCATION
One Dupont Circle, Suite 360
Washington, DC 20036-1110
ph 202/293-6440, fax 202/293-0073
www.aahe.org

ISBN 1-56377-022-9
ISBN (18-vol. set) 1-56377-005-9

Contents

Section III
Service-Learning in Local and International Communities

Appendix

About This Series

by Edward Zlotkowski

The following volume, *Construyendo Puentes (Building Bridges): Concepts and Models for Service-Learning in Spanish,* represents the 13th in a series of monographs on service-learning and academic disciplinary areas. Ever since the early 1990s, educators interested in reconnecting higher education not only with neighboring communities but also with the American tradition of education for service have recognized the critical importance of winning faculty support for this work. Faculty, however, tend to define themselves and their responsibilities largely in terms of the academic disciplines/disciplinary areas in which they have been trained. Hence, the logic of the present series.

The idea for this series first surfaced late in 1994 at a meeting convened by Campus Compact to explore the feasibility of developing a national network of service-learning educators. At that meeting, it quickly became clear that some of those assembled saw the primary value of such a network in its ability to provide concrete resources to faculty working in or wishing to explore service-learning. Out of that meeting there developed, under the auspices of Campus Compact, a new national group of educators called the Invisible College, and it was within the Invisible College that the monograph project was first conceived. Indeed, a review of both the editors and contributors responsible for many of the volumes in this series would reveal significant representation by faculty associated with the Invisible College.

If Campus Compact helped supply the initial financial backing and impulse for the Invisible College and for this series, it was the American Association for Higher Education (AAHE) that made completion of the project feasible. Thanks to its reputation for innovative work, AAHE was not only able to obtain the funding needed to support the project up through actual publication, it was also able to assist in attracting many of the teacher-scholars who participated as writers and editors.

Three individuals in particular deserve to be singled out for their contributions. Sandra Enos, former Campus Compact project director for Integrating Service With Academic Study, was shepherd to the Invisible College project. John Wallace, professor of philosophy at the University of Minnesota, was the driving force behind the creation of the Invisible College. Without his vision and faith in the possibility of such an undertaking, assembling the human resources needed for this series would have been very difficult. Third, AAHE's endorsement — and all that followed in its wake — was due largely to then AAHE vice president Lou Albert. Lou's enthusiasm for the monograph project and his determination to see it adequately supported have been critical to its success. It is to Sandra, John, and Lou that the monograph series as a whole must be dedicated.

Another individual to whom the series owes a special note of thanks is Teresa E. Antonucci, who, as program manager for AAHE's Service-Learning Project, has helped facilitate much of the communication that has allowed the project to move forward.

The Rationale Behind the Series

A few words should be said at this point about the makeup of both the general series and the individual volumes. Although Spanish may seem a natural choice of disciplines with which to link service-learning, given the size and growing importance of the Spanish-speaking community in the United States, "natural fit" has not, in fact, been a determinant factor in deciding which disciplines/interdisciplinary areas the series should include. Far more important have been considerations related to the overall range of disciplines represented. Since experience has shown that there is probably no disciplinary area — from architecture to zoology — where service-learning cannot be fruitfully employed to strengthen students' abilities to become active learners as well as responsible citizens, a primary goal in putting the series together has been to demonstrate this fact. Thus, some rather natural choices for inclusion — disciplines such as anthropology, geography, and religious studies — have been passed over in favor of other, sometimes less obvious selections from the business disciplines and natural sciences as well as several important interdisciplinary areas. Should the present series of volumes prove useful and well received, we can then consider filling in the many gaps we have left this first time around.

If a concern for variety has helped shape the series as a whole, a concern for legitimacy has been central to the design of the individual volumes. To this end, each volume has been both written by and aimed primarily at academics working in a particular disciplinary/interdisciplinary area. Many individual volumes have, in fact, been produced with the encouragement and active support of relevant discipline-specific national societies. With regard to the present volume, the American Association of Teachers of Spanish and Portuguese has given its enthusiastic endorsement.

Furthermore, each volume has been designed to include its own appropriate theoretical, pedagogical, and bibliographical material. Especially with regard to theoretical and bibliographical material, this design has resulted in considerable variation both in quantity and in level of discourse. Thus, for example, a volume such as Accounting contains more introductory and less bibliographical material than does Composition — simply because there is less written on and less familiarity with service-learning in accounting. However, no volume is meant to provide an extended introduction to service-learning *as a generic concept.* For material of this nature, the reader is referred to such texts as Kendall's *Combining Service and Learning: A Resource Book for Community and Public Service* (NSIEE 1990) and Jacoby's *Service-Learning in Higher Education* (Jossey-Bass 1996).

I would like to conclude with a note of special thanks to editors Josef Hellebrandt and Lucía T. Varona. Their openness to suggestions and their commitment to strengthening the volume in every way possible have made working with them a pleasure. I would also like to acknowledge the generous assistance of Roxana Pages-Rangel, of Bentley College, and Virginia Gonzalez, of Northampton Community College, for their feedback on the manuscript.

May 1999

Foreword

by Carmen Chaves Tesser

On behalf of the American Association of Teachers of Spanish and Portuguese (AATSP), I am happy to endorse *Construyendo Puentes (Building Bridges)*, developed and published by the American Association for Higher Education. This text is a sound approach to the many conceptual and methodological changes that have taken place in the teaching of languages and cultures. In reviewing what Spanish teachers have accomplished and what theory informs us, the editors have compiled a series of suggestions to help students and teachers "connect with communities in order to facilitate learning *with* each other rather than *about* each other."

The AATSP has been a major player in the development of the foreign language standards that emphasize the "weave" of learning and teaching without neglecting students' communities. Those who have written for the present volume have anchored their remarks on the standards document — a visionary text that promises to revolutionize the way we teach, learn, and communicate with each other. The ultimate goal of language teaching and learning, as reflected in the standards document, is to provide the learner with the ability to continue developing language and cultural knowledge through lifelong experiences within the context of, in this case, Spanish-speaking communities. The learning will continue to take place through the reading of literature as well as through the appreciation of other cultural products from the communities involved.

We are happy to be part of this effort by the AAHE and will continue the dialogue begun through this volume. Ours is a common goal — that of building collaboration among all organizations whether discipline- or teaching-level specific.

Carmen Chaves Tesser is 1998 president of the American Association of Teachers of Spanish and Portuguese.

Introduction

by Josef Hellebrandt and Lucía T. Varona

> "My grandfather speaks Spanish [then the student added quickly] [sic] but not naturally. He had a lot of wetbacks working for him. He would say, 'I want you to plant the seeds over there. . . . I want you to pick that.' . . . He was good at giving orders in Spanish."
> — Robinson 1988, cited in G. Robinson-Stuart and H. Nocon (1996: 431)

Construyendo Puentes (Building Bridges) aims at helping teachers and administrators, as well as students, realize the potential of service-learning in Spanish and incorporate it into their curricula. As editors of this volume, we believe that becoming proficient in a second language cannot be separated from learning the culture of the people who speak that language. More important, perceiving one as separate from the other is divisive as is obvious from the quote above. Robinson quotes a supposedly enthusiastic and accomplished Spanish student from a private California university who, when asked why he studied Spanish toward the end of his academic program instead of at the beginning, responded "I doubt I'll have to use it" (Robinson-Stuart and Nocon 1996: 433). To those familiar with the history of teaching second languages, the testimony by Robinson's student may not come as a surprise, given the scant attention the foreign-language profession has paid to the potential of collaborating with language-minority communities in promoting the learners' linguistic and cultural competencies. Despite a slew of approaches, methods, and strategies for teaching and learning a second language that have emerged in the last 20 years, student learning has basically remained confined to the classroom. Most likely, Robinson's student did not see the cultural connections made available to him through the study of Spanish. Or perhaps he did, but did not receive sufficient incentive during his studies to pursue this possibility. While we will never know, this case illustrates the necessity to help learners recognize that language takes places in a sociocultural context in which language acquires and conveys meaning among individuals and communities. Meaningful language study and training then requires that learners participate in these processes by interacting with community members, participating in their pursuits, and learning *with* them as opposed to learning *about* them.

Proficiency-based and communicative approaches, with their emphases on context, function, and task performance, have been credited with replacing seat-time with performance criteria, as have efforts of language immersion. Still, very few of those have led to off-campus experiences with ethnic communities that go beyond mere visitation. As Genesee (cited in Omaggio-Hadley 1993) and Omaggio-Hadley (1993) report, efforts designed to integrate language and content through immersion and content-based instruction have been limited in this country to the early grades and to assisting learners with limited English proficiency integrate into English-based instructional contexts at the secondary and university levels. Both indicate that these efforts are mostly classroom-based and emphasize subject-matter areas. Only in 1996, with the publication of *Standards for Foreign Language Learning: Preparing for the 21st Century* by the American Council for the Teaching of Foreign Languages (ACTFL) did the profession reach a national consensus and acknowledge the important role of language communities in preparing linguistically and culturally proficient students for the 21st century.

As part of this brief tour d'horizon about language teaching and learning in the United States, we wish to emphasize the role of culture in both second-language and teacher-education settings. Like a bridge, culture has become a linking device that integrates the other four language skills and connects language classrooms with the surrounding communities. Galloway (cited in Omaggio-Hadley 1993) ironically describes one of the traditional ways of teaching bits and pieces of cultures as the *4-F Approach* (fiestas, folk dances, festivals, and food). In contrast, Seelye's (1984) seven goals of cultural instruction and learning activities offer learners an integrated approach to building cultural competence. Among other things, he expects students to critically assess statements about a culture and to research cultural phenomena. In 1996, the five goals of the national foreign language *Standards* — cultures, communication, connections, comparisons, and communities — reflect some of Seelye's perspectives and are published as an interconnected set of performance standards. The goals of cultures and communities, particularly, are aimed at providing the student with immediate and contextualized cultural experiences at home and abroad. Next to emulating specific cultural goals, the *Standards* promotes what Nostrand (1991) refers to as *direct* as opposed to *indirect* cultural experiences. Knowledge about another culture, he explains, lacks the personal, in-depth experience students gain only from personal immersion into that culture, experience they need to protect against ethnocentrism.

If we were to reevaluate the attitude displayed by Robinson's student toward learning Spanish, could a service-learning experience have helped him avoid forming such a compartmentalized view quoted earlier? If so, what degree of cultural awareness and maturity could he possibly have acquired? The response to the first question could be "perhaps, yes." Even though administrative regulations and interventions — such as a second-language requirement — have been found ineffective in influencing attitudes toward Spanish speakers and the language itself (Nocon, cited in Robinson-Stuart and Nocon 1996), the formal and informal evaluations that accompany several of the essays in this volume suggest that community-based learning can positively influence the manner in which students perceive the study of Spanish and its cultures. Interacting directly with community members might also help them go beyond an abstract and generalized view about Hispanic people.

How much could a service-learning component have widened the cultural awareness of Robinson's student? Had he had an opportunity to participate in a community-based program and learned how to show "self-awareness before other-awareness" (Smith 1995), his cultural maturity most likely would have improved. His learning experience would have been guided by teachers familiar with the latest pedagogical advice regarding the learners, affective domain and techniques to promote cultural understanding (Omaggio-Hadley 1993; Richard-Amato 1996). The progress of Robinson's student could have been assessed by using Hanvey's (1976) system of cultural awareness. Learners are assessed according to their ability to demonstrate cultural awareness regarding given information from a specific source or situation and how they interpret it. For example, by working with textbooks or travel brochures, students at Level 1 tend to focus on the very visible cultural traits and interpret those as unbelievable and exotic. At Level 2, learners react in a frustrating, irrational fashion when exposed to culture conflict situations and become aware of those cultural traits that are quite different from theirs. Ideally, while one might be tempted to adopt Hanvey's recommendation to aim for Level 4, at which learners experience cultural immersion and are able to demonstrate awareness from the insider's perspective, Level 3 might be more attainable, according to Hanvey. At that level, learners are not immersed, but rather they engage in intellectual analysis of culture, which allows them to become aware of significant and subtle traits different from their own culture. If one considers Level 3 the threshold for prospective language teachers and Spanish majors, could Robinson's student have reached a level higher than Level 1 in cultural awareness? Perhaps — had he participated in a service-learning component.

In light of the conceptual and methodological changes to teaching languages and cultures and to help avoid similar student experiences, *Construyendo Puentes (Building Bridges)* seeks to provide teachers and administrators with suggestions on how to connect students and teachers with communities to facilitate learning *with* each other rather than *about* each other.

When we invited contributions for this volume, our goal was to receive numerous submissions for our three main categories: theoretical essays, pedagogical essays, and bibliographical annotations to the literature representing the main Hispanic groups and populations in the United States. However, after reviewing all the contributions, we found that service-learning has found only limited acceptance in the field of teaching Spanish language and literature. This might be due to several factors. Hale, for example, suggests there is a missing link between service-learning in Spanish and the second-language and foreign-language curriculum. Moreover, we discovered that programs in Spanish with a service-learning component do exist, but it has not been until recently that language teaching has opened its door to the community. Furthermore, we realized that we also needed to modify our initial categories to (1) *service-learning as theory,* (2) *service-learning from the classroom,* and (3) *service-learning in local and international communities,* to better reflect the diverse and rich experiences of service-learning projects in this country and abroad. Although we were very pleased that the volume attracted essays about service-learning projects in the United States with Mexican-Americans/Chicanos and Cubans, as well as international examples from Mexico and Ecuador, we were surprised to notice the absence of any contribution devoted to Puerto Ricans in this country. Unfortunately, despite calls to members of the Hispanic Caucus and to specific institutions in the Northeast, our efforts to remedy this shortcoming were unsuccessful.

Finally, the diverse theoretical perspectives in many essays forced us to reflect on goals, content, and scope of service-learning programs in Spanish. We feel quite ambivalent as to where exactly to draw the line between programs that emphasize experiential learning, immersion learning, community learning, and service-learning.

At a session we conducted at the 1998 Annual Meeting of the American Association of Teachers of Spanish and Portuguese (AATSP) in Madrid we encountered a similar hesitance as to what should entail service-learning as compared with the aforementioned educational programs. Based on the apparently diverse theoretical facets regarding service-learning, we did not want to confine service-learning to a strict definition, but rather offer our readers different perspectives, ranging from projects to meet local community needs to international projects aimed at promoting cultural collaboration and understanding as well as the protection of the environment. Of course, our endorsing such a flexible definition does not mean that anything can fit under the rubric of service-learning, such as study abroad or immersion programs. Instead, the articles in this volume do embrace a set of clear criteria that constitute service-learning, such as the promotion of civic responsibility, academic rigor, reflection, planned and evaluated experiences both either formal or informal. Clearly, our intent is to encourage colleagues at other institutions to experiment with community programs that serve a common good and meet most of the above criteria.

Theory, Classroom, Community

The authors in the first section, "Service-Learning as Theory," reflect on several theoretical perspectives and discuss the implications of service-learning in relation to critical pedagogy, second-language acquisition, and the creation of cultural knowledge. The article by Hale invites the reader to reflect on a missing link between language teaching and cultural proficiency. According to her experience, service-learning was the connection that helped bridge the gap between language and culture. Arries uses a critical theoretical approach to service-learning, which brings to our attention the need to enhance independent, creative research, and critical analysis through language. Mullaney presents a theoretical reflection on how community input can help a student's language acquisition. The essay by Varona reflects on the three different levels of knowledge from a critical pedagogy perspective where students and teachers develop an awareness of their own culture, which in turn allows them to become more intercultural.

The articles in the second section, "Service-Learning From the Classroom," describe how to implement concrete projects from the perspective of the classroom. Expanding on the theoretical tenets presented in the first section, the authors report how the various collaborations benefited from a variety of community settings and methods and provided a valuable service-learning experience in Spanish to all participants. The first essay in this section, by Baldwin, Díaz-Greenberg, and Keating, gives an account of how service-learning in secondary teacher programs can connect course work to the students' field experience. As already suggested by Hale, providing connections between campus and off-campus learning increases cultural awareness. In the second article, Irizarry makes a case for including community service into advanced Spanish literature courses. She argues that reading a work on the subjects of altruism and service prepares a student for community work, as students working in the community helps their understanding of complex literary works. The article by Lizardi-Rivera summarizes her experience with using service-learning in a translation class. Clearly, as Mullaney emphasizes in the first part of the volume, such learning in the community enhances the students' overall language competence. In the essay that follows, Varas introduces the idea that service-learning is a process that bridges the gap between abstract theoretical and experiential learning. She emphasizes that service-learning develops analytical thinking and personal growth, an observation also made by Varona. The last article in this section, by Boyle and Overfield, reports on a service-learning experience that helped attract upper-division students from other disciplines to interact with Cuban refugees. As a result of this exchange, students conducted research that brought them to discuss inconsistencies between what they had read in books and what the refugees told them. Similar to Arries, a reflection on the diverse Hispanic cultures and service-learning in Spanish and other disciplines helps students become critical thinkers.

The essays in the final section, "Service-Learning in Local and International Communities," illustrate how service-learning from the community to the university leads to empowerment. The article by Darias, Gómez,

Hellebrandt, Loomis, Orendain, and Quezada summarizes a collaborative community-university video course and offers an honest, dialectical reflection on the nature of *working with each other* as opposed to *learning about each other*. It is an example of how two community members and two students became coauthors of this essay. Smith follows with an essay describing how teachers from California and Oaxaca, representing two cultures with different characteristics, are able to maintain a level of respect and admiration for each other. The author reflects on critical theory, and describes the methodology necessary to prepare the participants in their journey to learn to read the world of others. The essay by Strang concludes this volume. Her article offers a new perspective to the discussion of service-learning and the environment. She discusses how a social foundation in Ecuador responds to the needs of local communities to preserve natural resources. Students from different universities come to work, serve, and learn with the community participating in a mutual empowerment process. Indeed, while the academic emphasis of the students' involvement in community projects may be less structured and subject to less formal evaluation compared with other service-learning projects described in this volume, their committed work in Ecuador merits our attention from our perspective of service-learning.

An Invitation

We hope that this volume encourages further service-learning projects in Spanish. Clearly, this is not a handbook on service-learning with a how-to-do approach on the design, implementation, and evaluation of service-learning in this country and abroad. Instead, this volume is an invitation to colleagues and departments to take the plunge and experiment with this form of academic-community collaboration on behalf of a common good. Of course, as many of the contributors have indicated, reaching out to communities and inviting their collaboration requires careful planning and ongoing encouragement on both sides. The transformative character that underlies many service-learning projects allows students and teachers to realize that in the process, we find mutual benefits that enhance our cultural perspectives. Service-learning helps all participants become aware of, understand, and celebrate culture.

References

Hanvey, R. (1976). "Cross-Cultural Awareness." In *The Spanish-Speaking World: An Anthology of Cross-Cultural Perspectives*. (1992). Edited by L Fiber Luce, pp. 22-33. Lincolnwood, IL: National Textbook Co.

National Standards in Foreign Language Education Project. (1996). *Standards for Foreign Language Learning: Preparing for the 21st Century*. Lawrence, KS: Allen Press.

Nostrand, H.L. (1991). "Basic Intercultural Education Needs Breadth and Depth: The Role of a Second Culture." In *Critical Issues in Foreign Language Instruction*. Edited by Ellen Silver, pp. 131-159. New York and London: Garland Publishing.

Omaggio-Hadley, A. (1993). *Teaching Language in Context*. 2nd ed. Boston, MA: Heinle & Heinle.

Richard-Amato, P. (1996). *Making It Happen: Interaction in the Second Language Classroom*. 2nd ed. White Plains, NY: Longman.

Robinson-Stuart, G., and H. Nocon. (1996). "Second Culture Acquisition: Ethnography in the Foreign Language Classroom." *The Modern Language Journal* 80(4): 431-449.

Seelye, H.N. (1984). *Teaching Culture: Strategies for Intercultural Communication*. 3rd. ed. Lincolnwood, IL: National Textbook Co.

Smith, A.N. (1995). "Prerequisites to Teaching and Learning Culture." In *Broadening the Frontiers of Foreign Language Education*. Edited by G.K. Crouse, pp. 57-76. Lincolnwood, IL: National Textbook Co.

Service-Learning and Spanish: A Missing Link

by Aileen Hale

Service-learning, the union of community service with academic reflection and analysis, has been gaining increased attention in recent years. Although related concepts have existed for years in the form of internships and practica, service-learning has emerged as an especially vital part of the educational curriculum today. Thus far, the integration of service-learning into mainstream curriculum has primarily been for the purpose of developing in students a sense of citizenship and democratic ideals. A missing link yet to be extensively explored is the application of service-learning to the foreign- or second-language curriculum. For example, few universities have integrated the concept of having students work in Spanish-speaking communities as a means of learning Spanish. Those institutions that have taken the initiative to help their students acquire communicative competence in a second language through applying service-learning as a methodology have experienced remarkable success, not only in their students' acquisition of the language but also in their motivation for language learning and change in attitude toward native speakers of the language. Firsthand experience in coordinating service-learning programs for university students studying Spanish in Mexico, as well as research substantiating students' overall interest in the method, has personally influenced me to become a strong advocate for applying service-learning on a much broader scale throughout the nation.

This article will provide a brief historical background on the cultural and linguistic needs of the United States today, including the urgency for redesigning existing language curricula; the potential of applying service-learning as a means of addressing student and societal unrest in this field; educational theories supporting service-learning; and student voices, which have been gathered from researching the effects of service-learning, as applied to language and culture learning, to substantiate these educational theories.

General Background

In the last 50 years, the populations of cities throughout the United States and the world have become substantially more multicultural. With these changes — both national and international — comes an ever-increasing demand that Americans possess cultural competence and second-language skills to better prepare them for a world that has become known as the global village (Allen 1968; Bartlett 1988; Burn 1978; McLuhan and Fiore 1967).

> *The urgency for a world perspective has so accelerated that we can no longer afford to be satisfied by small, incremental change. . . . Human survival, as well as business competitiveness and defense capability, depends on the speed with which American educational institutions incorporate an international perspective. (Newell 1987: 139)*

Although an ability to deal constructively with people different from oneself is seen as increasingly necessary in a world in which international interactions and mutual dependencies are growing in scope and importance (Dunnett, Dubin, and Lezberg 1986), multicultural educators claim that U.S. citizens are ill-prepared to deal with the political, economic, and social issues of this global era (Burn 1978; Lambert 1987).

One area where Americans need preparation in this era of global interdependence is that of language and cultural competence — without which they will move increasingly toward parochialism and isolation (Lambert 1987). Second-language proficiency and cultural literacy are no longer simply matters of curricular importance, but rather issues of national importance (Frye and Garza 1979). Not only educators but also U.S. politicians have recognized this vital need. U.S. Senator William Fulbright (1979) charged the American population with "linguistical and cultural myopia" (15). Senator Paul Simon (1980) echoed Fulbright's thoughts as he declared America "linguistically malnourished" (5). Americans have assumed that the English language is universal since it appears possible to go virtually anywhere in the world and find English-speaking individuals. Thus, they find little need to bother learning a foreign language (Brown 1991). Yet, in placing the burden on others to learn English, Americans forfeit a great deal of linguistic and cultural understanding.

Increasing foreign-language proficiency among our college students necessitates the redesigning of language programs (Frye and Garza 1979). A component of redesigning programs involves improving teaching methodologies as growing dissatisfaction exists among students with the ways in which languages are taught (Harrison and Hopkins 1966). Students hunger for educational experiences that involve the whole person, that get to the heart of the matter, and that have a more direct connection with life and the context in which it is lived out in their surrounding communities. Confronted with the emptiness of rote learning and memorization in traditional learning models, especially in language classes, student voices are raising the need for building a relationship between what is taught in the classroom and what is utilized in the real world.

This growing dissatisfaction with current educational models, noted by both students and educators, necessitates an examination of the traditional methodologies of teaching in the United States. In particular, the teaching of language and culture at the university level, where most upper-level language and cross-cultural training occurs, needs to be reexamined in its detachment from contextual learning environments.

Traditionally, the learning of a foreign language has been regarded as the acquisition of vocabulary, syntax, morphology, and other aspects of grammar (Littlewood 1984; McDonough 1981; McLaughlin 1987). This grammar-translation approach, although at one time effective for learning to read and translate foreign texts, has proven ineffective in developing the true verbal and written proficiency needed in a second language today. A large percentage of current students who have been trained in this grammar-translation approach may be able to demonstrate reading and writing proficiencies; however, they rarely feel confident in their ability to communicate with a native speaker of the target language outside the classroom context (Brown 1991).

With the societal needs of today's linguistically and culturally diverse communities and workplaces, communicative competence, which refers to one's underlying knowledge of a system insofar as it is observable through performance, has become widely recognized as a goal of language teaching (Applegate 1975; Brown 1994; Grimshaw 1973; Hymes 1974; Paulston 1975; Taylor and Wolfson 1978). This type of competence transcends the limitations of traditional grammar-translation competence, as it includes a communicative factor. This communicative dimension has resulted in increased emphasis on the oral performance factor in foreign-language learning; that is, the ability to use a second language with conversational proficiency.

Publications and professional workshops on teaching foreign languages and cultures at the university level continue to focus on the use of cultural realia (authentic materials) in the classroom. This real language is seen as a necessary supplement to the traditional "patterned dialogues, one-sided conversations, and grammar substitutions so frequently used to develop grammatical competence" (Frye and Garza 1979: 225). In addition, many language programs are attempting to facilitate increased contact with native languages and cultures in domestic foreign-language classrooms through the incorporation of media: newspapers, radio, television, documentary materials, and other authentic materials. However, as Nostrand (1966) contends, personal interaction is also essential to language learning.

> No matter how technically dexterous a student's training in the foreign language, if he avoids contact with native speakers of that language and if he lacks respect for their world view, of what value is his training? Where can it be put to use? What educational breadth has it inspired? (5-8)

Neglecting to engage students in an authentic context for second-language learning will never allow them truly to develop their linguistic skills. Building rapport and sharing knowledge and experience are the most important factors in learning a language (Mead 1964).

The teaching of language, thus, needs to be increasingly interactive and context-based to address student and community needs. Similarly, the teaching of cross-cultural understanding needs to be context-based, as the two exist in a symbiotic relationship (Allen 1968; Bourque 1974; Jay 1968; Kaplan 1966). Although it is widely recognized that with knowledge of a language there must exist a similar knowledge of the social, religious, and economic attitudes of a people (Jay 1968), many language programs fail to incorporate in-depth study of the culture of the subject language (Seelye 1974). Over the years, those teachers who have worked to incorporate culture into the language curriculum have had to improvise in an effort to find effective means of making their students culturally aware (Valdes 1986). As one language professor has noted: "Typically, a professor teaches language separately from the culture(s) in which it is used. Maybe one day a week he or she reads or shows a movie about a culture which speaks this language, but that's about the extent of it."

But if we teach language without its cultural context, we are teaching meaningless symbols or symbols to which students attach wrong meanings (Politzer 1965). As one language student (Jan) remarked, "You don't fully understand a culture until you know their language. So many things don't translate just exactly how they're supposed to, with the intended connotations." Similarly, a professor (Kit) has contended, "I don't think you can really learn a language without learning the culture; nor do I think you can learn the culture without learning the language." Yet, a great number of university language courses continue to teach foreign languages isolated from an in-depth study of their corresponding cultures.

Service-Learning Applied to the Language Curriculum

One approach that attempts to address the weaknesses of current linguistic and cultural pedagogies involves integrating college students into their surrounding communities through experiential learning. The theory that forms the basis for this approach dates back to the early 1900s with John Dewey (1938). It has been paralleled throughout the world in the works of socially minded educators such as Paulo Freire (1970). Today, one common model of experiential education is known as service-learning: the union of public-community service with structured and intentional learning.

Service-learning is meant to foster civic responsibility and enhance the academic curriculum into which it is integrated. Service-learning also enables students to apply the theoretical knowledge they acquire in the classroom to real-life situations, further developing their practical skills. Acquiring communicative competence in a second language necessitates the practical application of course content in a culturally and linguistically appropriate setting. Many who have attempted to acquire a language through language labs or even through the use of language partners have voiced continual frustration at still being removed from the reality in which the language is spoken by native speakers. As one student (Jannet) stated, "I just can't handle sitting there anymore; I can't handle the conjugations. I feel like I've had it a million times and that's not what's helping me learn Spanish anymore. I want more hands-on. I need to be using it, practicing it."

Service-learning in a community of the language being studied provides the context in which to apply classroom knowledge. Additionally, if students aim to be successfully integrated into the community of a language they are studying for professional purposes, it is essential that they gain experience in this community before graduation.

One important objective of service-learning as a teaching method applied to the liberal arts curriculum is to foster civic and social responsibility in students. But beyond this democratic goal, Slimbach has identified several academic and humanitarian objectives of service-learning related to language and culture learning. These objectives seek to:

1. *Expand students' awareness and understanding of social problems and their ability to address or personally respond to such problems.*

2. *Enable students to learn from a different segment of society than that which he or she would normally interact with.*

3. *Break down racial and cultural barriers through the process of students' reaching out and building bridges between different demographic groups.*

4. *Introduce students to an experiential style of learning.*

5. *Teach students the meaning of service, patience, cross-cultural understanding, interdependence, humility, and simplicity.*

6. *Teach students tools for self-evaluation and critical analysis of institutions, social systems, and their own contribution to and effect on a given community.*

7. *Further the acquisition of a foreign language, when working in or with another culture. (1995: 10)*

In academic service-learning placements, students usually work with people of different cultures, genders, races, ages, national origins, faiths, languages, sexual preferences, economic, and educational levels. However, they are rarely required to speak or even learn the language of the community into which they are placed or to gain in-depth understanding of the culture in which they are working. Sometimes, this knowledge is absorbed at a sub-conscious level, but when language and culture are intentionally integrated into the curriculum, the transformative potential for meeting the afore-mentioned objectives grows exponentially.

The impact of service-learning on language acquisition and cultural understanding has yet to be extensively explored and documented. To date, service-learning has been predominantly utilized in social service and humanities classes — classes especially appropriate to teaching students what it means to be responsible, knowledgeable, and caring citizens (Astin 1994). Astin has, in fact, cited service-learning as the most effective means of accomplishing higher education's "stated mission: to produce educated citizens who understand and appreciate not only how democracy is sup-posed to work but also their own responsibility to become active and informed participants in it" (24).

However, in addition to preparing students for citizenship and democra-tic participation, higher education also seeks to prepare students for the working world (Boyer 1988). Since the working world today is both multicul-tural and multilingual, using service-learning as a method for teaching lan-guage and culture seems a natural next step toward adequately preparing future citizens to join this country's workforce. And yet, despite progress in incorporating service into the liberal arts curricula of many colleges and universities, thus far few of these institutions include in their work compre-hensive integration of the concept into language and culture classes.

Educational Theories Supporting the Application of Service-Learning

A number of renowned educators including Dewey, Freire, Gandhi, and Giroux have elaborated educational theories that provide a framework for the application of service-learning across today's curriculum. In addition, critical pedagogues, including Ada, McLaren, Park, and Walsh, have recog-nized service-learning as a pedagogically sound approach that meets the greater purpose of education; namely, developing critical thinkers able to apply their knowledge to the betterment of their community.

Dewey (1938) was one of the first educators to write about the impor-tance of experiential education as a way for students to develop their curi-osity, strengthen their initiative, and develop their intellectual and moral capacities. His theoretical and philosophical study of experience-based learning provides a broad rationale for the application of service-learning in college curricula today. Dewey affirmed that education, in order to accomplish its ends, both for the individual learner and for society, must be based on the actual life experiences of the individual. Although experiential learning, as defined by Dewey, did not necessarily imply service, the underlying theory of both forms of learning includes the same essential ingredients: experience, reflection, analysis, and application. These components have been strongly affirmed by transformational educators today (Ada and Beutel 1993; Delpit 1995; Freire 1970; Gilligan 1982; Giroux, Penna, and Pinar 1981).

Dewey's philosophy of experiential education arose out of the pedagogical discontent of both conservatives and radicals. In an effort to address both parties' frustrations, Dewey contrasted the underlying ideas of traditional education with more progressive ideas:

> [A]s opposed to the imposition of ideas in traditional education, exists the expression and cultivation of individuality in progressive education; to learning from texts and teachers, learning through experience; to acquisition of isolated skills and techniques by drill . . . acquisition of them as means of attaining ends which make direct vital appeal; to static aims and materials . . . acquaintance with a changing world. (19-20)

In contrasting these two philosophies, Dewey did not seek to prove the legitimacy of one over the other as much as to point out the necessity of integrating the two in the most positive and productive manner possible.

Educational emancipators including Freire (1970), Gandhi (1951), and Giroux, Penna, and Pinar (1981) have similarly criticized the traditional "banking system of education" that remains prevalent today throughout colleges and universities across the United States. This philosophy of education assumes that the professor possesses a body of knowledge that he or she imparts to or "deposits" in students through lectures during the course of a semester. Yet, because students do not take part in the creation of this knowledge, it becomes alienated from their experience of life, which in turn precludes most from applying it to the betterment of their community and society at large. Gandhi (1951) supported the theory that education should not focus on rote learning and memorization, but rather on service to the community. He believed that the traditional Western style of education was destructive because it trained people for certain occupations or filled them with a body of knowledge that did not help them solve their community problems.

One implication of these experiential theories is that, for knowledge to be usable through recall and application, it has to be acquired in a community setting; otherwise, it is forgotten or not available for transfer to new experiences. A key element of the learning situation involves the individual's interaction in that situation. The purpose of the interaction must be to derive learning from experience through reflective thinking, which in turn will lead to inquiry and a desire to resolve the question or problem being raised. The interaction in the learner must precipitate an active quest for information and for new ideas (difficult to achieve in the traditional classroom). The new ideas thus obtained then become the ground for further experiences in which new problems are presented, creating a continuous spiral of learning. In a linguistic and cross-cultural setting, this spiral of learning occurs naturally as students develop relationships in a given community. The desire for deeper and more effective communication with community members naturally provokes students to ask linguistic and cultural questions, seek answers, and apply newly acquired knowledge in a legitimate and tangible context.

This type of education goes beyond the traditional acquisition of a predetermined body of knowledge or set of skills, in that it allows for a critical pedagogy of educational transformation that includes dialogue, reflective thought, and social action. Counts (1932), Freire (1970), Gandhi (1951), and Giroux, Penna, and Pinar (1981) all argue that if humanity is to be liberated, there must be a link between reflection and action that empowers students to acquire the knowledge and skills needed to address issues of injustice in the world. In other words, they believe that higher learning should be an agent of social transformation. When incorporated into a language course, service-learning could offer a pedagogically sound method for students to acquire a level of proficiency in a second language and culture sufficient to facilitate their ability to address issues of injustice in surrounding communities.

The epistemology of service-learning is based on the assumption that knowledge is obtained in the interactive process of action and reflection. Critical pedagogy focuses on the sociopolitical forces influencing the structure of schools, the role of teachers, the goals of education, and the definition of knowledge — all integral to analyzing the role of service-learning in educational curricula. Critical pedagogues (Ada, Beutel, and Peterson 1990; Freire 1970; McLaren 1989; Park 1989; Walsh 1991) propose that the purpose of education is not merely to help people find their place in the existing society, but to empower people with the self-respect and understanding needed to form a new and more just social order.

It is essential that those implementing service-learning have an understanding of the pedagogy behind it, so that the service does not become disassociated from learning goals, but instead enhances the overall learning experience. Through the components of serving, reflecting, theory building, and theory testing, students develop critical thinking skills not usually found in the general education curriculum. Bing (1989), director of peace studies at Earlham College, believes that we must create a curriculum in which "theory gives meaning to experience and experience in turn produces a reconsideration of theory" (50). Kolb (1981) affirms that the problem of higher education is that direct experience and reflection are usually ignored in the learning process, while theory and testing are used extensively. Rather than empowering students through facilitating their creation of knowledge, traditional theory and testing disempower and disconnect students from the learning process.

Throughout our educational system today an assumption exists that,

> [w]ith motivation and effort, we can all learn the knowledge that textbooks and teachers pass down from one generation to the next — knowledge that is considered universal, unquestionable, and inclusive in scope, content, and orientation. (Walsh 1991: 23)

Critical pedagogues, however, question this assumption, convinced that educators need to approach learning as more than merely acquiring knowledge. Students also question this assumption — at least implicitly — when they graduate from high school or college with two years or more of Spanish classes behind them, but can demonstrate little verbal proficiency to substantiate their knowledge. As one student (Geena) stated, "I had about a year and a half of Spanish in high school, but almost completely forgot everything, so I had to start over in college."

The theory of critical pedagogy is particularly applicable to language learning, where the instructor can provide the foundations of linguistic knowledge, inclusive of grammar, vocabulary, syntax, phonology, and so on, but where, in addition, a community can provide a powerful setting for genuine communicative practice and skill building.

Student Voices Regarding Service-Learning: A Participatory Research Study

To substantiate this theoretical foundation, I have engaged in a participatory research process of dialoguing with a number of college students and a Spanish language professor, all of whom have used service-learning as a method for language and culture learning. Through documentation of their "voices," the strengths of employing service-learning in language and culture classes can be demonstrated.

The term "voice" is defined by some critical theorists of education (McLaren 1989; Soo Hoo 1991; Walsh 1991) as the personal and cultural histories and meanings the students bring to the classroom; the dialogue that ensues in their exchange of experiences; and their participation in relationships of power capable of transforming the larger social agenda. Since I regard students as a primary source of knowledge, I will highlight the voices of a group of students from Azusa Pacific University, who have participated in a service-learning language program in Zacatecas, Mexico. Through this process, I would like to bring student perspectives regarding the value of service-learning in language programs to the forefront of pedagogical discussion.

Overall Reactions to Service-Learning

When asked about their overall feelings regarding service-learning and its contribution toward language acquisition and cultural understanding, student and faculty unanimously approved the methodology and its powerful impact on the learning process:

(1) *Service-learning . . . it was great! I don't think professors in America or elsewhere emphasize enough the concept of integrating service-learning or any other type of hands-on experience for their students. That has yet to come. I think we're still stuck in that 'Western' style of learning in education of classes or seminars, which are great, but need a balance.* (Geena)

(2) *I think even if you just look at the concept of service-learning, you're doing a service and when you do a service, it just changes your whole attitude. I think you become a lot more humble. You're there to contribute something or to participate. You learn the language and culture kind of accidentally through your service work.* (Jan)

Motivation Through Building Relationships

Service-learning also gave students an increased incentive for learning, as they recognized that language is more than just vocabulary lists and verb conjugations; "language is communicating with people."

Service-learning definitely helped my language learning . . . it forced me to practice, to learn new vocabulary in a context where you needed to communicate with people . . . the practice of the language was what really helped a lot. (Ky)

Students commented on the motivating aspect of using language in a professional setting verses at home in a familial setting.

Service-learning is a very important part of my learning because it forces me to learn a different aspect of the Spanish language. Conversational Spanish, home and daily vocabulary are very important, but . . . being forced to put it to use with professionals adds a different kind of pressure for me. I slow down, speak more accurately, and try harder. It motivates me to learn when I know I have to communicate something important to individuals who want my opinion. (Jan)

This new motivation for learning came primarily from the relationships students built with individuals at their service-learning sites. As one student (Ky) reported concerning the people in her service-learning project, "The people were just so incredible and the relationships I built were definitely the most important to me, more so than the classes or grades or anything like that."

The traditional language learning classroom rarely offers this kind of relationship-building opportunity for students. Although some language classes have incorporated the concept of using outside language partners, students seem to strongly prefer a service-learning setting for relationship building. In a service-learning context a student has the opportunity to work with more than just one person to learn the language, thus gaining more than one perspective on the language and its culture(s). Additionally, in a service-learning setting, a student is required to work in a context in which the language being learned is spoken by the majority, rather than in a university setting in which a language partner comes to help the student in an English-speaking context.

Self-Confidence Gained Through Service-Learning

One important result of relating to so many people through service-learning was the amount of self-confidence students gained through expressing themselves orally in a variety of contexts. Prior to this experience, many students had been intimidated or very unsure of themselves when trying to converse with a native speaker. However, the exposure they gained to people of different socioeconomic backgrounds within society increased their confidence and ability to converse with a wide range of people in a number of diverse contexts.

> Working in the high school has been a huge confidence builder. Before I went, I used to think, how can I ever learn this language? It's totally foreign to me. I can't really talk with anybody and I don't really have that much knowledge. It seemed insurmountable. But having lived there for two months, I did learn Spanish and I can carry on basic conversations now with somebody in Spanish. It showed me that it's not an impossibility to learn a foreign language. (Ernie)

This confidence carried over to the students' lives in the United States as well. After returning from their two-month service-learning experience in Mexico, students reported a newly discovered interest and confidence in initiating conversations with native Spanish speakers on the streets of Los Angeles. Geena reported: "I have more confidence in approaching people and being more assertive in speaking Spanish now; I almost run to anybody who can speak Spanish as I try to pursue more opportunities to interact with them."

Connecting Language and Culture Learning

This exposure to different contexts for language use also enabled students to see aspects of the culture they would not otherwise have experienced. This exposure, in turn, led them to appreciate the essentiality of learning language simultaneously with culture. Through experience, they learned how language can be misused without a proper cultural understanding. After learning the hard way, one student (Jan) stated,

> You don't fully understand a culture until you know their language. So many things don't translate just exactly how they're supposed to, with their connotations . . . I remember misusing a word in Mexico and not fully appreciating its connotation until it was explained to me.

The students also gained a deeper appreciation of the cultural implications of language use through using the pronoun "usted" or "tu" in their places of service with superiors or people younger than they are. In language classrooms, cultural implications of a second language tend to be taught outside any contextual basis on which to build a concrete understanding. Firsthand experience of a language in its context allows it to become a usable part of students' lives rather than a kind of abstract knowledge they don't know how to apply.

Students commented that if there was in the traditional classroom any exposure to the culture(s) of the language being taught, it was largely superficial and lacking in comprehensiveness. A language professor (Kit) even noted, "In your typical classroom, you teach language separately from culture. Maybe one day a week you read about another culture or see a movie, but even then students are not able to understand any depth of cultural values by short readings from different countries."

In contrast to this lack of cultural understanding in traditional language classes, one noteworthy result of the service-learning approach was the amount of cultural awareness and understanding students acquired. Indeed, they explicitly commented that even though they learned a great deal about Mexican culture through living with Mexican families, they experienced important additional aspects of the culture through their service placements. Many felt that just a family homestay experience with language classes would have resulted in substantially less cultural understanding than they had gained through their service placements and the completely different perspective on Mexican society those placements provided. For example, a student who lived with an upper-middle class family would never have experienced the other side of life had she not worked at a homeless children's shelter. Other students working in public schools were surprised to learn about the politics involved in the educational system — something they experienced firsthand when classes were shut down for political rallies.

Change of Attitude

This deeper understanding of culture acquired through service-learning profoundly affected student attitudes toward Mexico and the Mexican people. Students acknowledged having had stereotypes of the people and the country before going to Mexico, but were quick to recognize the erroneousness of many stereotypes once they began to understand the language and culture. Working side by side with a woman manager, for example, significantly changed a student's perception of the roles of men and women in Mexico. In addition, seeing how hard many people worked greatly altered false assumptions of the Mexican work ethic. As one student (Ernie) commented, "I feel it's not fair how Mexicans are labeled as lazy in the U.S. They work very hard. Many of them work longer and harder hours than Euro-Americans."

Student attitudes also shifted as they experienced through their places of service a number of cultural values contradicting what they had learned through U.S. textbooks about Mexican culture. As they began to more fully understand and appreciate Mexican values, they gained a greater awareness of their own cultural perspectives and biases. Through the process of becoming more acculturated, they even began adopting some Mexican values for themselves, such as giving priority to being with people over accomplishing tasks.

In adopting Mexican values, students' attitudes toward the Spanish language also changed significantly. This change was particularly evident in the students' new-found love of learning the Spanish language and the culture of Mexico. Several students described their indifference, at best, toward learning Spanish or learning about Mexican culture before going to Mexico. Ky reported: "Before I went to Mexico, I would never have called myself prejudice [sic], but I also wouldn't go out of my way to get to know any Mexican people. Now, I have a completely different understanding of who they are and I absolutely love them!" The relationships students built both within their Mexican host families and service-learning sites dramatically changed their perceptions of and attitudes toward the Mexican people, their culture, and the Spanish language.

Recommendations to Educators

Finally, when asked what recommendations they would give to language educators, students unanimously endorsed service-learning as an effective method for teaching language and culture. They criticized the boring structure of the traditional classroom style of teaching, acknowledging how much more they learned through this type of experiential, hands-on learning.

When you're sitting in a classroom, you're very concentrated on what you have to learn and do. It's a very different mindset than if you're learning in a community setting. . . . even the surroundings of sitting in a desk versus standing next to someone on the side of the street — it's hands-on — I think that's where the connection comes. (Jan)

After having experienced this method of learning, none of the students wanted to enroll in traditional language classes again. They became critically aware of the weaknesses of traditional teaching methods, to the extent that they chose not to participate in this type of learning any longer. Although several tried to enroll in Spanish classes upon returning to the States, they ended up dropping out due to "boring book work, labs, and repetitive out-of-context drills." The students all commented on how readily they would have taken another Spanish course in the United States if there had been a service-learning component. But without that, they would rather go back to Mexico or another country to further their linguistic abilities.

Conclusion

As professor of language and culture courses who has used both traditional and more progressive methods, I must concur with my students that service-learning is one of the most effective methods I have ever employed. I myself learned a great deal of Spanish nearly 10 years ago while engaging in community service work in Quito, Ecuador. Although at that time I was unaware of service-learning as a formal method for teaching, I now wholeheartedly embrace this pedagogy, having experienced it firsthand as a student and having applied it as a professor.

Service-learning, when applied to the teaching of language and culture, has the potential to reach far beyond the acquisition of academic subjects. It has the power to reshape attitudes not only toward these subjects but, even more important, toward the people those subjects reference, thus alleviating some of the significant cultural and linguistic barriers that prevail in our society today.

References

Ada, A., and C. Beutel. (1993). "Participatory Research as a Dialogue for Social Action." Unpublished transcript.

————— , and C. Peterson. (April 1990). "The Educator as Researcher: Participatory Research as an Educational Act Within a Community." Workshop conducted at the National Association of Bilingual Educators Conference, Tucson, Arizona.

Allen, E. (1968). *Modern Foreign Languages*. Washington, DC: Association for Supervision and Curriculum Development.

Applegate, R.B. (1975). "The Language Teacher and the Rules of Speaking." *TESOL Quarterly* 9(4): 271-281.

Astin, A. (October 1994). "Higher Education and the Future of Democracy." Inaugural lecture as Allan Murray Carter chairholder, University of California, Los Angeles.

Bartlett, T. (1988). *Educating for Global Competence*. Report of the Advisory Council for International Educational Exchange. New York, NY: CIEE.

Bing, A. (1989). "Peace Studies as Experiential Education." *The Annals of the American Academy of Political and Social Science* 504: 48-60.

Bourque, J. (1974). "Study Abroad and Intercultural Communication." In *The Challenge of Communication*. The ACTFL Foreign Language Education Series, Vol. 6. Edited by Gilbert A. Jarvis, pp. 329-351. Lincolnwood, IL: National Textbook Co.

Boyer, E.L. (1988). *College: The Undergraduate Experience in America*. New York, NY: Harper Collins.

Brown, H.D. (1994). *Teaching by Principles: An Interactive Approach to Language Pedagogy*. Englewood Cliffs, NJ: Prentice Hall Regents.

———— . (1991). *Breaking the Language Barrier*. Yarmouth, ME: Intercultural Press.

Burn, B., ed. (1978). *Higher Education Reform: Implications for Foreign Students*. New York, NY: Institute of International Education.

Counts, G. (1932). *Dare the Schools Build a New Social Order?* New York, NY: Arno Press.

Delpit, L. (1995). *Other People's Children: Cultural Conflict in the Classroom*. New York, NY: The New Press.

Dewey, J. (1938). *Experience and Education*. New York, NY: Collier Books.

Dunnett, S., F. Dubin, and A. Lezberg. (1986). "English Language Teaching From an Intercultural Perspective." In *Culture Bound: Bridging the Cultural Gap in Language Teaching*. Edited by J. Valdes, pp. 148-161. Cambridge, NY: Cambridge University Press.

Freire, P. (1970). *Pedagogy of the Oppressed*. New York, NY: Continuum.

Frye, R., and T. Garza. (1979). "Authentic Contact With Native Speech and Culture at Home and Abroad." In *Teaching Languages in College: Curriculum and Content*. Edited by Wilga Rivers, pp. 225-241. Lincolnwood, IL: National Textbook Co.

Fulbright, W. (July 30, 1979). "We're Tongue-Tied." *Newsweek*, p. 15.

Gandhi, M. (1951). *Non-Violent Resistance*. New York, NY: Schocken Books.

Gilligan, C. (1982). *In a Different Voice: Psychological Theory and Women's Development*. Cambridge, MA: Harvard University Press.

Giroux, H., H. Penna, and W. Pinar, eds. (1981). *Curriculum & Instruction: Alternatives in Education*. Berkeley, CA: McCutchan.

Grimshaw, A.D. (1973). "Rules, Social Interaction, and Language Behavior." *TESOL Quarterly* 7(2): 99-115.

Harrison, R., and R.L. Hopkins. (1966). The Design of Cross-Cultural Training, With Examples From the Peace Corps. (EDRS: ED 001 103)

Hymes, D.H. (1974). *Foundations in Sociolinguistics*. Philadelphia, PA: University of Pennsylvania Press.

Jay, C. (1968). "Study of Culture: Relevance of Foreign Languages in World Affairs Education." In *Toward Excellence in Foreign Language Education*. Edited by Pat Castle and Charles Jay, pp. 84-92. Springfield, IL: Office of Public Instruction.

Kaplan, R.B. (1966). "Cultural Thought Patterns in Inter-Cultural Education." *Language Learning* 16:18-20.

Kolb, D. (1981). "Learning Styles and Disciplinary Differences." In *The Modern American College: Responding to the New Realities of Diverse Students and a Changing Society*. Edited by A. Chickering and Associates, pp. 232-255. San Francisco, CA: Jossey-Bass-Hall.

Lambert, R.D. (1987). "Durable Academic Linkages Overseas: A National Agenda." In *The Fulbright Experience and Academic Exchanges*. Edited by Nathan Glazer, pp. 140-153. The Annals of the American Academy of Political and Social Science, Vol. 491. Newbury Park, CA: Sage.

Littlewood, W. (1984). *Foreign and Second Language Learning*. New York, NY: Cambridge University Press.

McDonough, S. (1981). *Psychology in Foreign Language Teaching*. London: Allen and Unwin.

McLaren, P. (1989). *Life in Schools: An Introduction to Critical Pedagogy in the Foundations of Education*. New York, NY: Longman.

McLaughlin, B. (1987). *Theories of Second Language Learning*. London: Arnold.

McLuhan, M., and Q. Fiore. (1967). *The Medium Is the Massage*. New York, NY: Bantam.

Mead, M. (1964). "Discussion." In *Approaches to Semiotics*. Edited by Thomas Sebeok, Alfred Hayes, and Mary C. Bates. The Hague: Mouton Publishers.

Moll, L.C. (1990). *Vygotsky and Education; Instructional Implications and Applications of Sociolinguistic Psychology*. Cambridge, NY: Cambridge University Press.

Newell, B. (1987). "Education With a World Perspective." In *The Fulbright Experience and Academic Exchanges*. Edited by Nathan Glazer, pp. 134-139. The Annals of the American Academy of Political and Social Science, Vol. 491. Newbury Park, CA: Sage.

Nostrand, H. (1966). "Describing and Teaching the Sociocultural Context of a Foreign Language and Literature." In *Trends in Language Teaching*. Edited by Albert Valdman, pp. 1-25. New York, NY: McGraw-Hill.

Park, P. (1989). "What Is Participatory Research?" Unpublished manuscript.

Paulston, C.B. (1975). *Developing Communicative Competence: Role-Plays in English as a Second Language.* Pittsburgh, PA: University Center for International Studies and the English Language Institute, University of Pittsburgh.

Politzer, R. (1965). *Foreign Language Learning: A Linguistic Introduction.* Englewood Cliffs, NJ: Prentice-Hall.

Seelye, N. (1974). *Teaching Culture: Strategies for Foreign Language Educators.* Lincolnwood, IL: National Textbook Co.

Simon, P. (1980). *The Tongue-Tied American: Confronting the Foreign Language Crisis.* New York, NY: Continuum.

Slimbach, R. (1995). "Revitalizing the Liberal Arts Through Service-Based Learning." Unpublished manuscript.

Soo Hoo, S. (1991). "Lessons From Middle School Students About Learners and Learning." Los Angeles, CA: The Claremont Graduate School. (University Microfilms No. 91-35, 389)

Taylor, B.P., and N. Wolfson. (1978). "Breaking Down the Free Conversation Myth." *TESOL Quarterly* 12(1): 31-39.

Valdes, J.M. (1986). *Culture Bound: Bridging the Cultural Gap in Language Teaching.* New York, NY: Cambridge University Press.

Walsh, C. (1991). *Pedagogy and the Struggle for Voice: Issues of Language, Power, and Schooling for Puerto Ricans.* New York, NY: Bergin & Garvey.

Intercultural Service-Learning Practicum
Zacatecas, Mexico--Summer '96
GLBL 335 (3 units)
Professor: Aileen Hale

COURSE DESCRIPTION:

The Intercultural Service-Learning practicum course provides specially-arranged opportunities for students to work with a Mexican service organization or development project (e.g., in a government or mission-sponsored institute, hospital, orphanage, school, clinic or church). Students learn about the process of social change through their contribution to this agency. Readings, writings, and critical reflections facilitate the learning process of the service activity.

COURSE OBJECTIVES:

The Intercultural Service-Learning course involves the collaborative efforts of students, faculty advisors, and field site supervisors. The course recognizes these field supervisors as the primary providers of intern orientation, training, and oversight. Thus, the course objectives are directed toward preparing both the students and the site supervisor for the practicum assignment.

1. To provide students practical opportunities for linking self and others, study and service, theory and practice, cognitive and affective learning, and abstract and experiential education;

2. To provide a contextual learning environment for the acquisition of Spanish;

3. To provide students the opportunity to participate in a foreign service-learning project and research aspects of service compatible with his/her interests and life goals;

4. To increase students' intercultural awareness and understanding, enhance their experiential knowledge of a particular social problem, and promote personal transformation through the integration of action and reflection.

5. To provide structure to the practicum experience through applicable required readings, field site supervision and service monitoring; the keeping of a weekly learning log/journal, supervisor-learner meetings, and a final evaluation of experience.

6. To encourage APU students to give concrete expression to the Christian mandate to "love our neighbor as yourself" by meeting the needs of people with different racial, ethnic, social class, religious and ideological backgrounds from that of the student him/herself.

REQUIRED READINGS:

Robert Coles. The Call of Service: A Witness to Idealism. Boston: Houghton Mifflin Co., 1993.
Anthology of Service-Learning Articles. (to be distributed to students).

Intercultural Service-Learning Practicum
cont.

WEEKLY READING ASSIGNMENTS:

Week 1: Introduction to Field Study
In Class: Experienced Hand, pp. 55-57, 66-68; Pre-Field Questions & Goal Setting (Handout); Anthology: Hersch "Learning through Questions"
Readings: Coles, Chp 1: Method
Anthology: Wagner, "Field Study as a State of Mind"
Experienced Hand, pp. 45-47

Week 2: Defining Service
Coles, Chp 2: Kinds of Service
Anthology: Neuser, "Righteousness not Charity"; King, "On Being a Good Neighbor"; Joseph, "Cultivating Compassion"

Week 3: Finding Oneself within Service
Coles, Chp 3: Satisfactions
Anthology: Dass & Gorman, "Walking Each Other Home"

Week 4: Helping or Disabling?
Coles, Chp 4: Hazards
Anthology: McKnight "Professionalized Service and Disabling Help"

Week 5: Learning through Doing
Coles, Chp 5:Doing & Learning
Anthology: "Three Wonders"

Week 6: We Can Make an Impact!
Coles, Chp 6: Young Idealism

Week 7: Are we _really_ making a Difference?
Coles, Chp 7: Older Idealism
Experienced Hand, pp. 79-83

Week 8: The Bigger Picture
Coles, Chp 8: Consequences

LEARNING ACTIVITIES:

1. **Statement of Personal Learning Objectives:** During the first week of placement in a service organization, students will propose 3-5 key objective or goals for their service-learning experience. These goals will be assessed throughout the 8 week term to determine if and how they are being met. Goals may include areas of personal growth, skill development, deepening of cultural understanding, and acquisition of the Spanish language.

2. **Weekly Service Log:** The successful completion of this course requires at least 48 hours of instructor-approved service activity. Students will need to log their time--i.e., keep a record of the days and hours they are

engaged in service. Each week your service site supervisor should be asked to validate your time log by "signing off" next to each entry, perhaps at a regularly-scheduled "debriefing" time. The log will also be submitted weekly to the course instructor for an on-going verification of hours. (*see addendum for schedule of hours)

3. Weekly Journal: (6 Entries @ 5 pts. each = 30 pts.) Journals provide a method of reflecting on and recording learning experiences. They have two primary aims: a) to facilitate the learning process itself by helping the student identify the key elements they have learned, encouraging evaluation of those elements and planning of future activities which would build on them; and b) to provide a permanent record of what the student has learned (which will also form a part of his/her course assessment). The journal can be thought of as forming a structured diary of learning events. We will call these events "critical incidents", meaning events that have a strong impact on the student in terms of his/her predetermined objectives. (*see pp. 66-68 *The Experienced Hand*)

Each journal entry should be approximately 1-2 pages in length and include a description of:

1) how this week's reading and service helped you to better understand some aspect of *your own life--* personal growth;
2) how this week's reading and service helped you better understand the *Mexican people and their culture*;
3) how this week's service helped you in your process of *language acquisition--* i.e., new idioms or vocabulary learned; understanding of expressions in use, etc.
4) how this week's reading and service *inspires or discourages* your desire for future community service involvement.
   All entries must be typed!

4. Weekly Class Meetings: As a class, all students participating in service activities will meet on a weekly basis to debrief their experiences, make presentations, and discuss readings.

5. Agency Profile: (10 pts.) Each student will be required to produce a 2-3 page profile of their agency which describes the purpose of the agency, the needs it is meeting in the community, its source of funding, its perceived success, structure, etc. (*see p. 71 The Experiences Hand). This will be submitted by week 4 for evaluation by instructor and then included in your final paper.

6. Weekly Readings & Questions: (6 @ 5 pts. ea. = 30 pts.) Questions related to each weekly reading will be assigned prior to each class, with one week to be completed and submitted for the following class meeting and discussion.

7. Class Presentations: (10 pts.) Each student will be assigned **one** week to make a presentation of the readings as they relate to his/her service. Students will be expected to lead a class discussion based on his/her preparations.

8. Self-Evaluation: (20 pts.) Each student will evaluate his/her own progress made toward realizing his/her service-learning objectives (as proposed during week one). This will be a final paper of 4-6 typed pages, following the guidelines from Week 6 Reading: pgs. 79-83 of The Experienced Hand.

Intercultural Service-Learning Practicum
cont.

GRADING:

1. Weekly Journal: (6 Entries @ 5 pts. each = 30 pts.)
2. Agency Profile: (10 pts.)
3. Weekly Questions: (6 assignments @ 5 pts. ea. = 30 pts.)
4. Class Presentation: (10 pts.)
5. Self-Evaluation: (20 pts)   **Total = 100 pts.**

The above assignments will be graded according to the following scales:
1-5:   5=A, 4=B, 3=C, 2 or 1=D
1-10:   9-10=A; 7-8=B; 5-6=C; 3-4=D; below 4=unacceptable
1-20:   18-20=A; 16-17=B; 14-15=C; 12-13=D; below12=unacceptable

The following is the criteria for determining grades:
A: Papers/assignments are well-written & organized, showing completion of assigned task, thoughtful reflection integrated with experience, lectures, and readings.
B: Shows less thoughtful reflection and integration of experience, lectures, and readings, than an A paper.
C: Does not show adequate reflection and integration of experience, lectures, and readings.
D: Incomplete & unsatisfactory assignment.

1. ¿De qué manera contribuyó el alumno en su servicio?

2. ¿Está lo suficientemente satisfecho como para recibir el próximo año un alumno? Sí-no, comentario.

3. ¿Tiene algunas sugerencias para mejorar el programa de servicio?

7 de junio, 1995

Estimado Supervisor:

Nos complace saber que se encuentra bien. Mucho le agradecemos su hospitalidad al recibir a un alumno(s) de la Universidad de Azusa Pacific, para el seguimiento de su servicio social y el mejor aprendizaje en la vida y cultura de la ciudad de Zacatecas.

Ha llegado el momento de su amabilísima cooperación en la evaluación de su tiempo con ustedes. Siendo así posible el ayudarnos al contestar el siguiente cuestionario. Muchas gracias.

Kim Mac Donald

Coordinadora de Servicio Social
Azusa Pacific University

7 de junio, 1995

Estimado Supervisor:

Nos complace saber que se encuentra bien. Mucho le agradecemos su hospitalidad al recibir a un alumno(s) de la Universidad de Azusa Pacific, para el seguimiento de su servicio social y el mejor aprendizaje en la vida y cultura de la ciudad de Zacatecas.

Ha llegado el momento de su amabilísima cooperación en la evaluación de su tiempo con ustedes. Siendo así posible el ayudarnos al contestar el siguiente cuestionario. Muchas gracias.

Kim Mac Donald
Coordinadora de Servicio Social
Azusa Pacific University

Maria Teresa Quezada de Zamora
Coordinadora en el Estado de Zacatecas para Azusa Pacific University

Critical Pedagogy and Service-Learning in Spanish: Crossing Borders in the Freshman Seminar

by Jonathan F. Arries

The College of William and Mary is a coeducational, four-year public university in Williamsburg, Virginia, with approximately 5,500 undergraduates and 2,200 graduate students in various programs. The 10 professors and two instructors in the Spanish section of the Department of Modern Languages and Literatures teach all levels of courses and instruct approximately 700 students each semester. Each fall Spanish faculty advisors encounter a small number of freshmen who have studied Spanish for four or five years and have traveled or lived in a Spanish-speaking country. Because these students are often orally proficient, placement in an intermediate-level conversation course is not appropriate. Yet these highly motivated students are not proficient enough in analytical writing to justify placement in a literature or advanced topics course. When asked what they want from their first college Spanish course, they typically describe their travel in Latin America or Spain and say they want to learn more about Hispanic culture. However, the students' use of that noun in the singular form suggests that they have not had an opportunity to think critically about culture as a concept; they seem unaware that there is no such thing as a single Hispanic culture. Also troubling in these students' comments is the connotation of "foreignness" that their travel experience leads them to associate with the concept of Hispanic cultures; they may easily overlook the more than 20 million Hispanic Americans in the United States.

Such observations about the language and assumptions of these proficient, well-traveled students convinced me that what they really needed was a course in which they could thoroughly engage the cultures of Puerto Ricans, Chicanos, and Cuban Americans as seen in film and literature. This essay discusses my experience with service-learning in designing and implementing an introductory, special topics course in Spanish focused on the cultural perspectives of U.S. Hispanics. I first define critical pedagogy and explain the rationale that led me to use this critical theoretical approach. I then analyze the three-credit seminar as a curricular form that, although it creates a space in the curriculum for students to develop critical thinking skills, also erects barriers or borders that dramatically limit the applicability of critical pedagogy in the design of this course. I next discuss the revision of my expectations that these pedagogical borders seemed at first to require, and how a service-learning experience ultimately transformed the class into a critical cultural studies course. My concluding observations concern the implications of this experience for my own critical pedagogy.

The Curriculum and Critical Thinking

One of the designated spaces in the curriculum at William and Mary where students are supposed to begin to think critically and investigate concepts like culture is the freshman seminar. The 1995 *Viewbook*, a publicity brochure developed by the Office of Admissions, was probably the most likely source of information about freshman seminars to which 1996 freshmen had access when they began applying for admission as high school juniors. It provides a clear vision about the nature and purpose of the freshman seminar at William and Mary:

> Freshman seminars have maximum enrollments of approximately fifteen students. They are taught by faculty from twenty-six departments and programs, including almost all the departments in Arts and Sciences, and the Schools of Business Administration, Education and Law. All freshman seminars are reading-, writing-, and discussion-intensive, with the goal of initiating students into the culture of critical thinking and independent inquiry that is at the core of William and Mary's undergraduate program. . . . The objective of the freshman seminar program is to begin the challenging and rewarding process of taking students from being passive consumers of knowledge to becoming active creators of knowledge. (11-12)

This passage in the *Viewbook* establishes the freshman seminar as the legitimate curricular form at the College of William and Mary for learning critical thinking skills and defines two primary objectives: independent, creative research and critical analysis through language.

Critical Pedagogy

It is the use of language as a means to understand power and knowledge that is also one objective of a radical theory of education known as "critical pedagogy" that seems to hold great potential for instructional design. According to Giroux (1992), critical pedagogy involves a conception of language as a process of symbolic forms, a process that creates and reflects cultural identity as well as communicates meaning. This notion of pedagogy recognizes that language or "symbolic presentations" can be used to either critique or legitimize "the organization of knowledge, desires, values, and social practices" (3). Giroux further defines critical pedagogy as radical education in the sense that it is "interdisciplinary in nature, it questions the fundamental categories of all disciplines, and it has a public mission of making society more democratic" (10).

Shor (1992) also acknowledges the goal of praxis, or student action, in critical pedagogy, and defines this as a change directed toward the self as well as the society at large: "Empowering education . . . is a critical-democratic pedagogy for self and social change" (15). One of the means by which this change can take place is through "desocialization," the critical examination of behaviors, values, language, relations of power and discourse in classrooms, in mass media, and in our lived culture (114). Desocialization thus defined is similar to the semiotic notion of the reader of myth as one who unveils a language process that acts to distort meaning and so "naturalize" unequal power relations in society (Barthes 1981: 128). Both semiotics and critical pedagogy, therefore, seem to hold great potential as ways to train students to use language critically.

A second aspect of critical pedagogy that corresponded to my initial conceptualization of the freshman seminar is a suspicion of canons, "master narratives" (Giroux 1992: 23) or "high culture" (Aronowitz and Giroux 1993: 135-175), because they tend to endow a Eurocentric version of history, for example, with the aura of legitimacy and truth. My freshman seminar, "Perspectivas culturales de los Hispanos en los Estados Unidos," would expand the canon with its focus on the works of American film makers and authors who write in Spanish.[1] The course would also be "anticanonical" in that it would enable my students to contrast the images of Latino identity produced in the works of Puerto Rican, Chicano, and Cuban-American artists with the images of Hispanics created in the media and historical texts. I therefore found Giroux's concept of "historical memory" (1992: 247) particularly helpful as I sought to identify the types of resources about U.S. Hispanics that would help my students "desocialize" or "read the myths" produced in their previous schooling in U.S. history. Many freshmen have little or no knowledge about historical events such as the Cuban Revolution, the treaty of Guadalupe Hidalgo, or Puerto Rico's Commonwealth status with the United States. It is imperative to provide students with that type of background knowledge or they will fail to understand allusions to pivotal historical events embedded in Latino literature, films, and popular culture. I think of this background knowledge as an instrument that can enable them to "recondense" a sense of history that "evaporates" in the production of myth and ideology (Barthes 1981: 117-128). The recovery of historical memory could also enable students to reflect critically on the gaps in their previous education about the history and cultures of U.S. Hispanics, fill these gaps, and bring this new knowledge and self-realization to bear on the study of the Latina/Latino Other. As Aronowitz and Giroux (1985) point out, a critical or radical pedagogy is one that "must analyze, critique and challenge the codes underlying the forms of signification found in schools" (148).

A third aspect of critical pedagogy that seemed applicable to the goals of Hispanic studies and the freshman seminar is the teaching of critical thinking through writing, a topic that Shor addresses at length in his description of his work in "empowering education" at the City University of New York (1992: 237ff.). Shor is quite clear about the importance of a student-centered classroom, by which he means the inclusion of students' knowledge and experience in the curriculum. Two specific classroom exercises illustrate how I planned to implement a student-centered classroom. Because most of the students who have studied four or five years of Spanish have either traveled or lived in a Latin American country, I envisioned their first assignment as a personal letter of introduction to a hypothetical or real host family. Students could write about anything, but their letter would have to include a description of a food related to a pleasant memory about Hispanic culture. The primary purpose of this assignment was to harness my students' personal interests and experiences to motivate their writing and so ease their acquisition of composition skills in Spanish. Another assignment that I anticipated using on the first day of class would foreshadow the topic of their research paper. I planned to list a variety of themes related to Hispanic culture that we would encounter during the semester and ask students to identify the one that would be of greatest personal interest to them and, if none were appealing to them, to describe what it was about Hispanic culture that most fascinated them. With these types of exercises, informed by critical pedagogy, I hoped to enable students not only to discuss literature, film, and their new sense of history and myth but to apply those critical skills and their experience to the writing of reviews, narratives, essays, and a research paper.

The Curriculum and Its Borders

There seemed to be a close fit between the goals of critical pedagogy, the needs of my students, and my objectives, and it was therefore with great anticipation that I began to list the tentative course components and assignments for a new critical cultural studies seminar. When I began to consider how much time to allocate to the course components and assignments, however, it became obvious that the three credit-hour freshman seminar would not provide sufficient time to engage highly complex material in a second language. But the course could not be designated a four-credit course because the language of instruction was to be Spanish rather than English, and the quality of the students' writing in Spanish could not equal that of writing in their native language. This meant that, unlike a course offered in

English, the course could not fulfill the college writing requirement.

The difference between four-credit and three-credit courses may at first glance seem to be minor, but its implications for the depth and breadth with which students can treat course content are profound. Three-credit classes do not have lab components, such as a list server to which students subscribe or weekly discussion groups to focus on issues of special interest. Such components could theoretically be included in the design of a three-credit seminar, but in instructional design the time factor resembles a zero-sum game: If I were to include such activities during the formal class hour, they would tend to replace content; if the design mandated extracurricular meetings, they would reduce students' preparation time outside of class. I concluded that freshman seminar, which seemed to offer an ideal space in the curriculum for the innovative, critical study of Hispanic cultures, was also an organizational structure that imposed time constraints on teaching and learning. As I pondered the dilemma and tried to map out possible solutions, these limits began to resemble borders that could prevent students from attaining higher levels of analysis and critique.

Course Design and Compromise

My analysis of the form of the freshman seminar suggested that it would be too ambitious to train undergraduate students to do semiotics or discuss myth, much less engage in praxis or desocialization. I nevertheless prepared a course syllabus that, if not exactly driven by critical pedagogy, would at least permit students to write in a variety of ways about literature and films by Latino artists, enhance their knowledge of current events, and even provide some historical background. A close reading of the syllabus (see syllabus) reveals three primary sources of historical knowledge: a weekly radio program from the University of Texas at Austin called "Latino U.S.A.," a video program on the Chicano civil rights movement, and classmates' oral reports ("informes") on specific historical events. Less obvious was a plan to match the assignment of these historical events to the personal interests or experiences that students report on note cards on the first day of class. To help them make connections between history and the canon, I scheduled these reports (and the video programs) to coincide with the three main ethnicities — Puerto Rican, Chicano, and Cuban American — that provided a thematic framework for the novel, short stories, and films covered. I also sequenced writing assignments according to complexity, beginning with description and ending with a research paper. I became convinced, however, that if students were to learn skills that would enable them to challenge myths about the Hispanic Other in media, mass culture, and their prior schooling, that learning would have to take place in a different, more advanced course outside the borders of the freshman seminar.

I anticipated an uneventful first day of class and a smooth if unchallenging semester. I handed out note cards and asked the 12 students who were present to fill them out with the usual information, to include any experiences they had had with Hispanic communities, and to identify a topic of personal interest related to the Hispanic world. I showed them a list of possible themes from which they could select one or more, but made it clear they could choose any other theme that appealed to them (my examples were based on themes we would encounter in literature and film). To further alleviate their anxieties and prepare them to introduce themselves to me and their classmates in Spanish, I told them about myself, my research, and my interest in the cultures of Latinos in the United States. I also chatted briefly in Spanish about a week-long volunteer project I had recently undertaken during the summer (I worked as a translator at a clinic serving migrant workers on the Eastern Shore of Virginia) primarily to provide them with a practical way to gauge their listening comprehension skills. I then handed out the syllabus, summarized it for them much as I did in the preceding paragraph, went over the second day's assignment, and dismissed class with a sense that everything had gone just as I had anticipated.

Service-Learning and Serendipity

What I had not anticipated, however, was the reaction of some of the students to an off-the-cuff suggestion I made about possibly basing their research paper on a service experience like my volunteer project on the Eastern Shore. Several students clustered around my desk after class on Day Two of the semester and barraged me with questions. Could I arrange a service experience for them with the clinic I had mentioned? Would it be acceptable to use the experience as a field study in other courses such as anthropology? When could it take place? What about transportation? I responded to the few questions for which I had answers, consulted my colleagues for ideas about the other questions, and immediately faxed a letter to the clinic explaining my students' interests. The medical staff responded quickly with an invitation, my colleagues helped me locate invaluable resources on campus, and I suddenly found myself on a journey with my students.

This journey from a small college town to a rural clinic in coastal Virginia was not just a field trip in which a professor and two students crossed geographical and economic boundaries. It was, instead, a shared crossing of cultural, linguistic, and pedagogical borders that dramatically altered the meaning of the seminar for the students and transformed my understanding of critical pedagogy. Three segments of our journey corresponded to each border: our trip to the site of the clinic some 90 miles from William and

Mary, our work with the medical staff as interpreters/translators, and our visits to several camps and our conversations with the migrant workers who lived there.

In the first segment the students could not help but observe a dramatic change in the landscape. The suburban four-lane highway, dotted with 7-eleven stores most of the way from Williamsburg to Norfolk, ended at a toll booth. We paid a $10 fee, the guard raised the gate, and we crossed the 20 miles of Chesapeake Bay that constitute the border between the Eastern Shore and the rest of Virginia. We emerged onto a two-lane road flanked on either side by fields, farmhouses, and low buildings shielded by trees. The change was so abrupt it seemed as if we had entered a different country. When I explained that vegetable crops were cultivated in this part of Virginia, the students initially reacted with surprise and noted how unaware we are as to where (and how) our food is produced — "You just take it for granted." As we drove along, I explained that some of the one-story structures that we could glimpse in the distance were barracks where migrant workers lived. They again expressed surprise, not at the structures themselves, but at the inconspicuous nature of the migrant presence. It was as if a veil had been removed from their eyes and the presence of the Hispanic Other suddenly made visible. In that moment of realization on the highway these students began to demystify the invisible intersection between labor and race and the "taking-for-grantedness" that characterizes our alienation from the means of production in our society.

The second segment of our experience consisted of our work as interpreters/translators and involved two similar border crossings. The students' first assignment was to translate some promotional/informational brochures produced by the hospital or corporation that finances the clinic. When I checked their progress, I saw that this linguistic exercise would be taxing even for a much more advanced language student, and the three of us were soon collaborating on the task. I found myself struggling alongside them, borrowing a small dictionary to search for the appropriate terms to express the meaning, or the "signified," of the words in the texts. After about 30 minutes, one of the students looked up from her toil and in one exasperated sentence unconsciously laid bare the entire myth that was making the work so difficult: "The problem," she spat out, "is that there is no *meaning* here. It's just empty words that advertise a bureaucracy." The students had once again crossed a border, this time linguistic in nature, as they engaged language critically and began "contesting dominant forms of symbolic production" (Giroux 1992: 3).

Even more surprising than their successful "reading of a myth" without the benefit of my stock presentation on semiological systems was the fact that our roles had changed from expert professor and nonexpert students to coworkers. This leveling of authority that began with the translation of documents continued even when our translation assignment was interrupted by the arrival of an outreach van carrying several Haitian workers. The only employee who spoke both French and Creole happened to be on assignment elsewhere at the time. The need was immediate and one of the students and I found ourselves cast as equally nervous interpreters of a third language that neither of us had studied for some time. Although it was an agonizing 20 minutes for both of us, the experience certainly removed the social barrier between professor and student as we struggled to help one another assist the patients and staff. Our collaborative engagement in a problem-solving effort to help real people had carried us across a second, pedagogical boundary that would have been much more difficult to cross in our regular classroom at William and Mary.

Although not all of the students enrolled in the seminar participated in this service project, and those who did had spent only a day and a night on site, the experience nevertheless profoundly altered the course for the entire class. Upon our return from the clinic we began a second phase of the course in which students were reading and writing about Chicano literature, film, and a 1996 documentary entitled "Chicano: The History of the Mexican American Civil Rights Movement." The students who had visited the camps and spoken with migrant workers on the Eastern Shore spoke to their classmates at length about their experience and could describe in vivid detail aspects of migrant worker life to which Tomás Rivera only alludes in the two short stories in our reader. All of the students benefited from the combined descriptions of the author-as-insider and their informed classmates who had translated for real migrant workers. The readings coincided with students' oral reports on topics I had assigned, such as the historical distortion in the presentation of the Alamo in many history textbooks, the process of dispossession in the Southwest after the Treaty of Guadalupe Hidalgo, and income and education data from the U.S. Census Bureau. Judging from comments students made in class and in informal writing assignments, I knew they were particularly moved by footage in the documentary that described the history of the National Farm Workers Union. I had expected that students would choose to write their research papers on some cultural theme from literature or film, but after the experience on the Eastern Shore several students changed their topics and wrote their research papers on migrant health or gender or labor issues.

Discussion

Several months after the service event I interviewed the two students who had participated and asked them whether their service experience had changed the way they approached the course content on their return and what, if anything, had come of that experience.[2] They remained enthusiastic about service and wanted more such experiences. One student repeatedly stated that more professors "should take the initiative" and arrange opportunities for their students to apply their learning off campus. They had both enrolled in advanced Spanish classes as well as in courses in anthropology the following semester. One student is contemplating a dual concentration in those two areas. The other student commented on the interesting inversion of perspective that she obtained by working on the "physician side of the clinic," whereas before she had always been a patient. She is currently planning to participate in a three-week excursion to Mexico and Guatemala that traces some of the routes that migrant workers take as they make their way to the Eastern Shore each year.

Conclusion and Implications see p. 36

My students' comments suggest that service experiences provided them with a radically different context that transformed our bordered introductory writing course in Spanish into a critical cultural studies course. The implications of my experience with service for my understanding of the borders that limit teaching and learning have been profound. First, the experience has redefined my understanding of the term "context"; I now see it as a personally lived event that gives a learner sudden insight or a discovery that becomes a memorable schema or subtext she or he can use to make sense out of experiences in different settings, like an internal guidebook or map. Second, I learned that context created by service can empower students, enabling them to demystify complex aspects of language and society. I learned that the borders imposed by institutional forms can and therefore must be crossed. The pleasure I myself experienced while crossing the borders of pedagogy, culture, and language *with* my students made the hard work we did on the Eastern Shore (and subsequently in the classroom) like no other experience I have had as a teacher or student.

Shor compares critical pedagogy to a road that "crosses terrains of doubt and time" and leads to "critical learning and democratic discourse" (1992: 263). My work with the students in that service-learning was for me, personally, a long overdue step on that road. Furthermore, if I am correct that our experience on the Eastern Shore has provided my students and myself with a map to chart our way, there can be no turning back for any of us.

Notes

1. I wish to clarify that most of my colleagues in the Spanish section routinely include literary works by Latino authors and artists in advanced courses such as Hispanic Cinema and Literary Criticism, but also in intermediate-level classes such as Cross-Cultural Perspectives. This diffusion, however, means that freshmen might deeply engage only a half-dozen representative works if they continue their advanced study in Spanish.

2. I wish to thank Julie Novack and Anne Carpenter for agreeing to participate in the interview and helping me understand their perspective about the service-learning experience, and also Kevin McCoy, coordinator of public and community service and student activities at William and Mary, without whose support the service-learning experience might have never taken place.

References

Aronowitz, S., and H. Giroux. (1993). *Education Still Under Siege: The Conservative, Liberal, and Radical Debate Over Schooling*. Westport, CT: Bergin & Garvey.

———— . (1985). *Education Under Siege: The Conservative, Liberal, and Radical Debate Over Schooling*. Westport, CT: Greenwood, Bergin & Garvey.

Barthes, R. (1981). *Mythologies*. Translated by A. Lavers. New York, NY: Hill & Wang. (Original work published 1957)

Galan, H., and National Latino Commuications Center (producers). (1996). "Chicano: The History of the Mexican American Civil Rights Movement" [film]. Los Angeles, CA: National Latino Communications Center.

Giroux, H.A. (1992). *Border Crossings: Cultural Workers and the Politics of Education*. New York, NY: Routledge.

Shor, I. (1992). *Empowering Education: Critical Teaching for Social Change*. Chicago, IL: University of Chicago.

Spanish 151
Cultural Perspectives of U.S. Hispanics
Fall 1996

Professor Jonathan F. Arries
231 Washington Hall   tel: 221-1393
Office Hours: M 11:00-11:50, W 12:00-12:50 F 11:00-11:50 & by appointment

---

Required Textbooks

Santiago, Esmeralda. Cuando era puertorriqueña. New York: Random House, 1993.
Olivares, Julián (Ed.) Cuentos hispanos de los Estados Unidos. Houston: Arte Público Press, 1992.
Dozier, Eleanor and Zulma Iguina. Manual de gramática. Boston: Heinle & Heinle, 1995.

Recommended Textbooks:

Lunsford, Andrea and Robert Connors. The St. Martin's Handbook. New York: St. Martin's Press, 1995.
Spanish-English, English-Spanish Dictionary.

Course Objectives:

1. To develop competence in the following types of writing in Spanish: a) descriptions b) summaries/reviews c) narrations d) essay exams e) expositions
2. To explore in different media and types of texts the following themes in the cultures of U.S. Hispanics: a) community identity b) family c) women and their stories d) war e) death f) humor g) exploitation
3. To gain an understanding of the structure of novels, films, short stories and poetry written by or about the Puerto Rican, Mexican and Cuban populations in the U.S.
4. To become familiar with key historical intersections between the U.S. and the homeland of these populations; also current events
5. To improve grammatical knowledge and practice speaking skills

Course Components & Weights: **Grading Scale:**

1) Preparation	= 10%	93-100	= A	73-76	= C
2) Assignments	= 15%	90-92	= A-	70-72	= C-
3) Portfolio	= 10%	87-89	= B+	68-69	= D+
4) Quizzes (4)	= 20%	83-86	= B	66-67	= D
5) Midterm Exam	= 15%	80-82	= B-	65	= D-
6) Research Paper	= 15%	77-79	= C+	0-64	= F
7) Final Exam	= 15%				

Preparation:

My subjective evaluation of your readiness to engage in discussion and analysis in Spanish each day.

Assignments:

1) Daily written assignments to practice material in the grammar manual or to demonstrate comprehension of short stories.
2) Written assignments, such as short essays, which we will generally begin in the language lab during class. These may involve collaboration with partners.
3) One formal report on an assigned historical topic.

Portfolio:

A three-ring binder in which you will file all of your course work. Sections you must include are:

1) index cards on which you will ask questions or else write answers to brief questions on a daily basis. The purpose of the questions is to help you organize your thoughts prior to classroom discussion.
2) assignments written on the Daedalus program in the language lab.
3) class notes
4) lists, summaries and in-class exercises
5) all quizzes
6) the preliminary drafts of written assignments
7) the midterm exam
8) your research paper

Quizzes:

There will be four quizzes, each approximately ten minutes in duration. There will always be two sections: 1) a fill-in-the-blank section on the grammar topic of that week and 2) true-false, multiple guess, or short answers to questions about the radio news program entitled "Latino USA" that I will leave for you in the language lab each Monday beginning September 2nd.

Midterm Exam:

You will take part one of this test in the language lab during the week of October 7th. It will focus on the grammar points that we study each week and also topics addressed on "Latino USA." Part two will be an in-class essay exam, the purpose of which is to permit you to apply your knowledge about writing essay exams (the topic of that week) and also to formally present your ideas about your research paper.

Research Paper:

During the first week of class you will identify an aspect of culture that is of particular interest to you. Your declared interest will be the topic of your research paper, and most of the writing exercises are designed to help you gain the skills you will need to complete this component of the course. Specific guidelines for this (as well as all other assignments) will be forthcoming, but in general the paper should

Spanish 151
-3-

---

be approximately five pages in length (double-spaced; one-inch margins). I would like one of your sources to be an interview of a cultural informant, preferably someone who is not a student at W&M.

Schedule:

agosto
mi 28   Introducción al curso. Tarea: comprarse los libros. Leer <u>Cuando era puertorriqueña</u> p. 1-5. En <u>Manual</u> estudiar 7-12; fotocopiar p. 229 y hacer ejercicios 1 - 4.

v 30   Discusión. Cómo escribir una descripción. Ejercicios. Tarea: Leer 10-22 en <u>CEP</u>. En <u>Manual</u> hacer ejercicios 5-6 p. 229-230; escribir una descripción según los criterios.

sep
l   2   Discusión. El silabeo. Entregar la descripción. Tarea: Leer 26-38 en <u>CEP</u>. En <u>Manual</u> estudiar 13-14, hacer ejercicios 1-3 p. 230.

mi   4   Discusión. Los acentos. Más sobre la descripción. Tarea: Leer 41-66 en <u>CEP</u>. En <u>Manual</u> estudiar , hacer ejercicios 4, 7, 13.

v   6   **Prueba 1**. Discusión. Los acentos. Tarea: Leer 69-91 en <u>CEP</u>. En <u>Manual</u> estudiar 24-25, hacer ejercicios 1-3 p. 235. Revisar la descripción para entregar 16/9/96.

l   9   Más discusión de la descripción. Discusión. A personal. Tarea: Leer 95-113 en <u>CEP</u>. En <u>Manual</u> estudiar 28, hacer primer ejercicio 236.

mi 11   Discusión. Ejercicios. Posesivos y demostrativos. Ejercicios. Tarea: Leer 117-128 en <u>CEP</u>. En <u>Manual</u> estudiar 29-31, hacer ejercicio B 1 & 2 p. 236.

v   13   Discusión. Ejercicios. Latino USA. Introducción a la narración. Tarea: Leer 129-142 en <u>CEP</u>. En <u>Manual</u> estudiar 32-34, hacer cuarto ejercicio 236. Comenzar una narración según los criterios.

l   16   Discusion. Ejercicios. Entrega de la segunda discusión. Más sobre la narración. Tarea: Leer 142-164 en <u>CEP</u>. En <u>Manual</u> estudiar 34-35, escribir los primeros dos ejercicios 237.

mi 18   Discusión. Ejercicios. Trabajo en la narración. Tarea: Leer 239-261 en <u>CEP</u>. Prepararse por la prueba. En <u>Manual</u> estudiar 36-39, escribir último ejercicio 237.

v   20   **Prueba 2**. Entregar la primera narración. Discusión. Tarea:Leer "Pollito Chicken" (on reserve). En <u>manual</u> estudiar 132-135, hacer ejercicios 1 & 2 p. 256.

l   23   Discusión. Ejercicios. Más sobre la narración. Tarea: Leer "Dioses, animalitos y maestros" en <u>Cuentos Hispanos</u> 28-36. En <u>Manual</u> estudiar 136-141 y hacer ejercicios 3&4 256-7.

mi 25   Discusión. Ejercicios. Tarea: Leer "Una caja de plomo" (on reserve). Comenzar la revisión de la narración empleando el pretérito e imperfecto.

----

v 27 Discusión. Trabajo en la narración. Comparaciones. Tarea: Leer "El día que fuimos..." en <u>Cuentos Hispanos</u> 70-74. En <u>Manual</u> estudiar 46-49, hacer los últimos dos ejercicios 239. Preparar la segunda versión de la narración.

l 30 Entregar la narración. Ejercicios. Discusión. Introducción al resumen. Tarea: Leer "Al pozo con Bruno Cano" en <u>Cuentos Hispanos</u> 122-129. En <u>Manual</u> estudiar 50-53 y hacer el tercer y quinto ejercicios en 240.

oct
mi 2 Discusión. Ejercicios. Más sobre el resumen. Tarea: Ver "Up in Smoke" en Charles Center (Tucker Hall, abajo). Escribir apuntes. En <u>Manual</u> estudiar 54-57 y hacer primeros dos ejercicios p. 241.

v 4 Discusión. Trabajo en el resumen. Ejercicios. Tarea: Escribir un resumen de "Up in Smoke" según los criterios. En <u>Manual</u> estudiar 59-61 y hacer ejercicios 3 y 4 p. 241.

l 7 Discusión. Introducción a la reseña. Ejercicios. Tarea: Ver "Milagro Beanfield War" en Charles Center. Escribir apuntes. En <u>Manual</u> estudiar 62-64 y hacer ejercicios 1 & 2 p. 242.

mi 9 Discusión. Trabajo en la reseña. Ejercicios. Tarea: Entregar la primera sección del examen de medio semestre. Comprarse una libreta azul en donde escribir el ensayo el viernes.

v 11 **Examen de medio semestre**. Tarea: Leer la biografía de Roberta Fernández 174-175 en <u>Cuentos Hispanos</u>. En <u>Manual</u> estudiar 67-71 y hacer ejercicios C, D, E 242 only.

mi 16 Ejercicios. Introducción a la exposición. Latino U.S.A. Tarea: Leer "Zulema" en <u>Cuentos Hispanos</u> 187-195 (secciones I-III). En <u>Manual</u> estudiar 72-74, hacer "F" 243.

v 18 Discusión. Más sobre la exposición. Ejercicio. Tarea: Acabar "Zulema." En <u>Manual</u> estudiar 75-80 y hacer ejercicio "G," Ejercicio1 243.

l 21 Discusión. Trabajo en la exposición. Ejercicio. Tarea: Leer "Naranjas" 20-26 en <u>Cuentos Hispanos</u>. Prepararse para entregar la primera exposición. En <u>Manual</u> estudiar 82-90.

mi 23 Discusión. Entregar la primera exposición. Preposiciones. Tarea: Leer "Las Salamandras" en <u>Cuentos Hispanos</u> 78-85. En <u>Manual</u> estudiar 91-102 y hacer ejercicios 1-3 p 244.

v 25 **Prueba 3**. Discusión. Ejercicios. Más sobre la exposición. Tarea: Ver "Salt of the Earth" en el laboratorio en Washington Hall 316. Escribir apuntes. En <u>Manual</u> hacer ejercicios 4-6 p. 245.

l 28 **Informe 1**. Discusión. Ejercicios. Tarea: Leer "Zoo Island" 87-92 en <u>Cuentos Hispanos</u>. En <u>Manual</u>, estudiar 118-119, hacer ejercicios 1-3 p. 251.

mi 30 **Informe 2**. Discusión. Más sobre la exposición. Ejercicios. Tarea: Revisar la exposición según el criterio. Ver "Chicano" en laboratorio y escribir apuntes. En <u>Manual</u> hacer ejercicio 6 p. 251-252.

<u>nov</u>

v   1   **Informe 3**. Discusión. Ejercicio. Más sobre la exposición. Tarea: Leer "El Turys" (on reserve). En <u>Manual</u> estudiar 120-122 y hacer ejercicio 1, p. 252.

l   4   **Informe 4**. Discusión. Ejercicio. Tarea: Ver "Zoot Suit" en Swem. Escibir apuntes. En <u>Manual</u> estudiar 150-157 y hacer ejercicio 2 & 3 p. 258-259.

mi   6   **Informe 5**. Discusión. Ejercicio. Tarea: Prepararse por la prueba. En <u>Manual</u> estudiar 158-163 otra vez y hacer "Ejercicio" y ejercicios 1 y 2 p. 259.

v   8   **Informe 6**. **Prueba 4**. Trabajo en la exposición. Tarea: Leer "Milagro en la 8 y 12" en <u>Cuentos Hispanos</u> 138-144. Acabar con la segunda exposición para entregarla el lunes.

l   11   **Informe 7**. Entregar la segunda exposición. Ejercicios. Leer "Raining Backwards" en <u>Cuentos Hispanos</u> 146-152. En <u>Manual</u> estudiar 163-168 y hacer ejercicio 1 al final de p. 259.

mi   13   **Informe 8**. Introducción al trabajo de investigación. Ejercicio. Tarea: Ver "Mambo Kings" en Charles Center. Escribir apuntes. En <u>Manual</u> estudiar 171-175 y hacer los últimos dos ejercicios p. 260.

v   15   **Informe 9**. Más sobre el trabajo de investigación. Ejercicios. Discusión. Tarea: Comenzar a elaborar la última exposición hacia un trabajo de investigación. En <u>Manual</u> hacer ejercicios 1-3 sobre el subjuntivo.

l   18   **Informe 10**. Trabajo en el laboratorio. Discusión. Tarea: Leer "Carta de Julio" en <u>Cuentos Hispanos</u> 231-241. En <u>Manual</u> estudiar 175-179 y hacer ejercicios 1 & 3 p. 261.

mi   20   **Informe 11**. Discusión. Ejercicios. Presentación: música o poesía. Tarea: Volver a leer "Carta de Julio." En <u>Manual</u> estudiar 181-183 y hacer ejercicios 1 &2 p. 262. Estudiar para la prueba.

v   22   **Prueba 4**. **Informe 12**. Música o poesía. Discusión. Tarea: Ver "Barrio Belen." Escribir apuntes. En <u>Manual</u> estudiar 183-191 y hacer ejercicio 1.

l   25   **Informe 13**. Discusión. Ejercicios. Trabajo en el laboratorio.

<u>dic</u>

l   2   **Informe 14**. Música o poesía. Tarea: En <u>Manual</u> estudiar 191-195 y hacer ejercicio al final de 263.

mi   4   **Informe 15**. Discusión de los trabajos de investigación.

v   6   Evaluación del curso. **Research Paper Due**.

Examen final: 20 de diciembre, 1:30

Service-Learning and Language-Acquisition Theory and Practice

by Jeanne Mullaney

When a colleague approached me about integrating service-learning into my classes, my first reaction was that I was much too busy already to take on another project. Nonetheless, I listened to his proposal and found it intriguing because it made so much sense from a theoretical perspective. Thus, in spite of my initial reluctance, I decided to pilot the initiative.

The project involved grouping Hispanic students of English as a Second Language (ESL) with my students of Spanish who were native English speakers. In that manner, all of the students would have conversational partners who were native speakers of the languages they were studying and the groupings would become two-way exchanges of information and expertise. When we began the project, we sought to further the linguistic development of all of the students and to integrate the ESL students into our community college. We hoped to make them feel more a part of the community-at-large, both by giving them the opportunity to practice speaking English and by enabling them to meet native English speakers with whom they would not normally interact.

Although it would seem that ESL students are immersed in American culture and language, they often juggle a busy schedule of family, work, and classes that does not leave time for socializing. Moreover, they frequently remain in communities in which their first language is spoken, rather than joining communities in which English is spoken. Since foreign language students also lack opportunities to interact with native speakers of the language they are studying, and ESL students do not interact a great deal with native English speakers, the groupings of Hispanic ESL students with my Spanish students seemed to present an ideal solution for all involved.

Of the many definitions of service-learning that have been formulated, the one that best exemplifies my understanding of the term is as follows: "Service-learning is both a program type and a philosophy of education. As a program type, service-learning includes myriad ways that students can perform meaningful service to their communities and to society while engaging in some form of reflection or study that is related to the service. As a philosophy of education, service-learning reflects the belief that education must be linked to social responsibility and that the most effective learning is active and connected to experience in some meaningful way" (Giles, Honnet, and Migliore 1991: 7). Thus, in this project, language students performed a service that was an identified need in the community and that enhanced their language-learning experience as well. They reflected on their service both informally in class during the course of the semester and formally in writing upon completion of their service. The project served to foster the development of a sense of caring for others and a sense of civic responsibility in the participating students. In short, this service-learning project fit in with my philosophy of teaching and learning because it afforded students opportunities to use newly acquired language skills in real-life situations in their own communities.

The emphasis on meaningful second-language use comes as a result of the proficiency movement that has become so important in the field of foreign-language education. This movement, with its focus on communicative competence in the second language, has focused foreign-language educators on "the development of functional skills for real-world use from the very beginning of classroom instruction" (Savignon 1997: 223).

The proficiency movement also clearly affected the development of the *Standards for Foreign Language Learning*. According to the *Standards*, "the United States must educate students who are linguistically and culturally equipped to communicate successfully in a pluralistic American society and abroad" (1996: 7). It states that "to study another language and culture gives one the powerful key to successful communication: knowing how, when, and why, to say what to whom" (11). It also affirms that "the approach to second language instruction found in today's schools is designed to facilitate genuine interaction with others, whether they are on another continent, across town, or within the neighborhood" (11). Although the *Standards* does not prescribe a methodology for teaching foreign languages, it does cite approaches that have proven to be ineffectual, and it describes practices that have been shown to be effective. It also articulates what students of foreign languages should know and be able to do in each of the "five goal areas that make up foreign language education: communication, cultures, connections, comparisons and communities" (23). Further, the *Standards* spells out how these five Cs of foreign-language education are all interconnected:

> Communication, *or communicating in languages other than English, is at the heart of second language study, whether the communication takes place face-to-face, in writing, or across centuries through the reading of literature. Through the study of other languages, students gain a knowledge and understanding of the* cultures *that use that language; in fact students cannot truly master the language until they have also mastered the cultural contexts in which the language occurs. Learning languages provides* connections *to additional bodies of knowledge that are unavailable to monolingual English speakers. Through* comparison *and contrast with the language studied, students develop greater insight into their own language and culture and realize that multiple ways of viewing the world*

exist. *Together, these elements enable the student of languages to partici-*
pate in multilingual communities at home and around the world in a
variety of contexts and in culturally appropriate ways. As is apparent, none
of these goals can be separated from the other. (27)

When I undertook the service-learning project described here, I anticipated that it would enable students to progress chiefly in the goal areas of
communication and communities. This paper will describe the theoretical
underpinnings of the project from the pedagogical perspective of a Spanish
language teacher. Therefore, it will outline aspects of current language-
acquisition theory and educational philosophy as they apply to the teaching
of languages. Although parts of these theories are somewhat controversial,
they constitute my philosophy of language teaching because it is my experience that instructional methods and techniques based on these theories
are effective with the community college population. The student reflections
included at the end of this paper also attest to the efficacy of this type of
pedagogy.

Language-Acquisition Theory

There are certain undeniable precepts now commonly accepted in the field
of second-language acquisition, even though there is still much research to
be done. First, Krashen's distinction between language learning and language acquisition forms the basis of many current theories. His hypothesis
(1982) asserts that adults have "two distinct and independent ways of developing competence in a second language" (10). The first way is language
acquisition, "a process similar, if not identical, to the way children develop
ability in their first language" (10). Krashen elaborates, "Acquisition is a sub-
conscious process; language acquirers are not usually aware of the fact that
they are acquiring language, but are only aware of the fact that they are
using the language for communication" (10). The second way to develop
competence in a language is by language learning. Krashen uses this term to
refer to "conscious knowledge of a second language, knowing the rules, being
aware of them, and being able to talk about them" (10).

Whereas some theorists claim that children acquire while adults can
only learn, Krashen's acquisition-learning hypothesis asserts that "adults
also acquire and that the ability to 'pick-up' languages does not disappear at
puberty (1982: 10). This means that "adults can access the same natural
'language acquisition device' that children use" (10). The question then
becomes, how do we acquire language? Krashen restates the question to
ask, "How do we move from stage I, where I represents current competence,
to I + 1, the next level?" (11). His input hypothesis claims that "we acquire

when we understand language that contains structure that is a little beyond where we are now" (11). In other words, we acquire when we are able, through the use of context and extralinguistic information, to understand language that is I + 1.

Krashen's work shows that "repeated exposure to meaningful language is necessary for maximal second language acquisition" (1982: 30), because learners gradually construct an "internal system or representation" (Lee and VanPatten 1995: 94) of the target language that they later access to produce language. The language-acquisition device in the brain processes the language that comes in, endeavoring to understand its meaning and using it as raw data to create a linguistic system. It is crucial that the language be comprehensible, because if the learner does not understand what is being said, the language will not be absorbed or processed by the language-acquisition device. Thus, the most obvious advantage of the service-learning project described here was that it encouraged the use of meaningful language between native speakers of Spanish and English and learners of those languages. One benefit of the small groups or pairings was that the language that the students used with each other could be made understandable through the use of gestures, facial expressions, sounds, and perhaps even drawings. In other words, the conversational partners were excellent sources of meaningful language input for each other.

The second part of Krashen's theory, his affective filter hypothesis, postulates that anxiety creates a filter that acts to prevent input from being used for language acquisition. According to this theory, affective variables act "to impede or facilitate the delivery of input to the language acquisition device" (Krashen 1982: 32); therefore, "our pedagogical goals should not only include supplying comprehensible input, but also creating a situation that encourages a low filter" (32), so that our students will be more open to input. Clearly, working in small groups or with a partner helps to ensure that the affective filter will be fairly low, thereby allowing much of the language to be absorbed and acted on by the language-acquisition device.

Further, Peregoy and Boyle (1993) assert that "language comprehension develops as a result of opportunities for social interaction with speakers of the new language" (56) and that "all language skills . . . are best developed when students are using those skills to achieve communication goals that are interesting and meaningful for them" (153). In other words, students learn best when they are using language for authentic, communicative purposes, instead of merely repeating phrases that have no meaning for them, as was common practice in traditional foreign-language classes. Dulay, Burt, and Krashen (1982) concur that "a natural language environment appears to enhance the development of communication skills in a second language" (15). Such a natural environment is said to occur when the focus is on the content of the communication rather than the form, and this has been shown to be the superior environment for learners to acquire and become proficient in a second language. This was precisely the kind of environment we created with the students because we were encouraging them to use the two languages as a means of communication, rather than as a subject of study.

Consequently, given the current emphasis on the necessity of comprehensible input and meaningful communication for language acquisition to occur, it is clear that such deliberate, communicative use of the target language is essential, not only at the input stage but also in subsequent practice exercises. Indeed, Brown (1994) affirms that "contextualized, appropriate, meaningful communication in the second language seems to be the best possible practice" (69) for second-language learners to engage in. In fact, meaningfulness seems to be more important than the number of times a certain form or grammatical structure is practiced. Accordingly, the conversational groupings seemed an excellent source of both input and authentic communicative practice in which the focus would be on the message expressed. Moreover, the conversations would assist the learners in their acquisition of grammar because, as Krashen (1982) puts it, "we acquire by 'going for meaning' first, and as a result, we acquire structure!" (21).

Service-learning is also consonant with the first-language acquisition research showing that mere exposure to input is not sufficient for acquisition to take place. Berko-Gleason explains that "in order for successful first-language acquisition to take place, interaction, rather that exposure, is required; children do not learn language from overhearing the conversations of others or from listening to the radio, and must, instead, acquire it in the context of being spoken to" (1982, cited in Brown 1994: 41). Thus, humans learn how to speak a language by speaking it and being spoken to by others. The groupings provided many opportunities for social interaction with native speakers of the languages that the learners were studying. Moreover, since the students were using their skills in a purposeful manner for real communication, they were motivated to continue developing those skills.

Long's interaction hypothesis is a theory that builds on Krashen's philosophy of language learning and teaching. Like Krashen's theory, the interaction hypothesis stresses the importance of input in language acquisition, and it too emphasizes the fact that learners "cannot simply listen to input, but that they must be active conversational participants who interact and negotiate the type of input they receive in order to acquire language" (1981, cited in Shrum and Glisan 1994: 9). Likewise, the *Standards* states that "students need to be able to use the target language for real communication, that is, to carry out a complex interactive process that involves speaking and understanding what others say in the target language" (21). However, Long's theory adds that interaction and negotiation of meaning with more proficient speakers of a language have a positive effect on the developing language system of second-language students because, according to Long, (1983, cited in Shrum and Glisan 1994: 9), "speakers make changes in their language as they interact or 'negotiate meaning' with each other." Long explains that speakers negotiate meaning to avoid conversational difficulties or to revise language when difficulties occur. In everyday conversational interchanges, people need to use phrases such as "I don't understand what you mean," "Could you repeat that?" or "Could you say that again more slowly?" As Lee and VanPatten (1995) point out, these communication breakdowns commonly occur in many second-language contexts because of underdeveloped linguistic or cultural knowledge (148). It is therefore vital that students learn how to negotiate meaning in the second language to be competent in that language.

S.J. Savignon's definition of communicative competence maintains that it consists of four underlying competencies: "Grammatical competence, which is knowledge of the structure and form of language; discourse competence, which is knowledge of the rules of cohesion and coherence across sentences and utterances; sociolinguistic competence, which is knowledge of the rules of interaction; and strategic competence, which is knowing how to make the most of the language that you have, especially when it is deficient" (1983, cited in Lee and VanPatten 1995: 149). Social interaction and intercommunication, therefore, appear both to develop communicative skills and strategic competence as they provide learners with more comprehensible input that allows them to improve their language skills. In other words, even when the conversations broke down, the students were learning. Indeed, it gave them good practice for real-world conversations that are often full of misunderstandings. Thus, current second-language acquisition theory supported the service-learning project, because it offered both the meaning-bearing comprehensible input and the opportunities for negotiation of meaning necessary for language acquisition to take place.

Another theorist who has focused on the significance of social interaction in language learning is L.S. Vygotsky. His theory of learning is a sociocultural theory that contends that human development cannot be viewed independently of social context. For Vygotsky, humans are "thoroughly social" beings who learn and develop by having experiences. In Moll's words, Vygotsky's theory emphasizes the value of peer interaction and the "importance of activity and learning in the process of doing" (1990: 229).

On the subject of human communication, Vygotsky asserts that the "primary function of language and speech is social, for the purpose of communicating culturally established meanings" (1962, 1968, cited by Dixon-Krauss 1996: 17). Interestingly, the Standards also highlights the social aspect of language. It states that "language and communication are at the heart of human experience" (7) and that "to relate in a meaningful way to another human being, one must be able to communicate" (11).

According to Vygotsky, linguistic development occurs "as a result of meaningful verbal interaction . . . between experts and novices in the environment" (1962, cited by Schinke-Llano 1995: 22). He explains that language "is mastered at first in collaboration with an adult or a more competent peer solely with the objective of communicating. Once mastered sufficiently in this way, it can then become internalized" (1962, cited by Wertsch 1985: 25). After all, as Dixon-Krauss (1996) maintains, "social conventions such as language . . . could not be learned alone, because there could be no conventions in a world of one" (126). Furthermore, because of the social nature of humans, "mastering or developing mental functions must be fostered and assessed through collaborative, not independent or isolated activities" (1962, cited by Moll 1990: 3). Since humans are "thoroughly social beings" and language is a social convention, there can be no better way to learn it than in pairs or small groups.

A related idea is what Vygotsky has called the Zone of Proximal Development (ZPD). This can be loosely defined as the area in which learning takes place. Vygotsky describes it as "the distance between the actual developmental level as determined by independent problem solving and the level of potential development as determined through problem solving under adult guidance or in collaboration with more capable peers" (1962, cited by Schinke-Llano 1993: 123). What is interesting about this idea is the implication that what individuals can do today with the collaboration of a more capable peer, they can do competently alone tomorrow. Consequently, the potential developmental level of the learner becomes the next actual developmental level as a result of the expansion of cognitive abilities that comes from the learner's interaction with others. The new structures and vocabulary our students learned in collaboration with and under the guidance of their conversational partners represented acquired structures that they would be able to use independently in the future.

There are two important characteristics of the ZPD. The first is that the problem at hand has to be a little bit above the learner's current level of ability. In Krashen's terms, the language has to be I + 1, because it must stretch the learner's capabilities. The second characteristic of the ZPD is that there has to be a more skilled peer to mediate between the learner and the task or problem at hand. The language that the students used with their partners would almost certainly be I + 1, and the partners would assist each other in understanding it.

Another interesting aspect of the ZPD is that it allows performance to precede competence on the part of the learners. For instance, learners are able to use complicated language and structures that they have not yet acquired when they are working with a teacher or more competent peer. In the process of using the new structures for authentic, meaningful communication, they are actually learning and acquiring them.

The *Standards* also affirms that "active use of language is central to the learning process; therefore, learners must be involved in generating utterances for themselves. They learn by doing, by trying out language, and by modifying it to serve communicative needs" (37). Once again, it is clear that language learners have much to gain from participating in conversational groups in which they must use the language they are studying to express themselves.

To sum up, the service-learning project was consonant with Vygotskian theory in several ways. First of all, it capitalized on the thoroughly social nature of our language learners by providing a supportive instructional environment focusing on social interaction. Since there is growing evidence that collaborative learning between peers, regardless of ability, activates the ZPD, we knew that the project would mediate learning within the ZPD. Second, the service-learning project enabled learners to participate in speech and literacy events as well as authentic social transactions in which the second language was a tool for communication. In short, as Foley has advocated, it encouraged the teaching of the "second language not as an end in itself, but as a resource for achieving meaning" (1991: 36). The conversational groups afforded an excellent opportunity to apply Vygotskian theory and, in so doing, to expose students to all of the ensuing benefits.

Conclusion

The service-learning project succeeded because it was compatible with both prevailing second-language acquisition theory and current educational theory. It provided the participants with abundant comprehensible input for their developing language systems to work on, and it offered them plenty of opportunities to practice using the new words and structures they were learning for real communication in meaningful contexts. Furthermore, the service activity permitted students both to share their expertise in their native language and to benefit from their partners' expertise at the same time.

An unexpected outcome of the project was a heightened cultural awareness on the part of the students. Their interaction helped to break down the negative stereotypes of Latinos perpetuated in contemporary American society. As the attached student reflections indicate, the students also came to have a deeper appreciation of the difficulties of learning a new language, whether Spanish or English. Their reflections reveal that they learned much more than language as a result of the service-learning project. In fact, they touched on four of the five goal areas delineated in the *Standards*: the communication goal, which concerns communicating in languages other than English; the cultures goal, which pertains to gaining knowledge and understanding of other cultures; the comparisons goal, which relates to developing insight into the nature of language and culture; and the communities goal, which involves participating in multilingual communities at home and around the world. In short, they successfully used language systems as "a means for attaining the various outcomes described [in the *Standards*]: communicating [and] gaining cultural understanding" (29).

We judged the project a success because it enabled students to realize so many of the goals outlined in the *Standards for Foreign Language Learning* while providing a valuable service to their community. Indeed, the project supported and upheld the theories that it was based on. The emphasis on meaningful communication together with the supportive environment of these unique collaborative learning groups combined to provide a very positive language-learning experience.

References

Brown, H.D. (1994). *Principles of Language Learning and Teaching.* 3rd ed. Englewood Cliffs, NJ: Prentice Hall Regents.

Dixon-Krauss, L. (1996). *Vygotsky in the Classroom: Mediated Literacy Instruction and Assessment.* New York, NY: Longman.

Dulay, H., M. Burt, and S. Krashen. (1982). *Language Two.* New York, NY: Oxford University Press.

Foley, J. (1991). "Vygotsky, Bernstein and Halliday: Towards a Unified Theory of L1 and L2 Learning." *Language, Culture and Curriculum* 4(1): 17-42.

Giles, Dwight, Ellen Porter Honnet, and Sally Migliore, eds. (1991). *Research Agenda for Combining Service and Learning in the 1990s.* Raleigh, NC: National Society for Experiential Education.

Krashen, S. (1982). *Principles and Practice in Second Language Acquisition.* Oxford: Pergamon Press.

Lee, J.F., and B. VanPatten. (1995). *Making Communicative Language Teaching Happen.* New York, NY: McGraw-Hill.

Moll, L.C. (1990). *Vygotsky and Education: Instructional Implications and Applications of Sociolinguistic Psychology.* Cambridge, NY: Cambridge University Press.

National Standards in Foreign Language Education Project. (1996). *Standards for Foreign Language Learning: Preparing for the 21st Century.* Lawrence, KS: Allen Press.

Peregoy, S.F., and O.F. Boyle. (1993). *Reading, Writing & Learning in ESL*. New York, NY: Longman.

Savignon, Sandra J. (1997). *Communicative Competence: Theory and Classroom Practice*. New York, NY: McGraw-Hill.

Schinke-Llano, L. (1993). "On the Value of a Vygotskian Framework for SLA Theory and Research." *Language Learning* 43(1): 121-129.

Schinke-Llano, L. (1995). "Reenvisioning the Second Language Classroom: A Vygotskian Approach." In *Second Language Acquisition Theory and Pedagogy*. Edited by F.R. Eckman et al., pp. 21-28. Mahwah, NJ: Lawrence Erlbaum Associates.

Shrum, J.L., and E.W. Glisan. (1994). *The Teacher's Handbook: Contextualized Language Instruction*. Boston, MA: Heinle and Heinle.

Wertsch, J.V. (1985). *Vygotsky and the Social Formation of Mind*. Cambridge, MA: Harvard University Press.

Student Reflections

The following comments are taken from the reflections that students wrote upon completing their service-learning projects.

"When we met, we would usually ask each other how we were doing and what we did over the past weekend. Usually in English and then later in Spanish. Most of the time, we would help each other out with understanding the homework we didn't know what to do with. After going over the homework, we would converse about the differences and similarities of both English and Spanish cultures. Sometimes we were not able to explain why each of us did certain things for certain reasons, but we did out best to help the other person understand. We would also ask each other why the language was so difficult to learn, and why we were learning this language. . . . By meeting with Maria, I found out things that you can't always teach in a classroom. Like the long line at immigration and how she liked the United States from a Spanish-speaking point of view, or if it is easy to find a job in an English-speaking environment."

-- Matt

"I learned many different things about the Spanish culture and was quite interested in most of them. . . . We had fun talking about some of our different customs. She was amazed at how young children get to stay up late in America and how children are not disciplined too much. She was very helpful in helping me study for my tests and was very useful in helping me with my compositions. . . I now have a newfound love for the Spanish culture and I can thank my project learning for that. Finally, and most important, was that she was extremely considerate of my feelings and she really cared about teaching me about her native language and culture."

-- Louis

"During this hour that we met, my classmates and I discussed many things. More often than not, we spoke and wrote Spanish for the first half-hour of our meeting. I found this to very helpful because I need all the practice that I can get. For the second half-hour of our meeting, we spoke and wrote English. This was very helpful to our partner because she needed all the practice that she could get also."

-- Richard

"Some of the things we talked about were Spanish and English compositions that were due and how well or how poorly we were doing in class. But we mostly discussed how difficult the transition was from speaking Spanish and having to learn another language, and vice versa."

-- John

"The experience was a positive one because we both learned a lot about each other and how very different the languages are. It is difficult, but also fun to help each other with different languages. I would definitely do it again. . . The service meant a lot to me because it definitely helps us to learn by forcing us to use the languages properly or we won't know what each other is saying. It is good to use Spanish outside of the classroom." -- *Karen*

"We talked about our families, hobbies, favorite foods and places to visit. Also we discussed the differences between both Spanish and English cultures. For example, one interesting fact we learned about Edison's country is that you have to be 18 to go out on a date without a chaperone. The weeks following we discussed any questions that anyone might have on homework, compositions, or tests.

"I feel that it was beneficial to have someone outside of the classroom to answer our questions. You can learn things about their culture that the textbook doesn't teach you. I enjoyed getting to know Edison, and I feel that group interaction may benefit those who have difficulty understanding Spanish or English." -- *Chrissy*

"It helped me a lot with my Spanish work and speaking. I was able to get to know the grammar better. I was also able to find out where to put certain words in sentences that confused me. I was also able to pronounce words better. It was a great experience while it lasted." -- *Bobbie-Jo*

"In the past few months, I have had a greater understanding of the Spanish language, thanks to our partner Maria. It was equally educating just to see how hard it is to learn the English language as compared to Spanish.

"The verbs, vocabulary and grammar all made a bit more sense with some explanation from a person who you can sit down with for a whole hour. It also made me feel good to help Maria understand the English language a little better and help her to become a more sociable person. The added time we spent, plus the additional class time has given me a better feel in the social Spanish culture." -- *Matt*

"Maria helped me the most when I was working on my Spanish compositions. Maria would help me with some spelling mistakes and verb tenses. She wouldn't just tell me the answer, I would have to guess or look them up in the book if I didn't know them." -- *Keith*

"We helped each other with homework and class work. We also talked about different cultures and how hard it is to adapt to a different country. . . I found the service learning to be a very positive experience. It helped me a lot when I had a question and when I needed help with anything. It was like having a free Spanish tutor and vice versa. . . Service learning meant a lot to me because it was an excellent experience. One of the reasons is I met some nice people and I learned a lot." -- *Michael*

From Instrumental to Interactive to Critical Knowledge Through Service-Learning in Spanish

by Lucía T. Varona

> *In living with other human beings we come to know them in an interactive sense. This knowledge does not derive from analysis of data about other human beings but from sharing a life-world together — speaking with one another and exchanging actions against the background of common experience, tradition, history, and culture.*
>
> — P. Park (1993:6)

Interactive knowledge comes from sharing, connecting, and including, whereas instrumental knowledge requires separateness and externalization. Furthermore, critical knowledge comes from reflection and action, deliberating what is right and just. In this chapter, I shall describe and analyze the process of creating knowledge through service-learning with students enrolled in Elementary Spanish. I shall also explain how service-learning is incorporated in the course based on critical pedagogy and changes or innovations in language learning. To illustrate the type of knowledge we acquire throughout this experience, I will let my students' voices be heard.

One of the many ways in which Santa Clara University connects the community and the university is through the Eastside Project. The name Eastside designates a geographical area in the city of San Jose covered by this university program. The mission of the Eastside Project is to create a lasting partnership between the university and the community that fosters continuing discussion between the two parties. Thus, the Eastside Project is directly responsive to and shaped by the community. At the university, service-learning is used first and foremost to foster a paradigm shift in the minds of students. Our purpose is to provide them with personal experiences of cultures other than their own so that their perceptions of the world will expand and become more accurate (Sholander 1994). Participants in the Eastside Project venture into the community as students, not volunteers. They go out to listen, explore, question and wonder, observe, feel, and experience as well as serve.

I have incorporated service-learning into my Elementary Spanish classes *(see pages 74-75)* as a cultural project that consists of four phases that move from interpretive to interactive to critical knowledge. The phases are descriptive, personal interpretive, critical analytical, and creative active. In the descriptive phase the focus is on information that describes places and

1) people involved in the program. In the personal interpretive phase it is on relating the project to students' personal experiences. The critical, analyti-
2) cal phase is where the students engage in a more abstract process of critically analyzing the issues or problems raised in their visits to the communi-
3) ty. The creative active phase is a stage of translating the results of the previous phases into concrete action (Ada, Beutel, and Peterson 1990).

In 1992 when I began using the Eastside Project, I could not require the participation of every student in this program due to departmental policies; I could only invite them to participate. The response was very positive. Thirteen of 18 students from one class enrolled in programs offered by the Eastside Project. One reason why many of the students did not get involved was lack of time. Other professors teaching the same level of Spanish required only four visits to places such as a school, a restaurant, and a library where students had to observe how Hispanics behaved, paying close attention to nonverbal language. This was in contrast to my requirement of visits of between two and three hours for eight weeks during the quarter, a journal entry after each visit, an oral presentation, and a final paper — all for only 5 percent of the grade. My first task, then, was to convince my students that points do not reflect the amount of knowledge one acquires and that the Eastside Project was beyond quantification. Students who decided not to participate in the Eastside Project were invited to visit for eight weeks with a Hispanic friend and his or her family.

First Quarter — Interpretive Knowledge

During the first quarter students achieve mostly instrumental and interactive knowledge. They are shy and timid in starting conversations with the clients of the various programs. In class we focus on statistics and descriptions of the people participating in these programs. Discussions revolve around what is meant by Hispanic culture, and students come to realize that it is inaccurate to talk about a Hispanic culture when there are so many cultures under the label Hispanic. Students also learn about different Latin American countries when community participants share stories of their childhood. Frequently this takes place in Convalescent Centers where Hispanic elderly constitute a high percentage of the population. However, the spontaneity of a young child or the frustration of a troubled teenager can also spark such reminiscences.

Use of Spanish is very limited at the beginning of the experience, because students generally do not feel comfortable with the language they are acquiring. Since the main goal of using the Eastside Project in my Spanish classes is not language acquisition but cultural awareness moving slowly to cultural consciousness, students are not pressured to speak only Spanish during their visits. It is interesting to note that most of my students experience the pleasure in understanding a few words in Spanish when participants interspersed them in their English conversations. Toward the end of the first quarter, students are able to share with participants descriptions of where they live, and this gives them a sense of accomplishment. As one student wrote: "I felt so proud when I was able to explain to Francisca where I live and how my school is in Spanish. She was smiling all the time. She never asked me to repeat a word or anything; we kept on going."

Many of my students work at schools where a high percentage of the student population is Hispanic, and university students interact with teachers and students on a regular basis. In these settings, however, it is a bit more difficult to learn about the background of participants because children usually say they do not know where they come from or as one of my students wrote: "I am beginning to wonder if these kids really don't know where they come from or perhaps their parents try to avoid letting them know due to problems with immigration." Through their visits to schools, homeless shelters, soup kitchens, community centers, rehabilitation centers, and law clinics — all of which are selected because of their high Hispanic population — Elementary Spanish students learn to read the word and the world (Freire and Macedo 1987).

Hess (1994) and Hale (1997) stress that one of the objectives of service-learning is to connect students with communities to help solve racial, ethnic, and social problems pervasive in urban societies. In their journals, students express personal views that often have been influenced tremendously by stereotypes. It has been very interesting for me to establish a dialogue with my students through their journals, because this has allowed me to accompany them in their process of stereotype clarification. I find it extremely important to allow students to write their journals in English and to invite them to comment on anything that comes to mind. "Working with Hispanics is not new to me, there are many Mexicans in my parents' farm and I work with them during the summer; therefore, I am looking forward to working with Mexican kids in the school where I have signed up," wrote a student in his first journal entry. As his experience advanced, he wrote, "It is amazing to see that there are some Mexicans kids that are so smart." I reacted to his comment with a short note on the margin of his paper: "Why is it so surprising to you to see that these kids are so smart?" When he received his journal back, he came to my office and told me that he had believed that Mexicans were not very smart, especially because the children he had seen on his parents' farm never displayed the kind of behavior he was observing at school. This incident opened the door to a discussion of stereotypes. At the end, my student felt he had been given an opportunity to analyze and to clarify those stereotypes.

My students' first reaction to what they find at the Eastside Project placement sites is that there are not many differences between their lives and community participants' lives. When they engage in deep conversations with these participants, however, their eyes open to another reality.

> *During my last visit to school, children were learning about food. The teacher asked me to work with a small group of students to review with them the different food groups, to make things more interesting. I asked them what they had for breakfast. Two of the children said, "Nothing." Then I asked them why and they said, "Because we didn't have anything to eat." I felt so sad for these two children and now I am beginning to think, how many children do not have enough to eat.*

At this point, students have begun to move from interpretive to interactive knowledge and, through their journal reflections, have started the process of creating critical knowledge.

Even though I allow students to write their journals in English, I also ask them to write a sentence in Spanish that describes that day's experience. In the classroom, I use Spanish even when my students are sharing their experiences in English. A technique I use when students pose a question to me in English, knowing that it requires an answer in English, is to ask another student, "¿Qué piensas tú de esto?" ("What do you think about this?"), allowing him or her to respond to the other student in English rather than using English myself. If I feel the student's question still has not been clarified, I respond in English.

I have noticed in this experience with the Eastside Project that students usually do not know what to call the person or people with whom they are interacting. Expressions such as "my patient," "my child," "the old lady/the old man," "the people" appear in their journals during the first weeks of the program. This gives me the opportunity to engage in a student-teacher dialogue on the way we refer to others. We discuss the cultural expression "vieja/o" and how this word is used among Latin Americans as an expression of affection within the family, but how we cannot use it when talking about the elderly in general. We also discuss the sense of respect implied by the use of "usted" and "tú." One of my students was very upset because a senior citizen had called her "mi'ja." She could not understand why that lady was calling her "my daughter." This incident allowed the entire class to discuss the use of terms to express familiarity, gratitude, etc. I purposely do not tell students at the beginning of the course what to call the people with whom they will be working during the eight-week project. It is only when they start writing and talking about "kids," "the lady," "the old man," "my patient," "my students," that we analyze the word *participant* and how it fits the objectives of service-learning as discussed by Slimbach (1995). It is very clear to students that the spirit of this program is to see the community people participating in it as their mentors and not as people they serve. At the same time, it is important that students and participants enter into a collaborative learning process.

Class discussion constantly refers to students' journal comments, and many students use their placements and participants as topics for descriptive compositions. Every student works at his or her own pace in the service process. There are some who quickly connect their Eastside Project experiences with their personal life, moving from a descriptive to a personal interpretive phase. As one student wrote:

> *As a Japanese, I never thought we discriminated against anyone; however, now that I am doing my cultural project, I have found that many Japanese people do not want to be taken for Vietnamese. I am glad I am doing this cultural project in a very multicultural placement because it has opened my eyes to the things we do in my country but we never discuss them.*

In this case, service-learning in Spanish proved to be an enlightening experience for a foreign student learning Spanish. Even though a few students move from interpretive to interactive knowledge during this first quarter, the majority remain on the first level of knowledge creation.

Second Quarter - Interactive Knowledge

My focus in the second quarter of Elementary Spanish is to move from interpretive to interactive knowledge creation. After students have discussed basic information about programs and participants, I encourage them to relate what they are seeing to their own experiences and feelings. I especially encourage them to use metaphors to express what they are experiencing. "I feel like a window that allows fresh air in," said a student referring to her work at a Convalescent Home. Another explained, "I feel like a red apple among many green apples," when he felt he could not relate very well to the experiences of participants at a center for youngsters with drug and gang problems. I ask students to share with the class not only their core metaphor but also what made them feel that way. In the beginning, the metaphor is given in Spanish and the explanation in English. Once a week, I use the first part of the class (about 5 to 10 minutes) to share metaphors and draw from their experiences examples that illustrate the content of the class.

Mantle-Bromley (1992) suggests that those teaching culture in language classes need to help students revise not only their linguistic patterns but their cultural patterns. Along the same line, Galloway (1992) asserts that to understand another culture, one must construct a new frame of reference in terms of the people who created it. She also recommends that students begin with an understanding of their own frame of reference, and then, with teacher guidance, explore the target culture through authentic textual materials. Interactive knowledge comes from sharing with the community not only what you do but who you are. Many students have admitted in their journals that through the Eastside Project they have been able to know themselves better. One student wrote:

> I have been going to the shelter for a few weeks now. All this time I have been avoiding direct contact with the participants. Before I entered the shelter, one of the clients was outside. When he saw me he smiled and asked me if I wanted a cigarette. Even though I do not smoke, I stayed with him for about 10 minutes. We shared a lot in that time. I think I want to write my final paper about him. Today I learned I can open myself to people I usually would avoid.

Another student wrote about a conversation she had with her elderly participant:

> Yesterday Francisca was very sad, she could not understand why her family did not visit her on Sunday, she told me she thinks they might be sick or maybe they had an accident. First I thought Francisca was taking this to the extreme, I also thought she was being too demanding from her family. Then I remembered what we discussed the other day in class about analyzing a culture from a distance or from within. If I look at this incident from my own culture, I might find it extremist but if I look at it from the Hispanic culture, perhaps I could also think that something bad had happened to my family if they did not come to visit.

During this quarter, students are encouraged to focus on one participant and write about this person in their final paper — completely in English. In the beginning I wanted all students to write about Hispanics, but the reflections some students were sharing in their journals convinced me I should allow them to write about any person who had impressed and inspired them in the process of their acquiring another language. Seelye (1984) maintains that the role of the teacher is not to impart facts but to help students attain the skills necessary to make sense of the facts they discover in their study of the target culture. For Seelye, it is more important to achieve cross-cultural understanding within a problem-solving context. The more the student moves from his or her culture capsule to a multicultural space, the easier it is for him or her to acquire other languages. I have had only two students who focused on non-Hispanic participants who really helped them change their perspective toward learning a second language. One of the students wrote:

Dow is a very interesting man, he is Cambodian, but he has lived in Germany, Belgium, Canada, and in the United States. He is confined to a wheelchair now but he was very active in the military. Dow has shown me that perseverance is what it takes to learn a language, but most of all he has taught me that respect and admiration for other cultures is what really makes it possible.

Students acquire interactive knowledge in this second quarter through sharing more closely with the community participants. One student who worked at a Convalescent Home wrote: "Before my experience at Winchester I thought of convalescent homes as a place where old people went to die. . . . Now I realize that the residents are very real humans, too." During this quarter, the student's uncle fell into a coma and later died. She wrote, "I realized that by talking with Alfredo, God had been preparing me for the possibilities of Mark's life or death; I was forced to contemplate death more than ever before." She summarized her experience by quoting from the homily offered at mass: "God will send people we least expect, people we might somehow overlook." Another student who had not shown great interest in his project wrote after his fifth visit to his placement:

Today I found a kid who shared with me that the best time in his life is when he is at school. He reminded me of my own life. I grew up in one of the worst parts of Sacramento, the constant irresponsibility of my father, his drug problems and seeing my mother suffering was too much for me. I used to love school because there I could forget about everything else.

Oral presentations in the second quarter focus on what individual students have learned from the Eastside Project. They work in small groups, first sharing their experiences and then finding ways to transmit their messages to the entire class in Spanish, using any audiovisual resources available. Two students who had worked at a convalescent home and at a rehabilitation center presented their experiences to the class, using slides showing the places and people who had inspired them while reading Pablo Neruda's poem "El piano." This was a perfect way to present to the rest of the class how they moved from feeling like objects, like instruments, in the student-participant relationship to being mutually inspirational.

Presentations such as this one are almost like magical moments when the students are able to connect their personal experiences with what they do in service-learning; it is at such moments that the whole project makes sense to them and the teacher. These moments are also highly emotional; hence, it is crucial to accompany the students during this transition time. I have learned that if we do not move from this phase to critical analysis, we risk trivializing the entire process. I learned this when, during final presentations, the presenters were asked: "¿Vas a seguir trabajando con las mismas personas?" ("Are you going to continue working with the same people?"). Behind that question lay the idea: And now what? The answer most presenters gave was affirmative. Many students went back to the same placement during their third quarter.

Third Quarter – Critical Knowledge

This experience has brought all people closer to my heart. All races are within me. I have always known that everyone is equal, but seeing people treated unequally has pained me, and I, as part of everyone, will try to never separate myself from anyone again.

These are the words of a student who through critical knowledge learned that she belongs to many races and how painful it is to be discriminated against. At the same time, she implies a complementary action by vowing not to separate herself from anyone again. "Critical consciousness is raised not by analyzing the problematic situation alone, but by engaging in actions in order to transform the situation" (Park 1993: 8).

During the third quarter, the question "Why?" is constantly asked of students in their journals. When comparing the journals of first-quarter students with those of third-quarter students, I can see the long road we have walked. In the first quarter, their first entry was about the place where they were going to meet with community participants. Third-quarter students pay attention not only to the place but also to the entire community. In third-quarter students' journals, it is not uncommon to find comments such as:

As I drive through the streets close to the placement, I see people walking with small children rushing to school. I wonder what goes through the mind of that mother who has to leave her child for the day. Does she have a husband to help her support that child? Where does she live?

Students in the third quarter are more conscious of social problems than first- and second-quarter students.

Spanish is widely used in class during this last quarter of the Elementary Spanish sequence. The use of English in their journals is optional and class sharing takes place in Spanish. The final paper is in English but the oral presentation is completely in Spanish. Classroom conversation is based on relevant life experiences rather than on the tourist-based topics common in language classrooms. Students learn the subjunctive through reflecting on the ambiguities and uncertainties of their Eastside Project experiences.

Many students who have been undecided about a career find their calling during this quarter. A typical response was:

I wasn't sure about what I wanted to study but now I feel I want to become a teacher. I have found that children and I get along well. I am happy sharing my life with them. Before I always thought about the money I would be making, now that seems not to be so important any more.

During this quarter I, as a teacher, feel that the experience of service-learning closes the circle of naming, reflecting, and acting. Although each student works at his or her own pace in this process, most of them move from the stage of being "my brother's or sister's keeper" to being "my brother or sister." During the first stage of their work, students tend to distance themselves from the community participants. The second stage is usually characterized by feelings of protection and extreme sensitivity toward the lives of those participants. The third stage is where students put their experience in perspective and move from interactive to critical knowledge, admitting equality between them and their partners. Only after this first year, perhaps, could we truly move from service-learning to participatory action research, a stage where members of the community become full partners and coworkers.

Conclusion

Three primary objectives of service-learning are to (a) connect students with their communities to help resolve some of the racial, ethnic, and social problems pervasive in urban societies; (b) overcome the barriers between different cultures; and (c) encourage active reflection and action on the part of students (Hess 1994; Hale 1997). One of the goals in Santa Clara University's mission statement is to prepare students to assume leadership roles in society through an education that stresses moral and spiritual, as well as intellectual and aesthetic, values; seeks to answer not only "what is" but "what should be"; and encourages faith and the promotion of justice. Service-learning represents an especially effective way to accomplish this goal. Students in Elementary Spanish are given an opportunity to see the world through a different perspective — the perspective of the community. When students are able to connect their lives to what they are learning through service-learning, they become capable of taking action, action that is reflected in the decisions they make in their own lives.

In a chapter in *Beyond the Monitor Model*, Wilga Rivers (1993) presents a comprehensive overview of language teaching. She takes us from audiolingualism's inductive approach to Suggestopaedia to Community Language Learning. As she evaluates these different methods of teaching, she warns: "Nor should we forget that knowledge of the culture of those with whom we wish to interact is also an important aspect of communication, whether absorbed aurally, visually, or from graphic materials" (72). The study of culture brings critical analysis to the language classroom but, so far, language classes have rarely been seen as places for the acquisition of critical knowledge. Although language learning has moved from grammar-based instruction to a more communicative approach, efforts to interact with the community still focus on bringing the community to the classroom rather than integrating the classroom into the community. But authentic cultural learning takes place through a process of cultural adaptation or, as one student put it, "Culture is mostly felt not learned."

Cultural learning in Spanish cannot and must not avoid discussing what is right and just, hence the need for service-learning in Spanish. The process of acquiring a language is quite different from the process of acquiring multiculturalism. Moving from being a monolingual to a bilingual person is not the same as moving from being an ethnocentric to a multicultural person; nevertheless, the two processes should not be separated. Language and culture are inseparable but are acquired at a different pace. It is simply not possible for a student to articulate the process of moving from being ethnocentric to multicultural in the language that he or she is acquiring. Therefore, I encourage students to write their journals and final reports in English.

Many theorists have written about the cultural learning process (Adler 1975; Gullahorn and Gullahorn 1963; Kleinjans 1972; Lysgaard 1955), focusing especially on language-immersion programs during which students experience culture shock. At this point they must decide whether to retreat to the comfort and familiarity of their own culture or endure the frustration of culture shock. If they endure and learn how to work within this new set of behaviors, values, and beliefs, they have begun the process of acculturation (Cummins 1981; Wong-Fillmore 1983). I have seen this process evolve in my students through their participation in the Eastside Project. I believe that my role as a teacher is to accompany my students throughout the process, establishing an open dialogue with them. Their skills in Spanish cannot keep pace with the depth of their acculturation process; therefore, they need to rely on their native language to facilitate the learning process.

Some of my students are Hispanics who have lost the native language of their ancestors. For these students, the Eastside Project brings mixed feelings. Some of them have said: "I don't need to do the Eastside Project because I come from there so I know everything about it." My reaction to this is: "What have you learned from it?" I have analyzed cases of reverse discrimination through many student journals. For most of them the process of integration into the university becomes the focus of their reflections. Hispanic students learn Spanish as a form of empowerment. Spanish classes help them make their voices heard. I have seen how many Hispanic students have changed from hiding their past to giving their final presentation totally based on their family history. I have also found students who have been told by their parents not to accept the label Hispanic, much less to identify with it. The Eastside Project provides these students with enough evidence to understand their parents, and at the same time opens their eyes to the suffering of those who are newcomers and are still struggling to achieve their goals. They also are able to see that poverty has no race or ethnicity. The Eastside Project is effective for everyone because through service-learning all develop a social conscience.

Service-learning helps to develop the ability to see the world from another point of view. While it facilitates collaboration and respect for differences, it alleviates prejudice and misunderstanding (Jacoby 1996). Recently, I received a message from a former student who is attending medical school:

> Looking back, I think the Cultural Project you assigned us in Spanish opened my eyes to who I am and who I want to be. I am on my way to becoming what I have always wanted but my eyes and my heart were opened in that soup kitchen where I met so many people from so many different cultures.

Another student sent me a card from Tucson, Arizona, where she was doing community service with the Yaqui people:

> I have seen many differences but also similarities between the Yaqui culture and mine. Most of all, I experienced the richness of the Yaqui People. My experience in Tucson reflected a lesson you helped teach me; people need to be appreciated for who they are, their customs, cultures, and differences. Throughout the past few months I have realized how important people really are to me. I will continue to learn about them, to travel and meet people, and be open to new experiences.

This type of education goes beyond the traditional acquisition of a predetermined body of knowledge or set of skills, in that it allows for a critical pedagogy of educational transformation that includes dialogue, reflection, and action. If there is to be liberation for humanity, there must be a link between reflection and action that empowers students to learn the knowledge and skills necessary to address issues of injustice in the world (Freire 1970; Gandhi 1951; Giroux 1988).

My ultimate goal as a Latina Spanish teacher is to help my students understand, respect, and celebrate not only Spanish-speaking people's cultures but all cultures by understanding, respecting, and celebrating their own cultures. Service-learning has given me the opportunity to know my students at a deeper level and to share openly with them who I am.

References

Ada, A., C. Beutel, and C. Peterson. (April 1990). "The Educator as Researcher: Participatory Research as an Educational Act Within a Community." Workshop conducted at the National Association of Bilingual Educators Conference, Tucson, Arizona.

Adler, P.S. (1975). "The Transitional Experience: An Alternative View of Culture Shock." *Journal of Humanities Psychology* 15: 13-23.

Cummins, J. (1981). "The Role of Primary Language Development in Promoting Educational Success for Language Minority Students." In *Schooling and Language Minority Students: A Theoretical Framework,* pp. 3-30. Sacramento, CA: California State Department of Education.

Freire, P. (1970). *Pedagogy of the Oppressed.* New York, NY: Continuum.

Freire, P., and D. Macedo. (1987). *Literacy; Reading the Word and the World.* Westport, CT: Bergin & Garvey.

Galloway, V. (1992). "Toward a Cultural Reading of Authentic Texts." In *Languages for a Multicultural World in Transition.* Edited by H. Byrns, pp. 87-121. Reports of the Northeast Conference on the Teaching of Foreign Languages. Lincolnwood, IL: National Textbook Co.

Gandhi, M. (1951). *Non-Violent Resistance.* New York, NY: Schocken Books.

Giroux, H. (1988). *Teachers as Intellectuals: Toward a Critical Pedagogy of Learning.* New York, NY: Bergin & Garvey.

Gullahorn, J.T., and J.E. Gullahorn. (July 1963). "Extension of the U-Curve Hypothesis." *Journal of Social Issues* 19: 33-47.

Hale, A. (1997). "Second Language Acquisition and Cultural Understanding Through Service Learning in Higher Education." Doctoral dissertation, University of San Francisco, California.

Hess, J.D. (1994) *The Whole World Guide to Culture Learning.* Yarmouth, ME: Intercultural Press.

Jacoby, B., and Associates. (1996). *Service-Learning in Higher Education: Concepts and Practices.* San Francisco, CA: Jossey-Bass.

Kleinjans, E. (1972). "On Culture Learning." In *Culture Learning: The Fifth Dimension in the Language Classroom.* Edited by L. Damen, pp. 211-234. Reading, MA: Addison-Wesley.

Lysgaard, S. (1955). "Adjustment in a Foreign Society: Norwegian Fulbright Grantees Visiting the United States." *International Social Science Bulletin* 7: 45-51.

Mantle-Bromley, C. (1992). "Preparing Students for Meaningful Culture Learning." *Foreign Language Annals* 25(2): 117-127.

Park, P. (1993) "What Is Participatory Research? A Theoretical and Methodological Perspective." In *Voices of Change.* Edited by P. Park et al., pp. 1-20. Westport, CT: Bergin & Garvey.

Rivers, W. (1993). "Comprehension and Production: The Interactive Duo." In *Beyond the Monitor Model*. Edited by R. Barasch and C. James, pp. 71-95. Boston, MA: Heinle & Heinle.

Seelye, N. (1984). *Teaching Culture: Strategies for Intercultural Communication*. Lincolnwood, IL: National Textbook Co.

Sholander, T. (1994). "Educational Philosophy of the Eastside Project." In *Eastside Project Santa Clara University; What It Is - How It Works*, pp. 14-17. Santa Clara, CA: Santa Clara University.

Wong-Fillmore, L. (1983). "The Language Learner as an Individual: Implications of Research on Individual Differences for ESL Teacher." In *On TESOL '82*, pp. 157-173. Washington, DC: TESOL.

Why do we use the Eastside Project in Elementary Spanish?

Research in second language acquisition shows that the attitude a person has towards the people speaking the language being learned affects the way a second language is acquired. In addition, there are many studies suggesting that stereotypes are being reinforced by textbooks in which cultures are not well represented.

While, the textbook used in our classes provides a very tourist-like view of the Spanish speaking world, the Eastside Project provides an opportunity to learn from the life of Spanish speaking people not represented in the book. Moreover, this program helps students see that poverty, homelessness, and unplanned aging are not the exclusivity of immigrants but rather serious problems we find in our society today.

How are we going to use the Eastside Project in our Cultural Project in Elementary Spanish?

The Eastside Project will be used as another resource to the content of the class as much as the textbook. We will use the Eastside Project experience in communicative exercises at the end of every class, adapting the communicative exercises in the textbook to the students real experience in their programs. Therefore, the grammatical content of the class will be translated to real life first only describing what surrounds us but later expressing our feelings, doubts, emotions, narrating, or describing what has happened in the students' weekly experience in the community.

What do we expect from every student in our classes?

We expect that every student will find a program where Spanish speaking people are part of the clientele, administrators, and/or educators.

While our student is expected to do what the Eastside program requests, we also require that every student keep a journal in English in which the student will reflect upon the following questions:

- What did impress me today? The student will write about anything that observed or experienced that day, even when the students thinks that *nothing* happened, he/she should reflect upon that fact also.

- Where does this come from? When reflecting upon this questions, students should make a personal connection to whatever they are reflecting. It is important that in this stage, the student think about previous experiences that have to do with the feelings he/she is having. This personal connection should be recorded in the journal in a brief manner.

- Where am I in this? To answer this question, the student must analyze his/her position as a responsible citizen, as a Santa Clara student, and also about his/her beliefs and values in relation to that day's reflection.

- Where does this lead me? This question has to do with what action will be taken at a personal level, as a community or as a nation. Probably most of the time the student's reflection will stay at the personal level but as the time passes, he/she will find it easier to see the role he/she plays in the global society.

AT THE END OF THE QUARTER

WRITTEN REPORT

Every student will write a report based on the following stages. This report must be written in English.

- **Descriptive Phase**: What, who, when, where, how? When answering these questions, students should make a reference to the Hispanic group that the people with whom they worked belonged. The Internet will be a useful source of information about the countries or ethnic groups for this part. Students must keep in mind that many times the people with whom they will be working may or may not know very much about their cultural background.

- **Personal Interpretive Phase**: How did it make us feel? How can we relate what happened in the different Eastside programs with previous experiences in our own lives or with people close to us?

- **Critical Multicultural Phase**: Why are things, like the ones we observed in our Eastside programs happening? What does language have to do with this? How does this affect us as a community of human beings regardless of our culture? Who benefits from this situation? How? and Why?

- **Creative/Transformative Phase**: What can we do to change this reality? What would I change and at which level (personal or social) to improve this situation? What could we do as a group to help the agency with whom we were working?

ORAL PRESENTATION:

Every student will find three or more students to form a group with whom they will share what they have learned from the community. This information might come from their personal journals and will help them prepare a final oral presentation in Spanish.

Every group will have 20 minutes to present to the class. Students are encouraged to use audiovisual aids for their presentation. They are also encouraged to be as creative as they can, bringing to this presentation all types of art expressions they think they can incorporate. **THE ORAL PRESENTATION MUST BE IN SPANISH.**

THE STUDENTS' ROLE AS AUDIENCE OF THE PRESENTATIONS

Students presenting are strongly encouraged to involve the rest of the class in their presentation. Every student in the audience must prepare two questions for the presenters concerning the group's experiences.

GRADING OF THE CULTURAL PROJECT

```
8 Journal entries ..............................4
20-minute oral presentation...................5
Two questions to the presenters............. 2
Written report ................................4

Total......................................... 15
```

Service-Learning With Bilingual Communities and the Struggle for Change: A Critical Approach

by Mark Baldwin, Rosario Díaz-Greenberg, and Joseph Keating

During the past two decades, the deplorable economic, physical, intellectual, and moral conditions within the public schools have caused an outcry for reform (Boyer 1987; Goodlad 1984; Kozol 1991; McLaren 1989; Poplin and Weeres 1992; Silberman 1970; Sizer 1984). The state of education in America has been the subject of many studies (Amidon and Flanders 1963; Kliebard 1966). Reports about the condition of American schools abound, and major reform documents have been presented, including *A Nation at Risk: The Imperative for Educational Reform* (National Commission on Excellence in Education 1983); *A Place Called School: Prospects for the Future* (Goodlad 1984); *A Nation Prepared: Teachers for the 21st Century* (Carnegie Corporation 1986); *Tomorrow's Teachers* (Holmes Group 1986); and *College: The Undergraduate Experience in America* (Boyer 1987).

There are two competitive bodies of literature attempting to promote educational changes: the excellence/reform/effective schools movement, and the transformative movement. The excellence movement reflects research that equates effective teaching practices with increased time on task and higher achievement test scores. It concentrates on reductionist pedagogical practices, such as teacher-student interaction, amount of time on task, objectives and outcomes, and the reproduction of a curriculum geared to the academic success of the dominant group. Neglected are what Weis and Fine (1993) refer to as "the dynamics of power and privilege that nurture, sustain, and legitimate silencing" (2). The transformative movement "struggles to define new possibilities by adapting newer world views" (Poplin 1991: 4). Poplin distinguishes three places within this continuum: constructivism, critical pedagogy, and feminist pedagogy, all of which share in common a desire to incorporate new and different approaches to education, such as service-learning, while departing from the back-to-basics trend.

One of the groups most affected by adverse conditions in the educational system is bilingual children, a statistically significant and increasingly large percentage of the public school population. According to the 1990 U.S. Census, a total of 31.8 million people — one out of every seven individuals in the United States — speak a language other than English at home. The majority of these people, whose numbers have increased from 11.1 million in 1980 to 17.3 million in 1990, speak Spanish:

> Reflecting the youth of the Spanish-speaking population in comparison
> with many other language groups, Spanish speakers are a larger propor-
> tion of the school-age HSNELS [home speakers of non-English language]
> populations than of the adult population. . . . In 1990, they constituted two-
> thirds of the five-to-seventeen-year-olds but only a little more than half of
> the adults. The growth in the number of Spanish speakers accounts for
> nearly 70 percent of the growth in school-age HSNELS population. (Wag-
> goner 1993: 6)

By the year 2000 the majority of students in public schools will be children
of color with approximately 80 percent of them being Hispanic (Trueba
1989). Latino children experience a higher drop-out rate than any other
group (Walsh 1991), and by the age of 17, many of them are classified as
functionally illiterate (Fueyo 1988).

The interaction between schools and families from diverse ethnic and
linguistic backgrounds has been the research focus of many scholars (Bronfenbrenner 1986; Cazden et al. 1985; Delgado-Gaitan 1992; Harry 1992; Ogbu
1982; Phillips 1983; Siegel and Laosa 1983; Trueba 1989; Wong-Fillmore 1990).
However, some educators in the United States still underestimate the contributions of Latino families to educational achievement and attribute the
underachievement of Latino students to the inferiority of their culture, the
organization of their family, their values, and their lack of interest in education (Dunn 1987). Latino families are bracketed as "minority," and their contributions to the educational system are not considered valuable (Diaz-Soto
1993).

In an effort to assist in breaking down some of these misconceptions
among future educators, the secondary teacher credential program at California State University San Marcos has initiated a service-learning
practicum that connects a course on service-learning to field experience
within the schools. Because this program integrates both bilingual and nonbilingual preservice teachers, there is an opportunity, especially for the bilingual preservice teachers, to model positive connections between the Latino
community and the schools.

Design

Cognizant that one of the major criticisms of teacher educational programs
is the isolation of pedagogy from typical practice, we designed coursework
that would integrate and link classroom assignments to field experiences.
For example, one of the major themes of the coursework highlights the
importance of connecting the school to the community. In support of this
concept, the service-learning practicum being discussed here is incorporat-

ed into one of the required courses about high schools of the 21st century (see syllabus) and provides the basis for an exploration of the program theme called "The Teacher and the Community Interacting." Service to the community is also an important component of the mission statements of both the university and the College of Education, as is evidenced by the large number of courses (64) in which service-learning is a component.

Added impetus for incorporating this theme arose from the personal experiences of the instructors within the secondary program. One was a volunteer teacher on the Colville Indian Reservation who later included service-learning projects with the Navajo high school science students he taught. He commented that

> most of my students came from relatively impoverished families and also had a non-mainstream culture and language (Navajo). The service-learning projects provided a basis to increase their self-esteem as well as apply their personal knowledge [of an American Indian community] into a real world perspective. These early experiences made me personally aware of the value of including service-learning into the training of prospective teachers.

Another member of the secondary team has done extensive work in El Salvador and in the inner cities of New York and Florida. She stated that "service-learning is essential to promote a paradigmatic change of attitude in preservice teachers. It is only when they realize that they can become effective agents of change in the community that true empowerment takes place."

Still another member was in the Peace Corps in Africa and stresses the value of service as a learning experience and the need for preservice teachers to become involved in community projects. One final member has been involved in the field of voluntarism for the past two decades doing extensive work with the St. Vincent de Paul group. He believes that "the best lessons of my life come from my years of service as a volunteer. It is imperative that preservice teachers experience service-learning firsthand as they prepare to enter the teaching profession."

The program's interpretation of this theme is that all teachers should be aware of the larger community that has either a direct or indirect impact on their schools. Experiences, such as service-learning, that promote this awareness can have a variety of multidimensional benefits for the preparation of teachers and long-term effects on the students they will teach. Some of the potentially beneficial aspects of incorporating service-learning into teacher preparation programs include:

1) an experience that can give them a perspective on the teacher-student interaction different from that of a school (Root 1994);

2) a real-world setting for incorporating and connecting concepts from one's curriculum (Boyer 1983; Cairn and Kielsmeier 1991; Dewey 1938);

3) a basis on which to assist the student in becoming an acceptable person who has an ethic of care (Noddings 1988) as well as an informed citizen (Aronowitz and Giroux 1985);

4) a reflective-in-action process model that allows the connection of classroom theory to practice (Schön 1987).

We believe that by infusing all of these concepts into a service-learning practicum we can have a powerful and important impact on the perception of what and how secondary teachers teach. Bilingual-bicultural teachers have a unique perspective on this process and potentially have much knowledge and experience to share with other students in a program. There is, moreover, broad support for the inclusion of school-student interaction with the community. Ernest Boyer (1983) in *High School* suggests that community service be a high school graduation requirement and supports this by adding that a "service component for all students will do much to help build a sense of community and common purpose within a school and to be fully human one must serve." John Dewey (1938) has written that "the radical reason that the present school cannot organize itself as a natural social unit is because just this element [community service] of common and productive activity is missing." In *Second to None,* one of the models used to design the single subject credential program, the California Task Force (1992) suggests schools "fully integrate the community into the curriculum by exposing students to real world problems."

Most prospective teachers understand philosophically the value of service-learning after they have read and discussed the issues related to it but are not sure how it can be implemented in diverse high school settings. There are, however, a number of examples and models of service-learning that can assist prospective teachers considering how they might proceed with implementation and integration into their high school classes (Cairn and Kielsmeier 1991). One example includes granting service-learning credit to those high school students who want to do this as an option or for extra credit within a class or who want to participate in a separate class devoted exclusively to service-learning. Such a unit might be organized with the teacher as the advisor and the student receiving release time to carry out projects. A second example would be a one-time, whole-classroom project such as a science class assisting in building a nature trail. A third, and we believe the most powerful, is for the teacher into make a direct connection between his or her curriculum and the community by integrating the students' knowledge and skill base in a discipline into a service project in the community. Some examples of this type of service and learning include working with a nutritionist at a homeless shelter (home economics), testing water at beaches (biology), publishing a newsletter for immigrants about the availability of social services (language arts and foreign languages), building ramps for the disabled (industrial arts).

Individual high schools offer great variety in the ways they incorporate service-learning. Appropriate experiences during teaching training programs can inform the prospective teacher of these options and address motivation, available resources, and mechanisms for applying service-learning in high schools.

Implementation of the Service-Learning Practicum

The specific types of community sites that preservice teachers identify as suitable for their projects depend somewhat on teacher interests and disciplinary areas and geographical considerations. To assist teachers in this process, a class instructor can utilize the CSU San Marcos Office of Community Service-Learning. Early in the course the office coordinator shares information about service-learning through readings, handouts, and databases about specific organizations that have been used for service-learning in the past. Students can then use this information as a starting point to assist them in initiating their projects as well as a base on which to develop their philosophy on service-learning. Bilingual teachers are encouraged to make connections which those Latino community organizations with which they are most familiar and, when possible, to collaborate with nonbilingual students. Subsequently, they are given a handout that contains a series of prompts within a framework that assists with their information gathering (see Fig. A). With this framework, they are asked to identify, contact, and interact with a community organization that in some way impacts students in the high school to which they are assigned.

Prior to actually starting their practicum, the preservice teachers schedule a miniconference with their instructor regarding proposed placements and activities. This is a valuable part of the process in that it offers both the student and instructor time to clarify the goals of an individual project before it actually begins.

After completing their practicum with the community organization, students must design curricular lesson plan(s) that they can implement and explore within the context of their field placements. More specifically, students are asked to consider the following perspectives in designing the objectives for this lesson plan:

1) *What services does this organization provide to my students (schools) or their families?*

2) *How could this organization provide career or mentorship opportunities for students within the context of a (my) discipline?*

3) *How could this organization incorporate (my) students as part of a service project that would provide them with a real opportunity to benefit the community?*

4) *In what ways could the learning, i.e., discipline-specific content or topics, of my course correspond to the community resource?*

5) *In what ways can I assess the effectiveness of all of these aspects of learning with my students?*

Expectations are that a minimum of 15 hours (built into the course syllabus) will be devoted to completing the preservice teachers' service-learning assignment. The additional time needed to incorporate the lesson plan into their field placement varies depending on the methods they use with their own students. Instructors often observe these student teachers in the field implementing their service-learning projects. During reflection classes, which are held upon completion of the field experiences at the end of each semester, they provide an overview of their findings and implementation procedures in oral and written presentations. An essential closure element of these is a reflective or assessment process that includes a personal perspective listing recommendations for modifications to their service-learning lesson plan (see Fig. B). In addition to this reflective assessment, some of the preservice teachers develop an action research project that more formally addresses the issues of assessing the implementation process. Each student supplies a copy of his or her service-learning overview, lesson plan, and reflection/assessment to other members of the class. This material is added to an ongoing database of service-learning activities made available as a resource to all future course participants.

The prompts of this assignment provide an opportunity for these preservice high school teachers to seek both information and interaction with local service organizations and also to reflect on, design, and implement ways to apply what they find within the context of their classrooms (or discipline). An additional benefit of this work is that it provides them with a strong model of an experiential approach teaching that is generalizable to a number of situations.

To summarize, preservice teachers complete a number of processes during their service-learning practicum that assists them in formulating a personal perspective on service-learning. This perspective is translated from concepts gained from personal experiences into a formalized lesson plan implemented during their field experience. Both written and oral summaries are presented and discussed during culminating reflection classes as part of the evaluative process.

Student Outcomes

This section will include three case studies of representative preservice teacher outcomes or products from bilingual student teachers. All these cases were derived from the service-learning practicum, drawing upon student voices captured during reflection classes.

In Case 1, Kaija, a bilingual (Spanish) student teacher, was extremely interested in networking with a local literacy group that worked with parents of students at her school field placement site. Her narrative is as follows:

> Using this model I sought out service opportunities that might provide my Spanish classes a chance to tutor adult migrants. I was able to locate a local migrant tutoring program and after interacting and participating within the organization I was able to conceptualize a potential subset of clients for this organization, one that was not being serviced — the tutoring of older Latino grandparents. I met with this small group of older Latino women and found them to be gracious and culturally very rich. I designed my lesson plans to reflect the active involvement of my Spanish classes in assisting them with their conversational English and in exchange I hoped the women would relate some of their own personal histories from the migrant experience. I felt that my students would get experience practicing their Spanish language skills (discipline connections/service) as well as techniques in the teaching of English (career exploration). Through these one-on-one relationships I hoped that both individuals would gain insight and understanding. In fact I observed many of these types of outcomes from the interactions and I felt very rewarded as a teacher and a human. My students practiced their Spanish, got a perspective on teaching as a career, and felt good about assisting someone else during the personal interaction with these elderly adults. I hope to continue this tutoring group in the future with my classes as I feel there are powerful benefits to all involved.
>
> I believe this was a valuable experience for me because when a teacher in training like me has opportunities to conceptualize and implement her own concept of service-learning, she is more likely to include this as an integral part of her future teaching.

In this case, Kaija explored an existing community organization and identified a peripheral need and addressed it to the benefit of her students and the adults with whom they interacted. It is very exciting that she would take the initiative to go beyond the premise of using a social service organization to create curriculum. She saw a critical need and established her own "organization" and included her students in this ongoing process.

In Case 2, Issac, a bilingual Spanish and social studies student teacher, also explored an existing organization — the Boys and Girls Club. He used their existing format, which provides activities for children during times when parents work, to provide a basis to get to know the youth and their parents. After familiarizing himself with the organization, he was able to design a curricular plan in which his high school students would have opportunities to interact in this setting. His narrative is as follows:

> This club services elementary through high school students. It focuses its attention and programs as advocates for youth at risk from such social dangers as gang and drug involvement, dropping out of school, teen pregnancy, and abusive homes. An extremely high percentage of the youth who attend are Latino. I was particularly interested in how I, as teacher, could assist them in these efforts. The administrators said they would welcome the utilization of my Spanish language students to assist the younger students in a variety of cultural and educational activities. They are typically understaffed and viewed this as a way for my students to improve their Spanish, feel a connection to the community, and serve as role models for these younger students. Using this as a guideline for my lesson plan, I created a project for my Spanish 2 and social studies classes in which they were to select one of the scheduled activities (or in some cases suggest new ones) that they felt they enjoy becoming involved [in]. They scheduled regular times over a nine-week period to attend and kept a journal documenting their application of Spanish language skills (for the Spanish 2 students) and social issues (for the social studies class) as well as the variety of other experiences they had. This journal would serve as a basis for my assessment of their experience and provide prompts for a culminating seminar in which they all shared their experiences with each other.
>
> I was very excited by the outcome of this experience for them. They truly felt they were role models for these younger children, improved their Spanish language and teaching skills and had many opportunities to meet and interact with the parents of their students. My students felt very gratified by this experience on two levels. On one level this provided a greater understanding and empathy for the variety of problems and potential problems they observed throughout their experiences for both individuals and the community at large. On another level my students felt a very positive sense that they had provided some positive impact on the youth with whom they had interacted.
>
> I too learned a great deal about the greater community in which I would be teaching from both my interaction with the Boys and Girls Club

and from the interactions and reflections of my students. In all it was a very powerful application of an assignment in two different courses (Spanish and social studies), which I will attempt to duplicate as a full-time teacher.

Issac was able to creatively adapt his service-learning assignment to different disciplines in which outcomes were both distinct (on the content level) and similar (on the affect level). He and his students appeared to have gained a better understanding of the problems that the Latino community in particular faced. They also came to understand that they could all assist in contributing to the solution to some of these problems through their involvement in this service-learning project. Issac will probably be more sensitive to these issues with his high school students and much more likely to introduce service-learning to his future students as he enters the teaching profession.

In Case 3, Marilyn, a bilingual Spanish math preservice teacher, explored the Mexican American Educational Guidance Foundation (MAEGA), a local organization that provides leadership, support for mentors and scholarships, in an effort to assist youth of Mexican heritage to gain educational access to universities or trade schools. Her narrative is as follows:

This organization was very open to new ideas from teachers on ways to utilize mentors in an effort to provide encouragement and support to Mexican-American students. My idea on how to incorporate service-learning into my bilingual math class was to have each student select a career interest that had some math component and attempt to match this interest with a MAEGA mentor (who was also a role model). Not all of the career choices had matching mentors so I had to seek new individuals who would be willing to participate. Students would meet with mentors on the school site or at the mentor work site to explore how math is applied to their careers. Students volunteered some time at the site to work with the mentor. My math students kept a journal on the math applications as well as the educational goals needed to pursue this area of math as a career.

Their outcomes included a final letter to the mentor in a report format that was also used to deliver a presentation to the class. This application of service-learning incorporated a very integrated approach to teaching math. During this assignment, as volunteer interns with the mentor, my high school students had opportunities to explore careers and at the same time to apply specific mathematics to real-world problems. I think they were especially excited to have the opportunity of working side by side with such powerful role models.

Marilyn sought an organization that would link a service-learning experience to her teaching and a career area (math/technology) typically under-represented by Mexican Americans. By incorporating this concept into her bilingual prealgebra class, she provided the students with a multifaceted experience with professionals that would encourage them to explore careers and demonstrate mathematics applications to local community businesses. Many minority students have faired poorly in classwork in mathematics.

Conclusion

Bilingual teachers, especially in high-impact areas where Latino students make up a large student population, can have a tremendous effect in connecting the school to the community. They can provide leadership in implementing service-learning with their own students. The service-learning practicum at CSU San Marcos can provide the type of training necessary to start on this process. These future teachers can have an immense impact on their students if one considers the perspective that each teacher, during a lifetime of teaching, has the potential to critically affect hundreds or thousands of individuals by providing opportunities for experiences in which they interact, relate, apply knowledge, and explore the communities in which they live. To this end, the Secondary Credential Program at CSU San Marcos will longitudinally track these graduates with a questionnaire focusing on the implementation of service-learning in their teaching practice (see Fig. C).

References

Amidon, B., and N.A. Flanders. (1963). *The Role of the Teacher in the Classroom: A Manual for Understanding and Improving Teachers' Classroom Behavior.* Minneapolis, MN: Paul S. Amidon & Associates.

Aronowitz, S., and H. Giroux. (1985). *Education Under Siege.* Westport, CT: Bergin & Garvey.

Boyer, E.L. (1987). *College—The Undergraduate Experience in America.* New York, NY: Harper & Row.

———. (1983). *High School: A Report on Secondary Education in America.* New York, NY: Harper & Row.

Bronfenbrenner, U. (1986). "Ecology of the Family as a Context for Human Development. Research Perspective." *Developmental Psychology* 22(6): 732-742.

Cairn, R., and J. Kielsmeier. (1991). *Growing Hope: A Sourcebook on Integrating Youth Service Into School Curriculum.* Roseville, MN: National Youth Leadership Council.

California Task Force. (1992). *Second to None.* Sacramento, CA: Department of Education.

Carnegie Corporation. (1986). *A Nation Prepared: Teachers for the 21st Century.* New York, NY: Author.

Cazden, C., A. Carrasco, A. Maldonado Guzman, and F. Erickson. (1985). "The Contribution of Ethnographic Research to Bicultural, Bilingual Education." In *Perspectives on Bilingualism and Bilingual Education.* Edited by J.E. Alatis and J. Staczek, pp. 153-169. Washington, DC: Georgetown University Press.

Delgado-Gaitan, C. (1992). "School Matters in the Mexican-American Home: Socializing Children to Education." *American Educational Research Journal* 29(3): 495-531.

Dewey. J. (1938). *Experience and Education.* New York, NY: Collier Books.

Diaz-Soto, L. (Winter/Spring 1993). "Curriculum and Instruction Research: Native Language for School Success." *Bilingual Research Journal* 17(1, 2): 83-97.

Dunn, L. (1987). *Bilingual Hispanic Children on the U.S. Mainland: A Review of Research of Their Cognitive, Linguistic, and Scholastic Development.* Research monograph. Minneapolis, MN: American Guidance Service.

Fueyo, J.M. (1988). "Technical Literacy Versus Critical Literacy in Adult Basic Education." *Journal of Education* 170(1): 107-118.

Goodlad, J. (1984). *A Place Called School: Prospects for the Future.* New York, NY: McGraw-Hill.

Harry, B. (1992). "An Ethnographic Study of Cross-Cultural Communication With Puerto Rican-American Families in the Special Education System." *American Educational Research Journal* 29(3): 471-494.

Holmes Group. (April 1986). *Tomorrow's Teachers. A Report of the Holmes Group.* East Lansing. MI: Author.

Kliebard, H. (1966). "The Observation of Classroom Behavior." In *The Way Teaching Is.* Washington, DC: ASCD and NEA.

Kozol, J. (1991). *Savage Inequalities.* New York, NY: Crown.

McLaren, P. (1989). *Life in Schools: An Introduction to Critical Pedagogy in the Foundations of Education.* New York, NY: Longman.

National Commission on Excellence in Education. (1983). *A Nation at Risk: The Imperative for Educational Reform.* Washington, DC: U.S. Department of Education.

Noddings, N. (1988). "An Ethic of Caring and Its Implications for Instructional Arrangements." *American Journal of Education* 96(2): 215-230.

Ogbu, J. (1982). "Cultural Discontinuity and Schooling." *Anthropology and Education Quarterly* 13: 290-307.

Phillips, S. (1983). *The Invisible Culture.* New York, NY: Longman.

Poplin, M.S. (1991). "A Practical Theory of Teaching and Learning: The View From Inside the Transformative Classroom: Contributions of Constructivism." Unpublished manuscript.

————, and J. Weeres. (1992). *Voices From the Inside: A Report on Schooling From Inside the Classroom. Part I: Naming the Problem*. Claremont, CA: The Institute for Education in Transformation, Claremont Graduate School.

Root, S. (1994). "Service-Learning in Teacher Education: A Third Rationale." *Michigan Journal of Community Service-Learning* 1(1): 94-97.

Schön, D. (1987). *Educating the Reflective Practitioner*. San Francisco, CA: Jossey-Bass.

Siegel, I., and L. Laosa, eds. (1983). *Changing Families*. New York, NY: Plenum Press.

Silberman, C.E. (1970). *Crisis in the Classroom: The Remaking of American Education*. New York, NY: Vintage.

Sizer, T. (1984). *Horace's Compromise: The Dilemma of the American High School*. Boston, MA: Houghton Mifflin.

Trueba, H.T. (1989). *Raising Silent Voices: Educating the Linguistic Minorities for the 21st Century*. New York, NY: Newbury House.

Waggoner, D. (Winter/Spring 1993). "The Growth of Multilingualism and the Need for Bilingual Education: What Do We Know So Far?" *Bilingual Research Journal* 17(1, 2): 1-12.

Walsh, C.E. (1991). *Pedagogy and the Struggle for Voice*. New York, NY: Bergin and Garvey.

Weis, L., and M. Fine. (1993). *Beyond Silenced Voices: Class, Race, and Gender in United States Schools*. New York, NY: State University of New York Press.

Wong-Fillmore, L. (Winter 1990). "Latino Families and the Schools." *California Perspectives* 1: 30-37.

Fig. A

Service-Learning Practicum Prompts
for Secondary Pre-Service Teachers in "High Schools of the 21st Century"
EDSS 530

1) Name of Organization:

2) Contact Person: (name, title, telephone #):

3) Address:

4) Overview of organizations' mission or purpose:

5) Narrative of experiences including any observations, interviews and participatory activities (use back or attach if necessary):

6) Highlights:
    A) In what ways is this organization supportive of schools?
    B) In what ways did this organization demonstrate limitations to working with students (schools)? If so, what recommendations would you suggest to improve these?
    C) How could this organization be used with your high school students for service-learning that would include elements of service, learning and career exploration. (You will expand on specifics in #7)
    D) In reflecting on this experience what is the most important impression with which you are left?
    E) Could the service-learning experience practicum in general (or your specific one) be improved? If so, in what ways?

7) Using all the knowledge YOU gleaned from the practicum, design a service-learning lesson plan for your discipline that incorporates the organization you studied as the main focus of the lesson. Into this lesson plan explain how you will integrate the three critical aspects of service-learning as discussed in #6C (service, learning/content connection, career exploration). This lesson plan should include all relevant components including appropriate adaptations for culturally and linguistically diverse students.

Fig. B

Evaluation of Service-Learning Project

Experience and response to practicum: (as evidenced by written and oral report)

Perceived quality of the experiences as indicated by responses to the Prompts #1#6. Specific comments on how these were completed discussed and evaluated. (10 pts.)

Lesson Plan:

1.　　Does it connect all three aspects-- service, discipline specific learning and career exploration opportunities? (3 pts) Specific Examples--

2.　　Are all basic elements of a lesson plan present? (including potential adaptations for culturally and linguistically diverse students) (7 pts)

- Objectives
- Context
- Procedures
- Organizational patterns
- Activities (engagement)
- materials/resources
- assessment(s)

Overall Score/Comments:

Fig. C

Service-Learning Follow-up Questionnaire
to Graduates of
the CSU San Marcos Single Subject Credential Program

Name _____

School _____

Position _____

1)   How would you rate the value of doing this assignment as part of the requirements of completing the single subject credential program? (on a continuum of 1 to 5 with 1 being not valuable and five being extremely valuable)

        Explain?

2)   Have you had the opportunity to incorporate service-learning into your classroom teaching assignment? If yes, go to #3. If not, explain -- What have been some of the impediments to incorporating service-learning? Will you attempt to incorporate it in future? Explain.

3)   a) Explain the manner in which you have implemented service-learning into your classroom. How have your students responded to their involvement in service-learning?

        b) How would you rate the overall effectiveness of service-learning in your classroom (on a scale of 1 to 5, with 1 being ineffective and 5 extremely effective)?

        c) In what ways, if any, will you change the format you used to incorporate service-learning?

Education EDSS 530:

Secondary Schooling in the 21st Century

Dr. Joseph Keating
Office Hours: Monday/Wednesday 8:30-9:00 AM
(CSUSM) and 12:30-1:00 PM (SDLA) or by appt.(Craven 1245) 619-7504321
email: jkeating@csusm.edu

SYLLABUS

Description:

Through observations, readings, discussions, modeling and practice. students will gain an understanding of the concept of the newly evolving model of the secondary school of the 21st century. This course will focus on characteristics and applications of: theory' research and practice related to the professional teacher and schools; **community service-learning organizations and their connections to.schools**; learning styles of linguistic and cultural diverse groups and exemplary teaching strategies that including assessment and communication skills involved in cooperative and interdisciplinary teaming.

Required Texts:

Schools of the 21St Century. Customized Text. Joseph Keating (1996).
Second To None: A Vision of the New California High School (CA. High School Task Force) (1994).
The Good High School—Portraits of Character and Culture (Harper) Sarah Lawrence Ughtfoot (1983).

Additional Readings: (see customized text)

Objectives:

Upon completion of this course the student will be able to demonstrate knowledge, understanding, practical skills and appreciation for
    1 . the characteristics of schools of the 21St century;
    2. cooperative learning;
    3. interdisciplinary teaching:
    4. service-learning and its connection to schools;
    5. authentic assessments:
    6. problem solving/creative thinking
    7. specially designed academic instruction in English (SDAIE):
    8. action research as applied to the classroom setting.

Syllabus
Page 2

Course Schedule and Related Readings:

This course consists of ten weeks of classes before student teaching and one or two classes during the week of follow-up reflections (12/9-12/13). The final evaluation will include an integrated portfolio presentation. Regular sessions will normally be on Monday and Wednesday AM or PM (9-11 or 1-3) with a few exceptions. Jigsawing of articles will be done as the topic is presented in class and these dates will be discussed with the syllabus.

Schedule and Assignments:

Mon: 8/26 Syllabus / Introductions / Dine Philosophy of Learning (Benally)

Wed: 8/28 *Second to None* overview, discussion and Video School Culture
Assignment / Service-learning Assignment
Overview / explanation Mon. 9/2 Labor Day -- no class

Wed: 9/14 Technology in 21st Century Schools -- Dr. Joan Hanor (CSUSM)
Location and times TBA

Mon: 9/9 **Service-Learning Practicum, Overview (private conference time by arrangement)**

Wed: 9/11 The Good High School jigsaw presentation*

Mon: 9/16 Action Research Project Overview

Wed: 9/18 Action Research Project Planning

Mon: 9/23 SDAIE end Multicultural Overview/Planning

Wed: 9/25 SDME Lesson Presentation*

Mon: 9/30 **Independent Field Work Time for Service-Learning Practicum (no class)**

Wed: 10/2 School Culture Assignment Team Presentation*

Mon: 10/7 Science Education Overview

Wed: 10/9 Generic Interdisciplinary Problem Solving Models that are used in Science. Introduction to Odyssey of the Mind (Superlinks)* and Invention Convention

Mon: 10/14 Overview of Authentic Learning Techniques

Wed: 10/16 Performance Based Exams an example of implementation and scoring rubrics

Mon: 10/21 Overview of Cooperative Group Dynamics

Wed: 10/23 Preparation Time for Invention Convention Presentation

Mon: 10/28 Invention Convention Team Presentations *

Wed: 10/30 Service-learning Practicum, Presentations and Reflections * /Collect Journals *

Mon: 12/11 Action Research Project Presentations *
Reflections on Student Teaching/Coursework Portfolio Items connected to EDSS 530 Concepts

Overview of Assignments:

Specific details of each assignment are included in the text and will be given in class at the appropriate time:

SDAIE Lessons and Presentations (10 pts.)
School Culture Team Presentation (10 pts.)
Odyssey of the N6nd Problem (Superlinks) (5 pts.)
Performance Based Exam (Authentic Assessment) (5 pts. ? I
Invention Convention(Interdisc. group problem solving) (10 pts.)
Journals including jigsaw of specific reading assignments (20 pts.)
Service-Learning Project (oral and written presentation) (20 pts.)
Action Research Project Design and Presentation (20 pts.)
Portfolio Enclosures (Final) (10 pts.)
Attendance/Participation (10 pts.)

(punctuality and attendance is essential and missed assignments and classes will be excused for highly unusual circumstances only)

Total = 100 pts. possible (except if action research project is completed first semester then 120 pts.)

Grading Scale:

Students must maintain a B average in the credential program and obtain a grade of no lower than C+ in any individual course in order to receive credit for that course.

A   = 90-100 (97-100 A+)
B   = 80-89 (87-89 B+)
C   = 70-79 (77-79 C+)
D   = 60-69
F   = <60

Altruism and Community Service in Hispanic Literature: Readings and Praxis

by Estelle Irizarry

Community service can be meaningfully integrated with advanced litera-ture courses in Spanish on all levels, even for graduate students. Such a course easily fits into existing department parameters for thematic sym-posia and can combine theory with textual analysis. The approach does not regard literature as sermons or didactic texts, but rather as works that intro-duce readers to examples of service that seduce us not by exhortation but by the power of the text itself. Students work in the community and relate their experiences to analysis of the works.

Theoretical Rationale for Linking Literature With Service

R. Eugene Rice challenges the hierarchical notion that esoterism and knowl-edge gained from analytical reasoning and theoretical knowledge are superior to "knowledge apprehended through connections grounded in human community-relational knowing" (1991: 11) Both types of knowledge are part of the course, which builds on János László's (1992) theoretical premises in the domain of psychological aesthetics, as described in "The Psy-chology of Literature: A Socio-Cognitive Approach." László provides empiri-cal evidence of the complexity and richness of literary comprehension based on a view of the text as information processed by the readers' cognitive schemata and personal experience. Research by Jeanne M. Yanes (1992) and by R.C. Schank and R.P. Abelson (1977) likewise supports the value of cultur-al and experiential schemata in reading.

Hispanic literature in particular offers outstanding readings on the sub-ject of altruism and service, for example, in religious writings by such early authors as Moisés ben Maimónides (1135-1204), San Ignacio de Loyola (1491-1556), and Santa Teresa de Avila (1515-1582), as well as in secular literature, from Cervantes's Don Quijote to contemporary works by major Spanish and Spanish-American authors. Women writers are amply represented. First and foremost is Concepción Arenal, the 19th-century founder of Spanish soci-ology, author of extraordinary essays on the history of beneficence in Spain and of manuals on service to the poor and the incarcerated.

A good way to begin a course linking altruism with Hispanic literature is with a working definition of altruism as the students understand the term and as the dictionary of the Royal Spanish Academy defines it, as "Diligencia en procurar el bien ajeno aun a costa del propio" ("Diligence in procuring others' welfare even at the price of one's own"). This is, by the way, the longest definition I have encountered in any dictionary, English or Spanish. At the same time, one of the purposes of the course should be to arrive inductively at a wider, more comprehensive concept of altruism as practiced by the students and as evidenced in the readings.

Literary Approach

László's structured social-cultural approach draws on psychological theories of art developed by Vygotsky, resonance of personal memories, and goal directedness, utilizing cognitive categories of self-knowledge and personal experiences in the interpretation of literature. László provides empirical evidence that personal experience and relevance are activated during the reading of literature and, more important, that they sharpen comprehension and contribute to complex interpretation of literary texts. László uses categories developed in the domain of social cognition to formalize literary analysis in concrete terms, such as goal directedness, intentionality, actions, emotional states, roles, and insider/outsider narrative perspective, all of which are illuminated by readers' experience. This is not a subjectivist approach in that it is carefully structured and thereby allows empirical comparison of one reader's interpretation with those of others.

A course in Hispanic literature and service, guided by László's theoretical approach, focuses on developing in students the schemata necessary for meaningful, goal-directed contact with Spanish-language literary texts on the subject of service to others. Some considerations arising from this interaction are:

• Cultural characteristics in the exercise of charitable service as depicted in Hispanic literature.

• Cultural schemata. Transferability from one culture, country, or time, to another.

• Settings for charitable endeavors. Institutional/personal, spontaneous/organized, social/political, religious/secular, direct/indirect contact.

• Attitudes of providers and recipients.

• Historical changes in needs, attitudes, and practices.

Texts in Spanish

Many Spanish-language literary works attack social evils, but it is more difficult to find works that provide examples of altruism in a positive light; witness poor Don Quijote, who finds himself continually mistreated for his acts of altruism inspired by knighthood's code of honor. Stories of saints exemplify altruism but to the pint of sacrifice, a supreme form of altruism (Palmer 1920: 39), certainly far beyond expectations for lay service to others.

One may ask whether models of altruistic behavior are scarce in literature or simply that critics have not noticed them. Altruism is decidedly a little-discussed theme in criticism, perhaps because it deals with a sentiment that, like all sentiments, does not lend itself to cold, intellectual analysis. Nevertheless, social scientists since the 1970s have talked about something they call "prosocial behavior" (Kohn 1990: 63), which can serve as a theoretical basis for discussing altruism. As Smetana, Bridgeman, and Turiel (1983) explain, these terms have been applied interchangeably, to a wide range of behaviors presumed to have a positive effect on others (163). However, Kohn points out that in the determination of what is prosocial, motivation is not taken into account, whereas it is a factor in determining altruism. This distinction proves useful in discussing how characters behave in literary works.

A problem in finding appropriate texts in any language is the reality that Paul Mussen alludes to in his analysis of prosocial development when he asks why the discipline of social sciences is concerned more with problems than with solution (Mussen 1983: 1). Mussen recognizes that actions that constitute an immediate menace to society, such as crimes and conflicts, require immediate attention before we can pay attention to the study of such positive actions as kindness, consideration, and charity. It is only natural to expect literature to reflect this tendency to focus on negative behavior, perhaps because it is viewed as more interesting than positive behavior, as is the case in picaresque, naturalist, testimonial literature and social realism.

At the same time, the capacity of a critic or reader also plays a part in recognizing what Thomas Nagel (1978) calls "the possibility of altruism," which does not depend entirely on the author's making it clear. Grasping altruism in literature depends in large measure on the preparation, sensitivity, and above all, the experience of the reader, as László demonstrated.

My own list of representative titles that respond to some of the considerations mentioned above is compiled from both peninsular Spanish and Spanish-American authors spanning several centuries and all genres. The instructor can choose core readings and let individuals select others for relevance to projects and interests, with a heavier reading load for graduate students. For advanced or graduate students, complete texts are advised, whereas advanced undergraduate students could read selections or even excerpts. The readings from earlier eras that are no longer under copyright can be reproduced from a number of available editions and bound in a course pack, as I have done in my course at Georgetown. Individual selections from books under copyright can be placed on electronic reserve for students to access in the library's electronic reading room, if such a facility is available.

Accompanying information shown in the list *opposite* includes for each author the country of origin, title, genre, and, in parentheses, suggested selections, where applicable, and particular themes for discussion and reflection arising from the text.

Service Projects

A minimum service commitment of 40 hours during the semester has proved to be reasonable for this type of course. It is appropriate that service-learning courses in Spanish tend to direct their efforts to the local Latino community; however, students in upper-level literature courses, especially on the graduate level, usually do not need practice with the language itself, so the service experience need not be limited to helping only Hispanics. In practice, students have served in a wide variety of settings as tutors, advisors to a student poetry group, workers in nonprofit foundations, consumer advisors, and hospital translators. A variety of service projects accommodate a diversity of student talents and preferences, so in a course of this type individuals with particular interests are encouraged to choose a project or several projects from the many possibilities listed in the university's Center for Volunteer and Public Service's *Community Service-Learning Resource Guide*.

Each student accompanies another student or group to their service site at least once to broaden the service experience. As a parallel to László's attention to insider/outsider literary perspective, visitor students ("outsiders") can learn from the insights of fellow students involved in the project ("insiders"), with the class readings providing a common ground.

Activities

Due to the literary component of the course, reflection activities involve an adaptation of the journal model described by Julie A. Hatcher and Robert G. Bringle (1996), in which students write two entries weekly, describing their reflections on the service experience in one entry and relating that experience to their readings in the other. The purpose is to contrast subjective reflection with structured social-cognitive inquiry.

Classroom activities focus on discussion of readings and analysis of original knowledge sources as related to experiential perspectives. Students read and discuss the reflection essays that relate to the texts.

Development activities go beyond the semester and provide the benefit of students' experience by contributing to the development of a cumulative

Readings

Aguirre Bellver, Joaquín. Spain. "El mudito alegre." Short story. (Community and the handicapped.)

Allende, Isabel. Chile. "Vida interminable" and "El milagro discreto." From Stories of Eva Luna. Short story. (Types of charity, temporary vs. long-term commitment.)

Arenal, Concepción. Spain. La beneficencia, la filantropía y la caridad. Essay. (History, concepts, and practice of community service in Spain, from earliest times.)

------ . El visitador del pobre. Essay. (How to treat the poor when you are not poor).

------ . El visitador del preso. Essay. (Helping prisoners of both sexes).

Ayala, Francisco. Spain. "San Juan de Dios." From Los usurpadores. Story. (Self-sacrifice, motivations for charity.)

Betanzos Palacios, Odón. Spain. Luisillo. Poetry. (Helping needy children in our community; becoming involved.)

Cabrera, Lydia. Cuba. "Vida o muerte." From Ayapá: Cuentos de Jicotea. (Helping "our own," the sense of community.)

Cervantes, Miguel de. Spain. Don Quijote. Novel. (Helping those who refuse help [Part I, Chapter 22]. Is altruism quixotic?)

Dieste, Rafael. Spain. "Carlomagno y Belisario." From Historias e invenciones de Félix Muriel. (The handicapped.)

------ . Viaje y fin de don Frontán. Drama. (Conscience and remorse for lack of charity; opportunities lost.)

Gutiérrez Solana, José. Spain. La España negra. Travel essay. (Treatment of the mentally ill, the infirm, criminals.)

Jiménez, Juan Ramón. Spain (Nobel Prize). "El niño tonto," "El loro," "El perro sarnoso," "Las tres viejas," "El burro viejo," "La carretilla," "El niño y el agua," "Amistad," "La tísica," "Navidad," "Los Reyes Magos." From Platero y yo. Lyrical prose vignettes. (Small acts of kindness toward people and animals.)

Laguerre, Enrique. Puerto Rico. Solar Montoya. Novel. (Child abuse, foster child care, mentoring.)

Loyola, San Ignacio de. Spain. Autobiografía. Essay. (Giving and receiving service: "There but for the grace of God go I.")

Maimónides, Moisés ben. Spain. Guía de descarriados. Essay. (Book 3: Chapters 38, 39, 52; charity as a moral imperative; different types of service to others.)

Palacio Valdés, Armando. Spain. "Polifemo." Short story. (Even "monsters" can be altruistic.)

Pardo Bazán, Emilia. Spain. "La Nochebuena del carpintero." Short story. (Unobtrusive altruism; helping receivers of services to maintain their pride.)

Pérez Galdós. Spain. Torquemada en la hoguera. Novel. (Motivations for charity.)

------ . Misericordia. Novel. (Ingratitude, pride, the homeless, poverty, beggars, the "new poor.")

Peri Rossi, Cristina. Uruguay/Spain. "La gratitud es insaciable." From Una pasión prohibida. Short story. (Expecting gratitude; how it feels to be on the receiving end of service.)

Santa Teresa de Jesús. Spain. Selected poetry, Autobiografía, El libro de las fundaciones. ("God is among the pots and pans." Founding institutions for charitable endeavors.)

Unamuno, Miguel de. Spain. "Caridad bien organizada." Short story. (Organized, institutional giving vs. personal, individual contact.)

database of literary texts and service projects.

For graduate students, a term paper may highlight theoretical aspects, focusing on a particular author or text in relation to (1) cognitive or cultural schemata and their transferability, (2) current theories of realism in light of "experiential realism," and (3) reader reception theories. They would also present a summary of this research with the class.

Assessment by the instructor is based on several factors. Personal reflections are not graded, but those that relate the service experience to the text are. Each student also prepares an individual or collaborative semester project, such as finding an additional text from the reading list, or another text they have discovered, and presents it to the class.

Arenal, Loyola, Santa Teresa, and Cabrera show the need for collaborative work, so a class project is especially appropriate as a shared experience to be discussed in terms of the readings. It provides a common, structured service experience, a common ground for discussion, in contrast to the individual experiences of each student. Last year we all joined in a collective experience by volunteering our service at Food and Friends, an organization dedicated to preparing and distributing of special diets for homebound AIDS patients. The homework assignment was to write a reflection paper guided by theoretical and practical reflections from our readings and based on the following premise:

> *Arenal sugiere que no todo el mundo es apto para llevar a cabo el mismo tipo de servicio, que el que hace cada cual debe ajustarse a su sensibilidad y talentos particulares. San Ignacio, en cambio, ejemplifica una voluntad de servicio más general, en cualquier situación que requiera ayuda.*

> *(1) Compare la experiencia colectiva en Food and Friends a la de sus projectos individuales.*

> *(2) ¿En qué sentido caben estas dos experiencias dentro del concepto del servicio ignaciano o arenalano del servicio?*

> *(3) ¿Puede usted relacionar la experiencia en Food and Friends con otro texto que hemos leído este semesstre?*

> *[Translation] Arenal suggests that not everyone is suited for the same type of service, that each person might well choose service projects in accordance with his or her sensitivity and talents. Saint Ignatius of Loyola, on the other hand, exemplifies a more general willingness to serve in any situation of need.*

> *(1) Compare the collective experience in Food and Friends with your individual project.*

(2) In what way do both of these experiences fit in with the Ignatian or Arenalan concept of service?

(3) Can you relate your experience in Food and Friends with another text we have read this semester?

Sometimes the students' comments exhibit extraordinary perception and ability to establish connections. One student commented that "each encounter in leaving food was brief but poignant, similar to an episode of Solana. Going from place to place made us feel like pilgrims or travellers, like Solana and San Ignacio who met people they had never seen before who needed their help."

Throughout the course, the readings provided a shared literary experience and basis for talking about service. Students became very adept at drawing analogies and likened people they were working with to the literary characters.

Preparing for Service: Theory and Practicality

A Spanish-language course linking community service and literature could not ask for better texts than Concepción Arenal's magnificent treatises *El visitador del pobre* and *La beneficencia, la filantropía y la caridad.* Arenal, whose works are fast becoming canonical, was the founder of Spanish sociology and a champion of the poor (Irizarry 1998, 1993). It is hard to believe that they were written over a hundred years ago. As corner pieces for the course, they are rich in both theory and practical advice. Indeed, *El visitador del pobre* is virtually a vade mecum ideal for László's goal-directed reading.

Arenal's books provide a solid theoretical base for community service from a Hispanic perspective. The first chapter of *El visitador* provides a model for the reflection process. The author begins with theoretical considerations about human suffering as an inescapable reality. She is as concerned with the service providers' self-examination as with the beneficiaries of their services, since providers and beneficiaries are inextricably related. We cannot understand "them" until we know "what we are" and why we are helping. In *La beneficencia,* Arenal gives a comprehensive history of institutional service to the needy in Spain, from earliest times to the end of the past century. She clarifies the terms "beneficence," "philanthropy," "charity," and defines the latter as a necessity theoretically based on moral obligation, a sort of noblesse oblige: Those who are better off than others have a duty to help.

Arenal proposes that not everyone is suited for every type of service; people should serve in capacities for which they are specially suited. She herself was government visitor of women's prisons and ministered to the poor, but she also inspired others by her writing. Her model for selected service based on interest and talents can be contrasted to that which emerges in San Ignacio de Loyola's *Autobiografía*. He exemplifies a rather different type of service, of the individual ready to minister to whatever need presents itself. Both texts invite discussion about women's charity in the past century and religious vs. lay service.

Much like Robert Bellah (1996) today, Arenal sees service as a habit that can be cultivated. She points out the need for division of work, organization, communication between local and national agencies, and publicity in the press. She offers practical suggestions regarding welfare reform, role of women, and legislation. For the individual case worker, she has lots of practical advice, from how to dress to how not to become discouraged, what to do when our help is not successful, how to work with members of the opposite sex, and how to be realistic in expectations.

For students whose primary emphasis is literature, there is much to study in Arenal's books, notably her clever manipulation of legal style to convince, exhort, and question the system (Irizarry 1995).

A New Reading of an Old Text

How the service-learning experience affects the reading process and results in a complex reading, as László postulates, is illustrated in the following classroom experience with *Torquemada en la hoguera* (1889), by Benito Pérez Galdós, Spain's foremost 19th-century novelist. This is a well-known work that can be found in many anthologies and studied on diverse levels, from secondary school through graduate school. It is the story of Torquemada, an avaricious widowed landlord who shows no mercy toward those who owe him money and bargains with God for the recovery of Valentín, his genius son stricken with meningitis. His friend, a defrocked priest, speaks to him of "Humanity" as a deity to be appeased, and Torquemada then tries to undertake charitable acts, which are only somewhat so. On the verge of giving his coat to a shivering pauper on the street, he goes home to get an old coat instead. He forgoes collecting rent from a consumptive artist, but takes some of his paintings as mementos. In conversation with Tía Roma, an old beggar who has lived off scraps from Torquemada's table, he offers to donate a pearl to the Virgin of the poor. Tía Roma upbraids him for his misguided efforts to "buy" his son's life and predicts that if Valentín did survive, the miser would return to his bad habits. The child dies, and the disconsolate Torquemada vows to be meaner than ever.

In my experience of reading the novel many times in courses during the past 30 years, students invariably see Torquemada as deserving of blame for his lack of charity, suggested in the name he bears, that of one of the cruelest Inquisitors of Spanish history. To my utter surprise, students in the service-learning course had a completely new perspective. They did not blame Torquemada, but rather Tía Roma! Why would they find fault with this poor beggar, who had known nothing but poverty her whole life and who had herself helped Torquemada's family, as they too suffered privations because of his avarice? The students — without exception — censured Tía Roma because she did not encourage Torquemada's change of heart but rather predicted his failure — a self-fulfilling prophecy. People can discover service to others at any point in their lives, they argued, and if they are not given encouragement, they are likely to fall back on self-preoccupation. Tía Roma turned down the charity Torquemada offered her and told him the pearl would be useless to the Virgin, but the old miser was acting on what he thought was charity and needed help, not chiding.

The service experience of the students undoubtedly brought to the fore an aspect of the reading that a disinterested academic reading of the text would not reveal. Some of them were doing community service for the first time. The course itself served as their encouragement, as did their contacts with each other. Without support, they argued, how could anyone change?

This in turn led to discussions about whether some people are naturally disposed to altruistic behavior, whereas others discover it at some point in their lives. Was it too late for Torquemada, who was already deeply entrenched in self-serving behavior? Concepción Arenal's essays suggest, rather, that it is something that can be learned with practice. Students cited other readings that contributed examples of sudden conversion: San Ignacio in his autobiography, the saint protagonist of Ayala's story, and Don Quijote's conversion as he approached 50. These readers were able to discover connections among the texts they had read as easily as a computer does among links in a hypertext program. This was certainly an example of the type of complex comprehension based on experiential cognitive schemata that László posits.

Galdós's novel proved particularly illuminating to a student who had complained about having to work alongside people sentenced to community service as a punishment. This was a very committed young lady who had done extensive work in her home community before coming to the university, where she had been admitted to the Alpha Phi Omega national service fraternity. She decried the fact that the motivation of those obligated to do service was not unselfish, as was her own. Torquemada's conduct brought up the whole question of motivation for, after all, he was doing good as a quid pro quo. This student's reflective essay focused on whether the motivation of the doer was really a factor. The motive for doing charitable service doesn't really matter, she reasoned, when there is so much need. After all, the important thing is that the pauper received a cape and the consumptive artist a reprieve and some hope. Posing this question to the entire class, an instructor can insert discussion of the novel squarely into the theoretical framework of the course by providing a graphic illustration of prosocial behavior as opposed to altruism.

Conclusion

If, on the one hand, as László demonstrates, experience prepares readers for complex understanding of texts, it is logical to conclude also that reading prepares them for experience. The role of reading in the formation of ideas and character is a factor recognized implicitly in pedagogy. It is implicit in moralist literature of all times. Proof of this is the protonovel in Spanish, in which Alonso Quijano el Bueno transforms himself into Don Quijote, inspired by the novels of chivalry he has been reading. The debate about whether violence on television fosters violence in life is another example. It would be cynical to say that only violence inspires action but not the literary experience of altruism.

The readings for this course do not suppose or propose a return to didactic literature but rather the idea that there is in reading simultaneous energy that goes in both ways, making it possible, in the case of altruism, that (1) the person who has practiced altruism sees more in the text than other readers who do not (as László proposes) and that (2) the text can reinforce or inspire altruistic feelings in the reader. The result is an accommodation of reader and text that enriches the former and helps him or her to develop as a human being in both academic and service settings.

References

Bellah, R.N., R. Madson, W.M. Sullivan, A. Swidler, and S.M. Tipton. (1996). *Habits of the Heart: Individualism and Commitment in American Life.* Berkeley, CA: University of California Press.

Hatcher, J.A., and R.G. Bringle. (June 20-24, 1996). "Reflection Activities for the College Classroom." Indiana University Purdue University Indianapolis, Office of Service-Learning.

Irizarry, E. (1998). "Concepción Arenal and the Essay of Advocacy: The Medium Is the Message." In *Spanish Women Writers and the Essay: Gender, Politics, and the Self.* Edited by K. Glenn and M. Masquiarán de Rodríguez, pp. 6-24. Columbia, MO: University of Missouri Press.

――――. (1995). "Weighing the Evidence: Legal Discourse in the 19th-Century Spanish Feminist Concepción Arenal." *Computers and the Humanities* 29: 363-374.

————. (1993). "Concepción Arenal." In *Spanish Women Writers: A Bio-Bibliographical Source Book*. Edited by L. Gould Levine, E. Engelson Marson, and G. Feiman Waldman, pp. 44-53. Westport, CT: Greenwood Press.

Kohn, A. (1990). *The Brighter Side of Human Nature: Altruism and Empathy in Everyday Life*. New York, NY: Basic Books.

László, J. (1992). "The Psychology of Literature: A Socio-Cognitive Approach." In *Emerging Visions of the Aesthetic Process: Psychology, Semiology, and Philosophy*. Edited by G.C. Cupchik and J. László, pp. 210-226. Cambridge, NY: Cambridge University Press.

Mussen, P. (1983). "Introduction." In *The Nature of Prosocial Development: Interdisciplinary Theories and Strategies*. Edited by D.L. Bridgeman, pp. 1-7. New York, NY: Academic Press.

Nagel, T. (1978). *The Possibility of Altruism*. Princeton, NJ: Princeton University Press.

Palmer, G.H. (1920). *Altruism: Its Nature and Varieties; The Bly Lectures for 1917-18*. New York, NY: Charles Scribner's Sons.

Rice, R.E. (Spring 1991). "The New American Scholar: Scholarship and the Purpose of the University." *Metropolitan Universities*: 7-18.

Schank, C., and R.P. Abelson. (1977). *Scripts, Plans, Goals and Understandings*. Hillsdale, NJ: Erlbaum.

Smetana, J., D.L. Bridgeman, and E. Turiel. (1983). "Differentiation of Domains and Prosocial Behavior." In *The Nature of Prosocial Development: Interdisciplinary Theories and Strategies*. Edited by D.L. Bridgeman, pp. 163-183. New York, NY: Academic Press.

Yanes, J.M. (1992). "Comprehensible Input via Culture-Schema: Preparation and Inspiration for Literary Study." *Hispania* 75: 1348-1354.

Learning the Basics of Spanish Translation: Articulating a Balance Between Theory and Practice Through Community Service

by Carmen Lizardi-Rivera

Assessing the adequacy of English-to-Spanish translations made available to the general public in the state of California is a task that, unfortunately, almost always unveils a rather dismaying picture. It is not uncommon to encounter signs such as the following bilingual announcement, displayed at the parking lot of a church in downtown San José, California:

> For food and clothing: park in white spaces only, or on the street.
> Por comida o ropa: poneis sus carros en los espacios blancos solamente.

Similarly awkward language is used to instruct bus passengers to yield their seats to the elderly and the handicapped:

> A la requesta del operador u otra persona autorizada favor de ceder los ascientos asi marcados para personas mayores de edad y fisicamente impedidas.

Yet another example is found in a flyer announcing an international film festival. It advertises "bolentos" for only $10 and a reception afterwards:

> Fiesta con alimento proveido y entretenimiento Flamenco siguen en el club Hi-Fi.

Finally, a health clinic asks patients to sign next to the following clauses to authorize release of their medical history and other information on work-related injuries:

> Con esta firma:
> • Yo dare el permiso para liberar toda mi informacion medica pertinente sobre mi abilidad para trabajar a mi empleado.
> • Yo dare el permiso para liberar todos mis documentos medicos que pertenesen a esta herida o lastimada.
> • Yo estoy de acuerdo que toda la informacion que he escrito es verdad y correcta a mi mejor conocimiento.

In all four of the examples cited above, (1) written accent marks have been consistently left out, (2) nonexistent Spanish words have been used that require knowledge of English to understand the source of the language interference (e.g., requesta), and (3) existing Spanish words have been used in ways that can severely hinder communication (e.g., "mi abilidad para trabajar a mi empleado").

After considering the frequent occurrence of such problematic translations, one can arrive at at least two conclusions. First, in this country there is a lack of respect for Spanish readers. Since severely faulty or "ugly and unfaithful" translations (to use Child's 1992 terminology) only ensure communication problems, making these available to the public implies that the sponsoring agencies don't really care about whether the intended message is clearly delivered to the Spanish-reading individual.

The second, more obvious conclusion is that qualified translators are not being hired in most cases. Instead, agencies are relying on employees who are not language specialists. The so-called translators may be chosen simply because they have been heard speaking Spanish at the workplace or, even worse, based solely on the fact that they have a Spanish surname! In either case, several incorrect assumptions are made by the employer, the first one being that bilingualism is a monolithic concept (i.e., that all bilingual speakers are equally competent in all domains of both languages; see Valdés 1997 for a thorough discussion of what she calls the "bilingual range"). The second assumption is that good translations result automatically when an individual with some knowledge of both languages is asked to render a text from the source language into the target language.

The Need for Service-Learning Projects in the Field of Translation

The scenario described in the previous section clearly constitutes fertile ground for service-learning projects. Not only does the community need translations of better quality, but classroom learners need to become aware and critical of the poor quality of the translations made available to the general public. Moreover, learners need to literally get their hands dirty with a real-life translation project to realize just how demanding and serious the responsibility of translating a text is. One must not forget that, in the near future, these learners may either be asked to translate for a public or private agency, or may themselves be employers in need of translation services. If they have, at least, been exposed to the basics of the translation process, they will most likely be in the position of being better translators or decision makers regarding whom to hire or how much money to allocate in the budget to ensure that a good translator is hired.

With this in mind, I developed a plan to engage the participants of the upper-division Basics of Translation class at San José State University in one or more community service projects, starting in the spring of 1996. The goals intended were twofold: to provide both technical training on the phases of the translation process and a real-life experience in translating for a worthy cause.

The Translators and Their Projects

From the beginning of the semester, participants in the class were asked to reach out into their communities and select agencies or individuals (1) who needed translations that would somehow benefit the local Spanish-speaking community and (2) who, for one reason or another, were not able to afford paying for those translation services. Learners were thus made responsible for laying the foundations for the project and for being the decision makers in the process.

This had an empowering effect in several ways. First, it made learners identify, assess, and become committed to a specific area of need within their communities. Second, by selecting an agency and negotiating with the contact person, learners became liaisons between their communities and the class. Within the class, all individuals were responsible for ensuring fair distribution of the workload and for contributing to problem-resolution discussions when necessary.

In the spring of 1996, four translation projects were selected. The class consisted of 33 students, most of whom were native speakers of Spanish, born and raised in the United States. One of the students worked at a day care center seeking accreditation by the National Academy of Early Childhood Programs. As part of the process, the center needed to compile evaluative feedback from parents, many of whom spoke only or mostly Spanish. A 16-item questionnaire needed to be translated, along with an extensive 30-item assessment of how the day care program had been implemented.

The second project was proposed by a student whose mother worked for Los Alamitos Elementary School in San José. The materials to be translated consisted of a series of letters and handouts to be sent to the Spanish-speaking parents of students attending the school. These materials included handouts on disciplinary rules, uniform policy, library check-out procedures, and the code of ethics for volunteers.

A third student worked for the P.A.S.S. (Portable Assisted Study Sequence) Program, which serves migrant students in Grades 9-12 throughout the state of California, and whose main purpose is lowering school desertion rates among children of migrant families. A 40-page information manual needed to be translated to serve as a guide in implementing the program, and also as a reference tool for administrators, counselors, and teachers. Areas covered included the curriculum, teaching and grading techniques, cooperative vs. individualized learning, the writing process, and test-taking strategies.

The fourth project was identified by a learner who knew a teacher at Fischer Middle School in San José, who was in the process of adapting a Spanish version of the book *Stories We Brought With Us* (1986). The class translated nine chapters, each of which included stories from different parts of the world, along with accompanying vocabulary, grammar, and writing exercises.

In the spring of 1997, the class consisted of 25 individuals, approximately half of whom were native speakers of Spanish, born and raised in the United States. This time, the students focused on two projects. Thirteen of them translated fact sheets featuring the animals that live at the Alum Rock Center in San José. The remaining 12 students translated a series of tests for the Mid-Peninsula Support Network for Battered Women in Mountain View. (One of the students did voluntary work for this organization.) The materials consisted of self-help handouts, information on Family Court services (restraining orders, child custody, visitation, etc.), and informative readings on the behavioral patterns of victims and perpetrators of domestic violence.

The Logistics of Selecting the Projects

Some considerations need to be taken into account when selecting such projects. While some factors are intrinsic to the texts themselves, others relate more to classroom logistics. Intrinsic to the texts to be translated are length (due partly to time constraints) and complexity. When translating texts about specialized topics, one needs to ensure that students can gain sufficient understanding of the subject by referring to glossaries, materials and contact persons, previously existing translations of related texts, and so forth. The students who translated the materials on domestic violence exemplify this situation, since they were able to acquire sufficient command of the topic after consulting a series of dictionaries of legal terms such as "restraining order," "hearing," and "in pauperis petition."

Students who translated the fact sheets about the animals at the Alum Rock Center also had to look in several dictionaries and encyclopedias to find Spanish translations for names such as Banana slug, Mexican red-knee tarantula, Western diamondback rattlesnake, Gopher snake, and so on. Since some of these animals are only native to the United States, common Spanish names were not found in any of the sources consulted. This problem was solved with feedback from the contact person at the Alum Rock Center, who stated that in the scientific community, Latin nomenclature is considered the most unambiguous identification label. For this reason, all translations featured the Latin name, as well as some generic translation or brief explanatory sentence to compensate for the lack of a Spanish equivalent for the common name in English. In the case of the Banana slug, for instance, the students used the generic word *babosa* and added a sentence that read: "Por su color y su forma se parece a una banana y por eso en inglés se le llama *Banana slug*."

Among the logistic factors that influence project selection are the length of the academic term (quarter, semester), the number of students in the class, their proficiency in Spanish, and the amount of their previous exposure to translation. In the case of quarter-long courses, projects should be short and feasible (e.g., letters or handouts). One important consideration to keep in mind is that projects need not consist of a first-time translation of a text, but may instead involve editing a faulty, existing translation or completing one that has not yet been finished.

Regardless of the length of the school term, the number of students in the class is an important variable, since larger classes can translate higher volumes of work. Nonetheless, much depends on the learners' proficiency in Spanish. Since individuals translate better into their native tongue, in the translation classroom it is most efficient to have a combination of native and non-native learners working in teams. The type of feedback that both parties give each other is really valuable because, overall, their linguistic strengths differ in systematic ways. For instance, while the native learner of Spanish is instrumental in ensuring idiomatic fluency and correct use of grammar, the non-native learner's contribution in pointing out accent and spelling problems is very helpful. This, in turn, facilitates the instructor's task of correcting the translation, since more attention can be paid to mistakes of a more subtle and sophisticated nature and to the overall quality of the translation.

Before Translating: Preparatory Readings on Translation

Prior to engaging in the actual translation projects, learners should be given sufficient background reading on the phases in the translation process, as well as some practice in translating short texts and editing faulty translations found in the community (see examples cited on the first page of this article). Since it is important that the final product be of good quality, approximately half of the school term should be devoted to preparing the translators. In other words, the importance of training should not be underestimated. For this purpose, several short and relatively simple readings in the theory and practice of translation should be thoroughly discussed. The following has proved very helpful to the Basics of Translation students at San José State University:

• Valentín García Yebra's *Teoría y práctica de la traducción* (1984), chapters 3-4, pp. 30-33, and chapter 6, pp. 40, 42-43

• Leonel de la Cuesta's *Nociones preliminares de traductología* (1987), pp. 35-36

• Jack Child's (1992) *Introduction to Spanish Translation* (pp. 15-17, 26-28, and 150-153)

García Yebra discusses two phases in the translation process; namely, comprehension of the original text and expression of that message in the target language. He states that although comprehension is a *sine qua non* condition for a good translation, by itself it is only a stepping stone in the translation process. He also discusses the differences between an average reader and a translator-reader. Finally, he addresses the concept of "equivalencia funcional"; namely, striving to achieve the same effect on the readers of a translation as the original text had on its readers. He concludes with the following golden rule for translators:

> *La regla de oro para toda traducción es, a mi juicio, decir todo lo que dice el original, no decir nada que el original no diga, y decirlo todo con la corrección y naturalidad que permita la lengua a la que se traduce.* (1984: 43)

> *(Translation) The golden rule for translation is, to my knowledge, to say everything the original says, not to say anything the original does not say, and say everything as naturally and correct as the language to which it is translated allows it.*

Jack Child's discussion (1992: 15-17) addresses similar concerns by presenting — in a very accessible way — two theoretical models for the translation process; namely, that of Larson (1984) and Nida (1975). Child (1992: 150-153) goes more into the actual logistics of the translation process by discussing eight practical phases. Phase 1 (preparation) involves a "quick scan" to determine whether the text and/or the deadline are within the translator's capabilities. During this phase the following factors are also defined: (1) the type of text (medical, literary, etc.), (2) the prime reader (sociolinguistic profile of intended reader), and (3) the possible need for special materials or consultation with experts. Also during this phase, the translator should investigate whether a previous translation of the text exists.

Phase 2 in the translation involves what Child calls "an initial close reading" that may entail reading the text several times to ensure full comprehension. Attention should be given not only to the deep meaning of the text but also to its style. In Phase 3, the translator may have to spend some time doing research. Because of the nature of the text, it may be necessary to read background material on the topic, preferably texts published in both original and target languages, including previous translations of the text in question. Child's Phase 4 is optional, since the translator may or may not need to rewrite portions of the original text, such as "implicit information that is not needed in the SL [source language] but will be needed in the TL [target language] translation" (151).

Phase 5, translation into a first draft, is "the heart of the process" in which units of meaning are carried over to the target language without one's bothering too much to polish the translation or to get rid of typographical errors. Child cautions: "If you do spend too much time on polishing and seeking the best possible phrase, you will lose the continuity of your effort and the train of thought of the deep meaning" (1992: 151-152). After letting the first draft rest for a few days, the translator then comes back to it during Phase 6, when she or he is to look for "a reasonable balance between faithfulness to the original (accuracy) and naturalness (style and readability in the TL)" (152). The translator is supposed to put herself or himself in the shoes of the prime reader and, if possible, should have a second person read the translation.

During Phase 7, the translator edits and produces a camera-ready, final draft containing no typographic errors or other inconsistencies. Finally, Phase 8 constitutes the stage in which the translation is certified or notarized, if necessary. At this point, the translator is encouraged to keep a copy of her or his work, mainly for protection "should it get lost or be challenged" (153).

All the possible outcomes of an actual translation project are presented by Child in the very helpful "Beautiful-Faithful Matrix" (1992: Fig. 4.2, pp. 26-27), which features four possibilities: (1) beautiful-faithful (the ideal case), (2) beautiful-unfaithful (i.e., "favors the esthetic element over accuracy and may be justified in translating poetry and literature"), (3) ugly-faithful ("favors accuracy over esthetics, and may be justified in translating scientific, technical or commercial material"), and finally (4) ugly-unfaithful (the worst and, it is hoped, most rare type of translation). Child reminds the reader: "Translations are like lovers: the faithful are not beautiful and the beautiful are not faithful."

Citing Katharina Reiss's work (1976),[1] Child also presents a useful, three-way classification of texts: informative, expressive, and operative. The emphasis of informative texts is on accuracy (science, business, etc.); in the case of expressive texts, esthetics and emotional impact are the main focus (creative works of literature); and finally, the purpose of operative texts is to convince the reader (e.g., advertising). To prepare students to identify texts according to this taxonomy, one can ask them to bring samples to class of what they think would be most representative for each category. After discussing them in groups of three to four students, each team then chooses the best example of each category and presents it to the class. The class chooses the best representatives from all the teams and proceeds to do a translation (at home) of the text selected. Finally, the translation is discussed in detail by the class as a whole.

As for the reading by de la Cuesta, it touches on the importance of determining the profile of the prime reader for whom the translation is intended. De la Cuesta establishes three categories to aide in this process: mediate vs. immediate, specified/specifiable vs. unspecified/unspecifiable, and homogeneous vs. heterogeneous (1987: 35-36). The immediate reader is the one who personally commissions the translation for his or her own use. (All other readers would fall within the "mediate" category.) As for the specified/specifiable vs. unspecified/unspecifiable feature, the criterion is whether the identity of the prime reader is known or inferable to the translator. Finally, the homogeneous vs. heterogeneous dyad asks if the readership is uniform in terms of traits such as gender, educational level, social class, and dialect.

De la Cuesta uses a helpful example to illustrate his classification: If someone requests a translation of a handbook on how to extinguish fires and the intended readers are all the firefigthers living in Spanish-speaking countries, then the prime reader is mediate, specified, and heterogeneous. Since the firefighters themselves are not commissioning the translation, they are mediate readers. Because they can be identified based on their profession, they are specified readers. They are, nonetheless, a heterogeneous group because they differ in the dialects of Spanish that they speak and may also differ in other aspects, such as level of education. Although in most cases the readership falls within the heterogeneous category, it is important that the translator determine in what ways and to what extent there is heterogeneity in the intended readership.

Putting the Readings Into Practice

Students should be given class time to meet with their teams and to perform the following tasks: (1) make a list of all the members of the group and their phone numbers (to be photocopied for each member), (2) make photocopies of the entire text to be translated so that each member can have a master copy, (3) divide the text to be translated among themselves in an equitable way, and (4) fill out the text profile sheet entitled "Descripción del texto que se va a traducir" (reproduced at the end of this essay).

The text profile worksheet is meant to ensure that students go through Child's Phases 1-3. The information requested on this sheet is of two types: descriptive (for text identification purposes) and analytical (crucial for the actual translation process). The first type includes facts such as the name and telephone number of the contact person within the organization or group that requested the translation, the number of pages to be translated, whether a previous translation exists, and a brief description of the thematic nature and purpose of the text.

In light of what they discover about their prime readers, students give preliminary answers to such questions as (1) whether it would be necessary to modify lexical choice or the structural complexity of the sentences in the translation, (2) whether the original text contains explicit information that would not need to be made explicit in the translation (due to the prime reader's cultural background or knowledge of the topic), (3) whether the original text implicitly presents information to be made explicit, and finally (4) whether it would be necessary to consult special reference materials to accomplish the translation task (and if yes, which materials).

The Outcome: Multiple Drafts

After learners complete a first draft translation of the text assigned to them, small groups of three to four individuals (strategically arranged by the instructor) engage in peer editing. Very specific guidelines are provided to lead learners through the process (see "Guidelines to Edit a Classmate's Draft" at the end of this essay). These guidelines constitute what could be called a checklist to ensure coverage of key grammar points and pitfalls in English-to-Spanish translation, such as the overuse of personal and possessive pronouns, the passive construction, and gerunds. Within each group, every individual reads everyone else's translations and gives feedback, as specified by the guidelines. In addition to receiving written feedback, team members have an entire class period to meet with their classmates and explain their suggestions, and ask or answer questions.

Using their classmates' feedback, learners prepare a second draft of the translation and turn in both the first and the revised versions to the instructor. The instructor compares the two drafts, and attentively looks at how closely the learners have followed the suggestions given by their classmates. Further suggestions and corrections are made by the instructor, who in turn asks for a third draft. At this point, it is technically possible for the next draft to achieve camera readiness, since all corrections have been explicitly noted on the second draft by the instructor.

Third drafts are turned in along with the second draft, and this facilitates the correction process for the instructor because it is merely a question of verifying whether specific items have been corrected. My experience in the Basics of Translation class is that it takes most learners a fourth draft to achieve a camera-ready version. At that point, one of the team members collects from each person a disk copy containing that individual's final draft. The person in charge of collecting the disks is in turn responsible for arranging all the individual documents into a whole that should correspond to the ordering in the original.

A printout is then given to the instructor, who reads the entire text again, looking not only for typographical mistakes but also for fluency, functional equivalence, and naturalness. Students are graded individually, based on thoroughness and attention to detail in their own work and in their class-mates' drafts; adherence to deadlines given; and the quality of the final product.

Finally, the instructor sends the translations (paper and disk copies) to the agencies that requested them, along with a letter specifying the names of the translators, their contribution to the project, and a brief description of the conditions under which the final product was completed. Unfortunately, past experience shows that a very low number of agencies actually acknowledge receipt of the translation and express gratitude to the translators. The ones who do, however, are very thoughtful in showing their gratefulness. For instance, in the spring of 1997, Ms. Barbara Schneider, at the Alum Rock Center, arranged to have a reception at the Nature Center for all participants in the class as a token of appreciation for their hard work.

Possible Drawbacks: Some Suggestions

Some difficulties may be encountered when pursuing service-learning projects in the field of translation. First, peer editing may not be effective if the teams are not well-structured. Strategic attention should be paid to the makeup of the teams, considering not only the participants' Spanish language proficiency (i.e., balanced ratio of native to non-native speakers) but also their personality and aptitudes (e.g., motivation and disposition to work, attention to detail).

Deadlines may also be a source of difficulty. Since the first half of the school term is spent on translator training, successful completion of the project requires strict adherence to a timetable. This is also crucial given the configuration of the project; namely, its sequentially arranged stage format and the number of collaboration techniques used throughout. Especially in the peer-editing stage, it is imperative that a strong emphasis be placed on timeliness. A possible scenario to avoid is the following: Learner X reads learners Y's and Z's translations, providing helpful and timely feedback to both, but either Y or Z (or both in the worst case) fails to do the same; thus X can't turn in his or her second draft to the instructor by the assigned date. Making it explicit that timeliness is a part of the grade is very important to ensure smooth working conditions, both for students and for the instructor.

On a more technical level, the issue of computers can play a role. Members of each team should agree on the type of computer and software package to be used, and even decide on a style format (font, size, page and footnote numbering, headers, and so on). The use of diacritic marks (accent, tilde, exclamation and question signs) is also crucial. (It should be noted that some or all diacritics can be lost when software translator programs are used.) If a plan is developed and followed by all team members, the person who will eventually collect all disks and merge all documents into one will be saved a considerable amount of time and effort.

Conclusion

Communities with large Hispanic populations in the United States constitute fertile ground for service-learning projects in the field of English-to-Spanish translation. These projects not only serve to fulfill a great need for good translations in the community but also serve as empowerment tools for the community itself to pursue a plan of action in collaboration with the university.

The pedagogical program outlined in this paper aims directly at addressing the inadequacy of two strongly held assumptions; namely, that bilingualism is a monolithic concept and that bilingual individual equals good translator. With step-by-step training on the fundamentals of translation theory, learners develop an informed awareness and test the theory's validity through firsthand experience in their actual projects.

By choosing their projects and dividing the workload among them, learners have an opportunity to show initiative and creativity while developing a truly motivated commitment to their local communities. Through peer editing, native and non-native speakers of Spanish learn from one another, using their differences in language proficiency as a source of union, rather than division or competitiveness. Finally, by turning in multiple drafts of their translations, participants also learn to pay attention to detail and professionalism in the delivery of a product.

Note

1. This reference is in turn cited in Marilyn Gaddis Rose's (1981) *Translation Spectrum: Essays in Theory and Practice* (Albany, NY: State University of New York).

References

Child, Jack. (1992). *Introduction to Spanish Translation*. Lanham, MD: University Press of America.

De la Cuesta, Leonel Antonio. (1987). *Nociones preliminares de traductología*. Mexico D.F., Mexico: Ediciones Guayacán.

García Yebra, Valentín. (1984). *Teoría y práctica de la traducción*. Vol I, 2nd ed. Madrid: Editorial Gredos.

Kasser, Carol, and Ann Silverman. *Stories We Brought With Us.* 2nd ed. Englewood Cliffs, NJ: Prentice-Hall.

Larson, Mildred. (1984). *Meaning-Based Translation.* Lanham, MD: University Press of America.

Nida, Eugene A. (1975). *Language, Structure and Translation.* Stanford, CA: Stanford University Press.

Valdés, Guadalupe. (1997). "The Teaching of Spanish to Bilingual Spanish-Speaking Students: Outstanding Issues and Unanswered Questions." In *La enseñanza del español a hispanohablantes: praxis y teoría.* Edited by M. Cecilia Colombi and Francisco X. Alarcón, pp. 8-44. Boston, MA: Houghton Mifflin.

Descripción del texto que se va a traducir (Description of the Text to Be Translated)

Título: _____

Autor: _____

¿Existe una traducción previa de este trabajo?   SI__ NO__

Número total de páginas del proyecto: _____

Naturaleza del texto (tema o de qué se trata, propósito):

Material a cargo de cada traductor (especificar número de páginas, título de las secciones, los capítulos, etc.).

¿Será necesario usar algún diccionario, glosario o material de referencia especial para este trabajo? SI__ NO__
Si contestó que "SI", especifique:

Nombre y teléfono de la persona que proveyó el texto y con la cual el grupo se comunicará para consultar dudas:

Caracterización del "prime reader" (usar De la Cuesta, pp. 35-37 y Child, pp. 199-200)
¿Quién encargó la traducción? _____
¿Cuál es el destinatario final ("prime reader") del texto?
Lector mediato ____ inmediato ____ EXPLIQUE

Lector homogéneo __ heterogéneo__ EXPLIQUE (Tomar en consideración el nivel de educación, la edad, ocupación, conocimiento del texto que se traducirá, grado de bilingüismo, dialecto (e.g., ¿lo leerán personas de diferentes países?)).

De acuerdo a lo que contestaron en la pregunta anterior, ¿será necesario hacer adaptaciones especiales en las siguientes áreas? Si ése es el caso, especifique lo más posible.

Selección de vocabulario

Selección de construcciones gramaticales

Información explícita que se debe eliminar porque resultaría demasiado redundante, dado el trasfondo cultural del destinatario

Información implícita que se debe hacer explícita porque no resultaría clara, dado el trasfondo cultural del destinatario

¿Será necesario añadir notas al calce, un glosario o algún otro comentario explicativo?

Guía para corregir el borrador del compañero (Guidelines to Edit a Classmate's Draft)

Nombre del traductor: _____

Nombre del que corrige: _____

• Tiene problemas con la comprensión del mensaje del texto.	Sí ___ No ___
• Usa los pronombres personales demasiado (Recuerde que en inglés es obligatorio que cada verbo tenga sujeto explícito (e.g., he/she/we), pero que en español no es así (e.g., habla, canta, dormimos.)	Sí ___ No ___
• Usa la forma o voz pasiva demasiado	Sí ___ No ___
• Usa los artículos incorrectamente (los usa cuando no hay que usarlos o vice versa; usa el artículo definido en lugar del indefinido o vice versa)	Sí ___ No ___
• Usa los pronombres posesivos demasiado (e.g., El se puso sus guantes.)	Sí ___ No ___
• Usa anglicismos y/o falsos cognados	Sí ___ No ___
• Traduce literalmente las expresiones idiomáticas	Sí ___ No ___
• Problemas con el uso de las preposiciones (e.g., por/para; anglicismos --> look *for* = buscar Ø preposición)	Sí ___ No ___
• Posición incorrecta de los adjetivos (e.g., una gran ciudad vs. una ciudad grande)	Sí ___ No ___
• No es consistente con el uso de "Ud." o "tú" (puede haber problemas con otros pronombres: por ejemplo, si empieza a hablar en singular y luego usa el plural)	Sí ___ No ___
• Usa el gerundio (e.g., comiendo, durmiendo, etc.) en lugar del infinitivo (e.g., comer, dormir, etc.)	Sí ___ No ___
• Mezcla los registros al usar palabras muy informales junto con palabras muy formales. (Usa palabras de la lengua hablada que no se usan normalmente en la lengua escrita: e.g., nomás)	Sí ___ No ___
• El orden de las palabras no es natural o no fluye bien.	Sí ___ No ___

2 -- Guía para corregir el borrador del compañero

• Tiene dificultad al conjugar los verbos   Sí ___ No ___
    (terminaciones incorrectas porque no selecciona el tiempo verbal
    apropiado o porque no sabe conjugar el verbo)

• Deletrea las palabras incorrectamente   Sí ___ No ___
    (incluyendo los acentos y el uso de minúsculas y mayúsculas)

• Problemas con errores de mecanografía.   Sí ___ No ___

Otros comentarios, además de los que ya haya escrito Ud. directamente en el borrador del compañero:

Raising Cultural Awareness Through Service-Learning in Spanish Culture and Conversation: Tutoring in the Migrant Education Program in Salem

by Patricia Varas

The following paper discusses raising cultural awareness through service-learning by addressing several specific areas. My findings indicate that through service-learning students not only increase their language competence and confidence but also develop positive relationships with the children in the Latino community. It proves itself to be a key instrument in helping students bridge the gap between abstract/theoretical learning and experiential processes to develop analytical thinking and promote personal growth.

I have organized this article in several sections to give an overview of my successes and struggles in meeting the needs of my students in Spanish Conversation and Culture through the adoption of service-learning.

Willamette University and Service-Learning: A Brief History

Willamette University (WU) is a small private liberal arts college in the Northwest. Willamette has a well-developed Community Outreach Program (COP) sponsored by the Office of Student Activities that has been responsible for organizing community service projects since 1991. During 1993-94, more than 500 students participated "in short- and long-term community service projects, dedicating more than 16,000 volunteer hours" (Willamette University's Service-Learning Task Force 1994: 9).

In 1993 a team of Willamette University representatives attended the Campus Compact Summer Institute at Boulder, Colorado. This initiative was followed by the creation of a service-learning task force. Among the goals of the task force was integrating of service-learning into the 1994-95 academic curriculum.

Special thanks go to Oregon Campus Compact and its support through a Service-Learning Course Development Mini-Grant; to Irma Dash-Fernández and Dan Coble, both from the Migrant Education Program at the Salem-Keizer Schools; to Professor Robert Hawkinson from Willamette University; to Deborah Maloney for her invaluable comments; and to all my students past and present who have made service-learning a reality.

Hence, when we look at Willamette's history, we can see that it is no stranger to community service. On the contrary, the institution has demonstrated a clear and consistent commitment to such activities. The COP states as its goal "to encourage and facilitate community involvement, in an effort to improve the quality of life for the greater Salem, Oregon, area, and to help the Willamette community become more aware of the needs and issues facing society" (WU 1997). Furthermore, even as the Service-Learning Task Force's statement of purpose emphasizes the important role service-learning could play at Willamette, it also makes us aware of Willamette's historical affinity for community service. If service-learning is not only a program type but also a philosophy of education, that philosophy directly reflects our institution's motto, "Non Nobis Solum Nati Sumus" ("Not Unto Ourselves Alone Are We Born"), and its mission (Willamette "embraces a commitment to service and leadership in our communities and professions").

The Migrant Education Program at Salem-Keizer School District

In the summer of 1996, I applied for and was granted an Oregon Campus Compact Service-Learning Course Development Mini-Grant. This grant allowed me to work more closely with Dan Coble, the instructional assistant in charge of placing students in the Migrant Education Program, acquire materials that could be used in the Migrant Education Program, review our assessment process more thoroughly, fund two workshops on service-learning, and financially support those students who have developed ties with their pupils and would like to invite them to visit Willamette.

The first year I taught Spanish Conversation and Culture (Spanish 332), the Migrant Education Program in the Salem-Keizer School District was brought to my attention by Irma Fernández Dash, the migrant program assistant who supervises its implementation. She described the program and suggested bringing it to Willamette so our students could serve. All the faculty in Spanish (we are a comprehensive Foreign Languages and Literatures Department) reacted positively and announced the program in their classes. Students responded eagerly and soon we had many participants, not only among the upper-division classes but also the lower ones (such as the intermediate Spanish sections).

The Migrant Education Program (MEP) was established by the U.S. Congress in 1966 and is implemented on both national and local levels. Locally, the program in the Salem-Keizer School District has as its mission "to provide supplemental education, guidance services, and support services" to the migrant students enrolled in 40 of the 48 district schools (MEP n.d.: 1). This program is federally funded, and to qualify, K-12 students must belong to migrant families who move "within the state or between states so that their parents may work in agriculture-related occupations. The program serves only children who have moved within the last three years" (MEP n.d.: 3). A migratory child, the recipient of this program, is usually identified and prioritized by the Migrant Education Program as most in need of the services it provides because the child is "failing, or most at risk of failing, to meet the state's content and performance standards" and her or his "education has been interrupted during the regular school year" (Oregon Department of Education 1996: 14). High school students are also included in the program and receive individual tutoring after school at a local community center called *Mano a Mano*.

Teaching Spanish Conversation and Culture

I have been teaching at Willamette for five years. I started teaching Spanish 332, Conversation and Culture, four years ago. This course emphasizes the development of oral and listening skills and knowledge about the culture of Spanish-speaking countries.

Students who enroll in this course have successfully completed the upper division grammar class, ensuring a level of fluency in the target language. At the same time, the students' skills vary immensely and a wide range of fluency is the rule. The course must be able to meet the needs of students who have traveled widely in Latin America or Spain or who might speak Spanish at home and whose language skills are excellent, as well as the needs of students who have never traveled abroad, are shy and feel uncomfortable speaking in the target language.

Because we do not have a standard textbook for this course, instructors have been able to choose and change texts according to their interests, making sections distinct, variable, and dependent on the instructors' interests. This latitude has meant that each instructor has the freedom to implement her or his approach to accomplishing the set goal of "vocabulary building and acquisition of oral communication skills" (WU 1997: 132). Instructors have employed different readings, videos, and exercises to motivate class discussion and have stressed the cultural awareness of Latin America or Spain, according to their backgrounds. We continue to permit such latitude, and so my narrative only describes my experience and does not describe other sections of Spanish Conversation and Culture.

Most texts geared toward initiating class discussion are based on topics of interest such as relations among women and men, the environment, technology in our times, the family, etc. Readings tend to be general and so generic that they almost become abstract in nature. Little is presented about contemporary cultural, political, or social issues that can raise concrete questions about the people we are studying and their history. I believe this can partly be explained by the fact that general topics need less updating and revising and that they may be more attractive for a wider public.

When I originally made an assessment of Spanish 332, I recognized three main issues that I would have to deal with immediately. First, it was necessary to choose a text that would make the "object" of our study — Spanish and Latin American cultures and peoples — not only interesting for the classroom but also a "subject" with which we could interact. Second, I would have to deal with motivation. Many students think that a conversation class means just talking, no written exams, and very few written assignments. Although this assumption is partially true, students soon realize that attendance and class participation are key elements in evaluation: If one does not attend class, one cannot participate! Motivation may be difficult to control, but attendance can be measured and is an important part of the student's grade. Third, I would have to address the problem mentioned above; namely, the varying levels of the students' language skills. The more fluent students might intimidate the less fluent ones and might even dominate class discussion. Through trial and error, I eventually realized that these concerns could all be addressed through a service-learning component.

From the first year I taught Spanish 332, I decided not to have a text. Although this decision potentially could have had some drawbacks, such as copyright concerns and the requirement of more class preparation, I felt that the freedom and spontaneity to develop or choose my own materials were worth the trouble. I have been able, in this way, to update the readings we use in class and to customize them according to the groups' interests and disposition. Furthermore, students have been welcomed and even encouraged to make suggestions and bring their own readings.

I also created working groups as a teaching and learning tool, which displaced learning as an individualistic and competitive activity. The working groups shifted the stress from *the student* to *a group* of peers with diverse skills and needs who had to work together and help each other accomplish their homework and presentations and succeed in the classroom. In this manner, students would have responsibilities not only to the class and themselves — i.e., their grades — but to their group. The members of the working groups would, I hoped, develop a symbiotic relationship in which they would take care of each other, offering support and making sure no one fell behind.

Varying levels of skills among students are a fact all those who teach have to grapple with, especially those of us who teach foreign languages. The working groups also made it possible to deal effectively with this diversity by allowing students to participate in cooperative learning experiences, including exchanging their knowledge openly when preparing oral presentations, discussing and familiarizing each other with the readings before studying them in class, and preparing vocabularies for class.

Implementing Service-Learning in Spanish Conversation and Culture

In the spring of 1995, after attending a workshop on service-learning at Willamette, I decided to formally incorporate my students' work in the Migrant Education Program as part of the Spanish 332 curriculum. The students were expected to serve a minimum of two hours per week and their main goal was to work not as mentors, but as tutors. Together with Irma Fernández Dash, I felt this difference was important to set the tone for the work the students would undertake. Irma's assessment of the program's needs was that the program required students to help instruct migrant children. Thus, the first step in the implementation of a service-learning program — "assessing community needs" (National Center for Service-Learning 1990: 19) — was met: My students would be "on target for the community" by tutoring migrant children.

There are several community service programs at Willamette based on mentoring. In this capacity the student acts as both role model and friend to the mentee, primarily through being a companion in games, walks, and excursions. In contrast to this, the students serving in the Migrant Education Program would not only be role models and companions but would also and primarily serve as tutors who could help migrant children with their homework and aid them with the skills their teachers had targeted as in need of help; for instance, reading or math.

A second question that arises when one implements a service-learning component is how precisely the community experience will benefit one's students. The first and most obvious consideration here was that the tutor would have to use her or his language skills in the target language. In many cases, the Willamette student would have to speak Spanish because the migrant child would not speak English and would have to give the child considerable attention. As we shall see, however, this experience turned out to be far more fruitful than just providing language practice for my students.

Because many students at Willamette participate in extracurricular activities, have part-time jobs and hectic class schedules, or lack transportation, I was concerned to give them ample opportunities to fulfill their compulsory tutoring assignments. From the first day of class, students were warned that tutoring was not a choice and that if they were unable to meet this requirement, they should transfer to the other section. Dan Coble was aware of the students' schedules and transportation limitations and preferences. With this information and his knowledge of the schools most in need of tutors, he was able to offer my students several choices regarding school placement. In this manner, "those being served control[led] the services provided" (Sigmon 1990: 57), while those who served were also in control of their learning environment, customizing it as much as possible to their needs.

Students, overall, enjoyed the experience and found it an eye-opener. Even though they were aware of the existence of a large Latino population, few had ever come into contact with it; service-learning became their chance to learn about and interact with this population. By the end of the semester the students completed their tutoring and received from the program a certificate for their work and a coffee voucher at a well-known establishment in town. All were delighted by these tokens of appreciation, and many cherished their certificates and used them as references when looking for jobs.

I mentioned above that service-learning has become an instrumental tool in addressing some of the problems I singled out: lack of a text and objectification of the subject of study, varying language skills, and student motivation. I have come to realize the full effectiveness of service-learning as a way of dealing with these issues through regular revision of my syllabus over the years that I have taught Spanish 332 (see three examples at the end of this paper). First of all, through service-learning the students come into direct contact with a population largely invisible to them. Many of the students believe that Spanish is a good career language that will concretely help them find better jobs. On the other hand, they have never truly been in touch with the population they intend to serve or work with. Through their work in the Migrant Education Program, students have been able to develop cross-cultural skills and become more sensitive to cultural and class differences. They start interpreting and thinking critically about culture, becoming aware of prejudice, intolerance, and racism in their community and within themselves. By following readings geared to the traditional conversation course, students continue to talk about the Spanish-speaking population as something foreign to them, as an object to be dissected and analyzed. The barrier between *them* and *us* is never crossed; it is simply discussed. Service-learning through the Migrant Education Program takes a step beyond exposure; it actively engages the students (Levison 1990a: 68).

My students' written and oral reactions to their pupils have been enlightening in this respect. They have had to understand that some students refuse to speak English in class because they have an accent and that some young girls are kept away from their classes and peer interaction because their parents are leery they will lose their way and become influenced by "American culture and values." Inevitably, students reflect on their own fears and values; they feel a sense of solidarity with the child who is afraid of being laughed at: Many have been there before. They see the young girls and realize that their culture is as rich as the students' cultures and that there is no reason to culturally colonize the other.

Although I am aware of the debate between elective and required service, I am convinced it should be mandatory in Spanish 332. There was a precedent for this at Willamette, and I believe service has been a key component of my teaching goals and style. I did not want students to view service-learning as the level of giving associated with voluntarism (Levison 1990b: 547). Those students who would not participate in service-learning would, practically speaking, be left at the margins of the class; they would not be part of it and would be missing an important element, just like missing an exam or not handing in an essay. Because the students are given ample opportunity to choose where they want to tutor and what preparatory readings and discussions we conduct in class, I have not had any problems with student support, attendance, or participation. On the contrary, many students have served more than two hours per week and have seemed very excited by their contact with a Latino child. There does not appear to be a negative connotation attached to the mandatory nature of the service, because the program targets a group that is related to our subject of study. Hence, it makes sense to be involved.

I also believe that the student engaged in service-learning tends to give the best of herself or himself. There is an internal shift to incorporate the other and her or his problems because there is a common goal. Thus, the student becomes less self-conscious of language limitations and more willing to use the skills she or he has. In this way, differences of language skills become a secondary issue in tutoring. The student must be able to communicate with her or his pupil, and all tutors are able to do so. The general comment I hear from my students is that their pupils are empowered when they can help their tutors and correct their Spanish. This creates an environment in which every one learns because the authority and power granted by knowledge are actively deconstructed, with both pupil and tutor functioning as learners and teachers.

Hence, we can see how service-learning helps solve many teaching issues in Spanish 332. However, it would be naive to believe that service-learning is a panacea and that it can solve any course predicament by itself. Service-learning must be integrated with the texts, discussions, and assignments conducted in class. On its own, it might be perceived as merely a charitable task that assuages consciences and may or may not raise students' awareness of the real world.

I regard this as my major challenge: to provide the support necessary for service-learning through class activities and readings. It is not enough to make service-learning an important component of the students' final grade. If teachers fail to incorporate service-learning, it could potentially be perceived as an imposition and mechanical requirement that must be satisfied to pass the course. Thus I am continually revising the readings, discussions, videos, and assignments for Spanish 332. I do not think I have yet fully integrated the service-learning component into Spanish 332, but I have made positive changes to achieve this goal.

Three Successful Assignments

I would now like to concentrate on three assignments that have been particularly successful in giving support to the service component in the course. In 1994 students were required to keep a journal in which they captured their thoughts and experiences in working with their pupils in the Migrant Education Program. Even though this work was rewarding, I felt that a large number of students did not make weekly entries but instead wrote what they could before handing in their journals. I also observed considerable variation in the quality or thoughtfulness of the entries. Some students reflected on their experiences and grappled with thoughts and contradictions, while others were satisfied simply to describe their time with their pupils. In 1995 I decided to conduct a brief interview with each student. I felt this was a more thorough form of evaluation and it allowed the students to be more honest about the highlights and shortcomings of the program. It was, however, very time-consuming and students appeared unnecessarily stressed because I required the interviews to be conducted in Spanish.

Thus, this year I decided to have oral presentations or updates in class instead of journals or interviews. In this way, students are able to discuss their feelings and experiences while practicing the target language. I have come to the conclusion that a combination of interviews and presentations might be the best way to develop discipline, analytical thinking, oral and listening skills in the target language, and interaction among the students.

A third assignment I would like to discuss is a combination of readings, video, and homework that is particularly successful in providing the necessary background and preparation for working with migrant children. This year we started the semester with an article on "The American Dream." We studied not only the vocabulary but also the implications of agency and point of view when defining what a dream or aspiration is. Inevitably, the discussion shifted to stereotypes, to cultural values, and to class. The students became aware of immigration in pursue of a better life and its meaning, the shortcomings of the American dream, and the advantages of the other culture.

The next readings were on the indigenous civilizations of Mexico and Central America. We saw a video on the architectural sites in these regions and studied the values these cultures cherished and the disruption and destruction the conquistadors brought with them. We also read a story by the Mexican writer Juan Rulfo, "It Is Because We Are So Poor," that allowed us to reflect on the impact the pre-Columbian past has had in shaping the values of today's Latino community, including the importance of family, land, and religion.

Finally, we watched another video in which the son of a migrant worker tells of his life. He reads a poem about his experiences as a migrant child. Since the vocabulary and the speaking speed were problems for the students, I gave them a copy of the poem so they could follow while the poet reads. Despite these difficulties, the students became more aware of migration patterns and of the migrant presence in many states. They became conscious of the hardship the children they tutor confront daily but seldom talk about. Questions of political identity among Chicanos and Latinos became a focus of discussion.

In response to this material, students had to write a composition on what is attractive about the Latin American culture. Most of them reflected on family values and intimacy, on festivals and food, on these cultures' respect for their elders and the land, and on their lack of materialism. These were elements that the students appreciated and desired to have in their culture. In some cases, however, stereotypes and the image of the other as exotic peoples with primitive beliefs resurfaced.

Overall, these assignments and texts fostered an environment of respect and openness. The students became aware that we are not value free in our judgments and that language acquisition is part of learning a culture. We cannot learn one without the other.

Conclusion

Because I believe that service-learning is not only a form of teaching but also a philosophy of education, my approach to it will continue to fluctuate as I grow and continue learning about this process through trial and error. For me, service-learning can never represent a finished process simply applied year after year to incoming students.

I find that my students have benefited immensely from their service at the Migrant Education Program in the Salem-Keizer School District. The benefits have been not only academic — benefits easy to evaluate and determine — but also personal and ideological — benefits subjective and difficult to assess. I am also aware that the students' level of integration, of self-awareness, and of consciousness of the real world has increased. Class discussions are more active and thoughtful; students are less willing to dismiss the power of stereotypes and more interested in engaging in exchange.

They are surprised at the conditions they find in public school classrooms and at the problems in promoting bilingual education. I should point out that many of my students, after this experience, are inclined to pursue degrees in education with an emphasis on bilingual or English-as-a-second-language education. They can be quite critical of classroom approaches they encounter when they perceive these as being unfair to their migrant pupils. They become quite attached to their pupils and learn about their personal lives and customs. The migrant child ceases to be merely an abstraction or social problem. Thanks to service-learning, the Willamette students in Spanish Conversation and Culture become more inclusive and develop a capacity for deeper personal and cultural rapport.

References

Levison, L.M. (1990a). "Choose Engagement Over Exposure." In *Combining Service and Learning*. Vol. 1. Edited by J.C. Kendall and Associates, pp. 68-75. Raleigh, NC: National Society for Experiential Education.

Levison, Lee M. (1990b). "Required Versus Voluntary: The Great Debate." In *Combining Service and Learning*. Vol. 1. Edited by J.C. Kendall and Associates, pp. 545-549. Raleigh, NC: National Society for Experiential Education.

Migrant Education Program. (n.d.). Migrant education handout. Salem, OR: Author.

National Center for Service-Learning. (1990). "The Service-Learning Educator: A Guide to Program Management." In *Combining Service and Learning*. Vol. 2. Edited by J.C. Kendall and Associates, pp. 17-38. Raleigh, NC: National Society for Experiential Education.

Oregon Department of Education. (1996). *Handbook for Directors of Migrant Education Projects.* Salem, OR: Author.

Sigmon, R. (1990). "Service-Learning: Three Principles." In *Combining Service and Learning*. Vol. 1. Edited by J.C. Kendall and Associates, pp. 56-64. Raleigh, NC: National Society for Experiential Education.

Willamette University. (1997). *College of Liberal Arts Catalogue.* Salem, OR: Author.

Willamette University. (March 25, 1997). Homepage of Willamette University: http://www.willamette.edu/.

Willamette University's Service-Learning Task Force. (1994). *Action Plan, 1994*. Salem, OR: Willamette University.

SPAN 332.01
Spanish Conversation and Culture
(1994)

The main goal of this course is to develop the student's oral and conversational skills. They way to do this is by introducing you to the culture (literature, cinema, music, food, etc.) of Spanish speaking countries.

Class participation and attendance is a must. Also tutoring at the Migrant Program is required.

Grading:

class presentations	35%
class participation	35%
tutoring	20%
journal	10%

All deadlines are final.

SPAN 332.01
Spanish Conversation and Culture
(1995)

The main goal of this course is to develop the student's oral and conversational skills in different context. They way to do this is by introducing you to the culture (literature, cinema, music, food, etc.) of Spanish speaking countries.

Class participation and attendance is a must. Also tutoring at the Migrant Program is required.

Grading:

Group presentation (20 min.)	20%
Homeworks (1 from 1-4 can be rewritten) (5x5%)	25%
Tutoring	25%
Oral Exam	15%
Attendance and Participation	15%

SPAN 332.01
Spanish Conversation and Culture
(1997)

El objectivo principal de este curse es desarrollar la habilidad oral de los estudiantes. Para lograr esto la clase se basa en discusiones sobre lecturas culturales que se llevarán a cabo en clase, presentaciones y tutorías de niños latinos a través del Programa de Educación Migrante en el distrito de Salem.

También se intenta desarrollar la capacidad de lectura de los estudiantes para prepararlos para los cursos superiores de la especialización y del "minor." Es por esto que leeremos con especial detenimiento una obra del escritor colombiana y premio Nóbel, Gabriel García Márquez.

La participación en clase, asistencia y 1-2 horas de tutoría en el Programa Migrante son **obligatorias**.

Grading:
       Tareas (1 de Tarea 1-2 puede ser reescrita) (3x5%)....18%
       Presentación de grupo (20 mins)...............................15%
       Grupos de trabajo de Eréndira...............................20%
       Tutoría 25%
       Examen Oral..12%
       Asistencia y Participación................................10%

Todas las fechas de entrega SON FINALES. Los trabajos entregados tarde recibirán una multa de .5 por día.

Community-Based Language Learning:
Integrating Language and Service

by J. Patrick Boyle and Denise M. Overfield

In an effort to expand traditional classroom space and emphasize the role of both the individual and the institution in off-campus communities, colleges and universities have been working to implement what is known as service-learning in their curricula. A growing number of articles (Hesser 1995; Palmer 1993; Permaul 1993) and journals (*Michigan Journal of Community Service Learning*) attest to this trend in higher education. Service-learning expands on previous experiential educational programs, such as internships, by combining traditional educational goals of intellectual and personal growth with the social value of community service (Berson 1993). Students must think about issues and people, then act on whatever knowledge or attitudes they possess (Permaul 1993).

This paper describes Crossing Borders, a collaborative effort of the Department of Modern Languages and the Student Affairs Division of a small women's college located in the urban setting of Pittsburgh. This project embraced many of the dimensions of a strong service-learning program, including the engagement of students in responsible and challenging actions, the provision of structured opportunities for reflection on the experience, and the matching of service providers and service needs through a process that recognizes changing circumstances. Service-learning adds a different dimension to the academic experience in that students see community service events, which have historically been the realm of student activities, integrated into the formal curriculum.

For the purposes of this paper, we prefer the term "community-based learning" (CBL) to service-learning. The former is a better descriptor of the type of activities used in the project presented here, because we believe it deemphasizes the traditional roles of service provider and service recipient and instead acknowledges all of the participants as coconstructors of the learning that takes place.

Theoretical Background

The learning experiences described in this paper were designed according to the tenets of sociocultural theory and prevailing notions of communicative competence. The latter stems from the research of Hymes (1972), who uses the term "communicative competence" to refer to the general communicative capabilities of an individual. This means that an individual's knowledge of grammar, for instance, includes not only an understanding of grammatical rules but also how those rules are used in speech performance. Canale and Swain (1980) propose a theoretical framework for communicative competence in a foreign or second language. In their work, there are three main competencies: grammatical competence, sociolinguistic competence, and strategic competence. The first of these consists of knowledge of lexical items and rules of phonology, morphology, syntax, and semantics. The second consists of two sets of rules: rules of discourse and sociocultural rules. Sociolinguistic competence focuses on language in use, such as politeness strategies and the ability to interpret utterances for social meaning, as when there is no apparent connection between the literal meaning of an utterance and the speaker's intention (Canale and Swain 1980: 30). Strategic competence refers to the verbal and nonverbal strategies used by an individual to compensate for breakdowns in communication due to insufficient linguistic competence or other variables. Traditionally, linguistic competence has been the focus of the foreign-language classroom, although the incorporation of cognitive theories such as sociocultural theory (see below) have expanded the way language and other subjects are taught in the classroom.

Sociocultural theory is based on the work of Vygotsky (1986) and states that learners develop cognitive processes by using language to mediate their experiences (see Wertsch 1978 for further explanation of this theory). Language is the symbolic tool that we, as learners, use to shape our thoughts and experiences. Given this, social interaction is a crucial factor in learners' development. Hall (1995) points out that all of our practices are sociocultural constructions developed and maintained by the members of the groups to which we belong. As we engage in these practices, we use the knowledge that we develop and share it with other group members. It is this common knowledge that makes group interaction possible (2). Initiating a CBL component in the language classroom expands the definition of what the group is to which we belong.

Foreign-language classrooms, however, are often teacher-centered environments that offer few chances for students to interact with each other. This may be due to a language program's strong emphasis on grammatical accuracy or to a lack of classroom time. In this kind of situation, the instructor may find it difficult to incorporate activities that offer meaningful opportunities for language mediation. The teacher is viewed as the expert, the individual who both knows the language and controls the environment in which it is spoken. Pica (1987) points out that in this kind of environment the students are well aware of inequalities in language ability. They are also aware of inequalities in their needs and obligations as participants in the interaction. The teacher asks most, if not all, of the questions, thus controlling both the nature of the language and the structure of any conversation that may take place, and the students may have little or no chance to actively engage in the development of the interaction. When the students are finally offered an opportunity to interact in a meaningful, realistic way with other learners, they may lack both the skills and confidence necessary to negotiate meaning.

Project Description

To address the above issues and incorporate an interactional perspective in the classroom that encouraged students to participate in both psychosocial and transactional uses of language, as well as expand the institution's use of service-learning to the foreign-language classroom, we sought to develop a CBL project in beginning and intermediate Spanish classes.

Quite by accident, we discovered a small colony of Cuban refugees recently arrived in the city. As newcomers, many spoke little to no English and therefore experienced problems in finding work. In addition, because many had left family and friends behind in Cuba, they felt lonely and isolated. Their sponsoring organization, Catholic Charities, was anxious to help them become more integrated into the community.

Crossing Borders[1] involved eight Introduction to Spanish 2 students and five Intermediate Spanish 2 students. Most of the students at the college come from Pittsburgh or its surrounding areas. Participation in this project was mandatory for the students, and the activities were an integral part of their coursework.

There is no language requirement at the college. According to questionnaires the students filled out at the beginning of the semester, all but two of the students were in the class because they considered Spanish "interesting." All of the students believed that studying Spanish would be useful in their future careers.

Language classes at the college meet three days a week, a schedule that does not allow for intensive interactive practice. Much of the homework has traditionally been workbook practice, in which the students listen to tapes and do grammar exercises. Classroom activities consist of pair work, peer editing, and homework review.

Because the city of Pittsburgh is not known for its Hispanic community, many students expressed the belief that Spanish is not useful for them in this city, but it might be if they moved to Florida or the southwestern region of the country. Given this assumption, many students view Spanish language acquisition as an intellectual exercise, not as a tool for the shaping of face-to-face interaction.

Matching the refugees with the students seemed an obvious choice of strategies. With the help of a grant from Pennsylvania Campus Compact, a state agency that funds service-learning projects, we developed a series of social events both on campus and off to facilitate interaction between the students and the Cuban participants. These included the screening of a Cuban film, "Strawberry and Chocolate" (Gutiérrez Alea and Tabio 1994), a visit to a campus art gallery, and a trip to a Latin American festival at a neighboring university.

Prior to the first event, one of the Cubans attended class and talked in Spanish of his experiences in Cuba. To gain some control of the guest's talk and thus enhance their understanding of his Spanish, the students prepared questions ahead of time about topics that were of interest to them. For instance, one student asked, "¿Cómo es la gente?" (What are the people like?) This is a simple grammatical structure for a student in the second semester of Spanish 1, yet the possible responses are laden with cultural and grammatical information. This is not to say that there were not communication breakdowns; however, both the students and the Cuban speaker had the opportunity to negotiate meaning in authentic conversation by asking for clarification and using repetition in addition to other strategies. The instructor and a volunteer from Catholic Charities were also present to clarify or translate when necessary.

At each social event, students arrived with a specific assignment. Prior to the visit to the art gallery, they prepared drafts of compositions. For this task, they had to imagine that they were refugees and were describing their typical daily activities in Pittsburgh. This exercise focused on uses of the present tense for the Spanish 1 class. The intermediate class practiced aspects of the past and present verb tenses by writing compositions in which they compared their imaginary prerefugee lives with their current refugee experiences in Pittsburgh. At the gallery, they were assigned to talk to at least one Cuban refugee about his or her daily activities. Afterward, they had to compare the information presented in the first draft with what they had learned in the course of the conversation. They then rewrote the compositions using the new information.

The instructor chose these types of assignments because they were appropriate for the study of whatever grammatical item was the focus at that point, and because they generated conversation in potentially awkward situations. It can be difficult enough for some individuals to make small talk with strangers; to do it in a foreign language can be downright frightening.

Students' Evaluation of the Project

The students kept weekly journals that gave them the opportunity to express their frustrations and satisfaction with the CBL component and other issues. Their responses were for the most part positive. Several expressed pride in knowing that their Spanish, while being far from perfect, could be used with people in real situations. Furthermore, more students participated in more CBL activities (even after they had completed the minimum number required) as the semester progressed.

The project had its challenges. Although the students were required to attend only three of the five scheduled events, a few found it difficult to schedule their work time around them. Some expressed frustration at their language ability and said it was difficult to manage a conversation, even with the assignments they had to prepare, in the face of so many communication breakdowns. Many of the Cubans expressed the same frustrations, and several students and Cuban participants were simply shy. Still, by the end of the semester, several of the students had volunteered to tutor the refugees in English on an individual basis and used terms like "amigo" to refer to the Cubans. Two students had even planned a trip to a local mall with a young Cuban woman roughly their age.

When asked whether the project should continue, nearly all of the students said that the practice with native speakers was both enjoyable and necessary and that it should continue in some form. Some wanted more flexibility in the kinds of activities, however. For instance, at least two students preferred not to participate in group events and wanted the option of doing one-on-one activities.

Other Learning Contexts

So far, we have described only activities designed for beginning and intermediate language learners. Several advanced students became aware of these activities in the lower level Spanish courses, and they wanted opportunities to meet the Cuban participants as well. To this end, the instructor designed with one student an independent study that focused on Cuba. As part of her coursework, the student read a basic text on Latin American history. Using the issues described in the book, she chose several areas that particularly interested her, including U.S. foreign policy regarding Cuba. Her assignment was to prepare research papers for each topic and in doing so to use, in addition to journals and newspapers, interviews with the Cuban refugees as resources. Much of the teacher-student dialogue centered on inconsistencies between what she had heard from the refugees and what she had read in other sources.

Assessment of Student Participation

In such a nontraditional format, nontraditional assessment procedures are necessary. In addition to taking tests, receiving oral grades, and completing homework assignments, the students prepared personal portfolios to document their development as language learners. As part of these portfolios, the students prepared material that specifically addressed what they felt they had learned as a result of nonclassroom interaction. (The portfolio guidelines appear at the end of this paper.)

Service and Reflection

It is important to return to a discussion of the issue of service and clarify further the role of reflection. Many of the students involved in this project did not feel they were providing a service to the refugees by attending social events and making small talk. However, coordinators at Catholic Charities frequently expressed their thanks and stated quite clearly to the students that they were providing a much-needed service to both the agency and the Cubans by helping them feel more comfortable in a strange city. The students, though, felt they were receiving the benefits of learning Spanish rather than providing any service to others.

For some individuals, the idea of providing service may elicit some feeling of superiority, thus leading to patronizing attitudes or an exclusive sense of "us" versus "them." This may be caused by one-day service events, in which students go out to perform a service for a community agency knowing that they will not have to return. When a service component is not integrated into the goals of a course and its scheduling discourages interaction between the so-called service providers and the so-called service recipients, the reflection element — a crucial part of any CBL component — cannot be used to its fullest potential. In other words, if the purpose of the CBL component is not clear within the framework of the course and the CBL experience itself is shallow or rushed, the reflection portion may be perceived as just another classroom task that the students have to fulfill to get their final grade. When this is the case, CBL may be viewed as charity and not as an essential part of an educational and community-building design. We believe that we cannot qualify such instances as successful programs according to the principles we use to develop such programs.

Furthermore, while reflection is a crucial element of CBL, research in the field rarely discusses its role within the community group, as opposed to that of the students in the classroom. While the agencies involved often express thanks and evaluate the effectiveness of the program, it is rare that the participants (or so-called service recipients) have a voice in the reflection process. In this case, the shifting makeup of the refugee community made it difficult to formalize such participation, but surely it is necessary to do so if a project such as this is to come close to achieving its goal of developing a language classroom and learning experience based on the principles of interactional competence and CBL.

The reflective dimension for the community participants should be yet another language experience for the students, as well as an opportunity for the participants to explore their attitudes and learning. Advanced language students, for instance, could interview the participants and summarize in writing what they hear, thus creating texts for reading purposes for both themselves and, possibly, less advanced students. The students and community group members might also develop oral presentations, artwork or videos, or explore other media for expression.[2]

Regardless of the form it takes, reflection proceeds "by questions and sustained dialogue — with self, with peers, with 'leaders' — that are designed to introduce, expand or resolve dissonance" (Morton 1993: 97). This dialogue allows the instructor, students, and community participants to move the objectives of a language course beyond the teaching of vocabulary and grammar to an examination of the individual's role in society — a role often determined by language background and use.

Reflections on CBL in the Classroom

The following conclusions are the result of this semester-long implementation of one kind of CBL component. They may help other instructors looking for ways to initiate a similar program.

Advantages of CBL

Some of the advantages of incorporating a CBL component included:

1. Learners become more aware of the communicative value of the target language as they use it in authentic situations in which each speaker is engaged in the outcome of the interaction.

2. Learners have opportunities to reflect on their learning and thus are given a more active role in the learning process.

3. Language learning is done in context.

4. Learners are literally taken out of the classroom space and into another venue. This gives them the opportunity to experience the dynamic, crucial role of language in the construction of social identity.

5. There is a two-way interaction between the community and the academic institution as both look for ways to improve the services and education they offer. The concept of the "ivory tower" becomes obsolete as the students apply what they learn in the community to their classroom experi-

ences. Similarly, the community agency that sponsors the students receives the practical benefits of the proximity of the college or university.

Challenges of CBL

Certainly there were challenges in implementing this program for the first time. These included:

1. Scheduling problems.

2. Students found it difficult to overcome tendencies toward shyness in talking to strangers in social situations.

3. Transportation problems. Some of the Cuban participants did not have transportation. The college provided transportation whenever possible, but occasionally it was unable to do so due to scheduling conflicts with other campus needs.

4. Developing a reflection component for the Cuban participants. The turnover rate in the refugee community is fairly high as the individuals involved move in a search for work and education. This means that the instructor must continue to introduce herself or himself and the college to individuals through the sponsoring agency. This process can be quite time-consuming as the instructor and the agency make introductions and explain the project. Furthermore, depending on the political reasons for the individual's refugee status, she or he may be unwilling to talk to anyone representing an unknown institution.

5. Continuing the program. See (4) above for a discussion of the reasons that make continuing the program difficult.

Conclusion

We have presented here a description of one kind of CBL language course. Certainly a need exists for studies to examine the long-term effects of such components on language learners. For instance, future studies might examine the ways these activities affect the development of learners' interactional competence or if interaction with native speakers in a nontarget cultural setting affects learners' attitudes toward the target culture.

Although not every course lends itself well to CBL, we cannot ignore the possibilities for language growth and cultural education that a good CBL component provides. As we rethink the traditional boundaries of the classroom, as well as the traditional divisions between the Academic Affairs and Student Affairs departments of an institution, we also rethink what it means to teach culture in a classroom and what the role of language is and will be in our society.[3]

Notes

1. The grant (#95HLC0007) described here was awarded by the Corporation for National Service. Opinions or points of view expressed in this document are those of the authors and do not necessarily reflect the official position of the Corporation for National Service or the Learn and Serve America Higher Education Program.

2. Depending on the educational level of the community participants, they might write their own thoughts for the students. In choosing appropriate activities, the instructor must consider issues such as literacy, political status of the group (do they have reason to distrust the consequences of public expressions of their thoughts?), and confidentiality required by the sponsoring agency.

3. The authors would like to thank several unknown readers for their thoughtful comments on this paper. All errors, however, are our own.

References

Berson, J.S. (May 1993). "Win/Win/Win With a Service-Learning Program." *Journal of Career Planning and Employment* 53(4): 30-35.

Canale, M., and M. Swain. (1980). "Theoretical Bases of Communicative Approaches to Second Language Teaching and Testing." *Applied Linguistics* 1: 1-47.

Gutiérrèz Alea, T., and J.C. Tabio, producers and directors. (1994). "Strawberry and Chocolate." Available from Suncoast Video.

Hall, J.K. (1995). "A Prosaics of Interaction: The Development of Interactional Competence in Another Language." Unpublished manuscript.

Hesser, G. (1995). "Faculty Assessment of Student Learning: Outcomes Attributed to Service-Learning and Evidence of Changes in Faculty Attitudes About Experiential Education." *Michigan Journal of Community Service-Learning* 1: 33-42.

Hymes, D. (1972). "On Communicative Competence." In *Sociolinguistics: Selected Readings*. Edited by J.B. Pride and J. Holmes, pp. 269-293. New York, NY: Viking.

Morton, K. (1993). "Reflection in the Classroom." In *Rethinking Tradition: Integrating Service With Academic Study on College Campuses*. Edited by T. Kupiec, pp. 89-97. Denver, CO: Education Commission of the States.

Palmer, P.J. (1993). "Is Service-Learning for Everyone? On the Identity and Integrity of the Teacher." In *Re-thinking Tradition: Integrating Service With Academic Study on College Campuses*. Edited by T. Kupiec, pp. 17-18. Denver, CO: Education Commission of the States.

Permaul, J.S. (1993). "Community Service and Intercultural Education." In *Rethinking Tradition: Integrating Service With Academic Study on College Campuses*. Edited by T. Kupiec, pp. 83-87. Denver, CO: Education Commission of the States.

Pica, T. (1987). "Second Language Acquisition, Social Interaction, and the Classroom." *Applied Linguistics* 8: 3-21.

Vygotsky, L.S. (1986). *Thought and Language.* Cambridge, MA: Harvard University Press.

Wertsch, J.V., ed. (1978). *Recent Trends in Soviet Psycholinguistics.* White Plains, NY: M.E. Sharpe.

Final Portfolio

Do not throw anything away this semester, including rough drafts of any writing assignments you do. If you keep your assignments on computer disk, keep a backup disk and do not change original documents when you revise. Instead, create a new document.

You should include the following in your portfolio:

1. Include at least two works (early and recent) that reflect your growth as a writer during this semester. These works must be written in Spanish and must have been produced for this class.
2. Include at least one item that you consider the most personally satisfying results of your work in this class.
3. Include evidence of how you have learned more about Spanish-speaking cultures.
4. Include evidence that you have developed at least one new strategy to help you deal with points, concepts, etc., that you have trouble with in this class. For instance, do you find it difficult to speak Spanish? Is test-taking a problem for you? Do you have trouble studying vocabulary? What kinds of strategies have you developed so that you can overcome these?
5. Include one item that reflects your strengths as a language learner. For instance, is writing your strong point? Is understanding grammar your strong point? Do you think you are best at speaking? Why?

Consider the following as possible pieces of evidence for the above: audiotapes of yourself speaking, compositions, journal entries, tests, notes you take in class, anything reflecting your work in the service component (photos, tapes, etc.). Be creative!

Organize your work in a folder and turn it in on the last day of class. Your portfolio will be returned to you when you take the final exam.

Community Video: Empowerment Through University and Community Interaction

by Teresa Darias, Arturo Gómez, Josef Hellebrandt, Amy Loomis, Marta Orendain, and Silvia Quezada

This chapter highlights some of the features of service-learning by present-ing the key components and experiences of a collaboratively taught course, Community Video. Span 118/Comm 138 was designed as a grant project at Santa Clara University (SCU) in Santa Clara, California. The course was developed (1) to increase student exposure to Spanish language communi-ties[1] and (2) to expose students to the process of providing instruction in cre-ating community video. The joint experience between university and com-munity members of Sacred Heart Parish was to focus on the potential of video to explore relevant social concerns. In this manner, students would learn about language and culture firsthand through an immersion and teaching process. Community members would, in turn, gain a voice in a medium normally denied to them.

Counter to traditional approaches to service-learning, this project was not based on outcomes determined by professors. Indeed, the very notion of what constitutes a service-learning experience was challenged when com-munity members were invited to work interactively with students in defin-ing course goals. This collectively interactive process was both frustrating and highly effective in evoking reflection on the progress of the class. Nei-ther students nor community members could escape the struggle to define and redefine course structure and goals on a weekly basis. "But what are we doing?" was a common refrain from students and community members alike. Community members were forced to formalize their thinking and "translate" who they were, whereas students were forced to expand their definitions of what counted as teaching and learning.

Redefining Terms and Identities in the Pedagogical Process

Traditionally, students have been very bound by their experiences in pro-duction classes to create a product. They are systematically encouraged to focus on the final video product as a measure of their success. Part of what is misleading in the term "community video" is that the word *video* is a noun commonly held to be a physical object, that is, a videotape. Perhaps a more accurate term for describing the course content would be the expression "community videography." Explained in this way, community video is a process of videography in which the learning phase is just as important as, if not more important than, the creation of an actual video itself.

Working within a community setting often hinders the smooth progress and development of an end product. Training others in the creation process challenges students even more because they are relinquishing control over authorship — and hence their sense of how to assess themselves and the situation. In this class, community members fought equally hard to gain a sense of who they were as both the authors and the subjects of their video. Students shared their struggle in witnessing the slowness of the process by which communities define themselves internally as well as externally.

The pedagogical challenges of such a situation expose commonly held assumptions about "who we are" for community members and students alike.[2] *Service* carries with it assumptions of power relations in which the community is implicitly defined as *other* — a group of people in need of external assistance. *Learning* is more of a mutual process that takes place between students and the community, though students are often assumed to gain more from the experience than their community partners. Community Video was designed to explicitly challenge these experiences on both sides in that members of Sacred Heart Parish would be responsible for defining the roles of university students as video teachers, translators, and facilitators. Students, on the other hand, were encouraged to become aware of the cultural distinctions and assumptions about learning they encountered.

Course Design

Community Video was developed as a team-taught, upper-division course for both communication and Spanish students. Working on campus as well as off campus, course participants collaborated with a local community organization — Sacred Heart Church — to facilitate a community-driven video project. According to the course syllabus, the goals of the class were (1) to introduce students to the development of community video as a cultural practice, (2) to train students in the critical examination of the mass media, (3) to immerse them in a culturally, and linguistically, authentic environment, and finally (4) to teach them to work in new ways that are collaborative and distinct from the parameters of an ordinary classroom setting. The goal of the on-campus component of the course was to have students examine the role of video in social and political contexts both in the United States and in Central and South America, and to have students study and develop strategies for cross-cultural interaction at the community site.

As originally designed, both Spanish and communication classes met regularly two times a week. Tuesday meetings took place on campus and addressed academic topics. The meetings on Thursdays were mostly off campus at Sacred Heart Parish and dealt with hands-on aspects of video production. On campus, Spanish students spent the first half hour of class comparing experiences and impression about the Sacred Heart community before discussing other topics. In class they discussed elements of cultural competence and learning focusing on the immersion component. Communication students discussed theories of narrative and other story-telling mechanisms applied to Hispanic and U.S. culture and media. For example, the narrative structure of local and national news broadcasts in English were similar in format to, and different in emphasis from, those of *Univisión* or *Telemundo*. An outside speaker from Univisión came to the class early on to explain concretely the struggles, both practical and cultural, of Latino journalists.

SCU students were asked to look at a variety of media contexts that precipitated the development of community video both inside and outside Latino culture. Beyond understanding the historical and political development of alternative media, students were asked to reflect critically on their experiences in the field — just as they would on an academic text. These experiences included reviewing the processes of teaching that they would be implementing, the video footage they would help others to shoot, and planning materials to be used in developing community video projects. Class screenings incorporated portions of "Noticiero Univisión," "The Grapes of Wrath," "Chulas Fronteras," "Nai: The Story of a Kung Woman," "Second Avenue," "Henry Honer," "Chicago video project," "Greenpeace," "Epes," and "Sewa." Excerpts were used both as technical examples of video documentary and as examples of Spanish cultural narrative. Language skills were crucial because a vast majority of the parish members knew very little English or felt more comfortable speaking Spanish.

The documentary and fictional videos selected for the class allowed it to focus on characters and stories. Students discovered that, like news format programs, soap operas in English and Spanish (*telenovela*) had similarities and differences. They compared cultural assumptions about characters and content as well as principles of story telling with the lived experiences of people at Sacred Heart. University-based classes generally ended by having Spanish students rejoin their classmates from communication to share insights and learn about communication practice and theory. The goal for communication students was to assist the community organization with the technical aspects of the project, whereas Spanish students took on the roles of mediator and translator between the collaborators. Community Video was designed to promote the development of language and video skills within a lived experience rather than in the artificial confines of a classroom or studio setting and to give students a deeper sense of the power of cultural and visual communication.

On the communication side, class participants discussed mainstream television as part of their initial planning for the various stages of video pre-production in the community. Working in small project groups, they examined issues such as: How many projects should there be? What is the video going to be about? Who should be in it? Who will be the audience? How will it be put together? The actual production stage of the class involved taping various community events; e.g., productions staged by the parish's Teatro Corazón,[3] video training sessions, and performance rehearsals. The students and community members also documented other, more spontaneous events that called attention to the learning process itself. In the editing stage of production, new videotapes were combined with archival footage of past Teatro performances for the final video. The script for the video was written by a single representative from the community, but images to accompany the script were collectively shot, logged, and chosen by a group of Sacred Heart parishioners.

The academic quarter ended with a screening of the near-complete (all but credits) video at Sacred Heart's recreational hall. Approximately 75 people from the parish attended the screening, which was supplemented by a panel discussion with students and community leaders. The follow-up discussion was videotaped, as well as spontaneous interviews with random audience members and key members of the SCU/Sacred Heart production team.

Design Modifications and Implementation

Over the span of the academic quarter, the course required several significant modifications. Logistics, transportation, and scheduling turned out to be the three major challenges. Changes in the campus portion led, in turn, to changes in the schedule of the last three weeks. Logistical challenges, community member and student time constraints necessitated condensing the production portion of the class. Limited access to equipment and transportation often delayed the start of on-campus and off-campus classes. Although initially enthusiastic, several community members failed to return to their project groups. Lack of community support and direction, along with a limited time frame, forced the class to work on a single project rather than on a more diversified group of projects. Although both sides were able to make the scheduled class times at the community site, it was difficult for the project groups to find time to work jointly during the preproduction and production phases.

Logistically, campus media services both helped and hindered the class's progress. The media lab with its multiple TV/VCR units allowed for efficient logging of recent and historical video. Unfortunately, editing facilities were far less technically and temporally accessible. This forced students and community members to work at the already crowded Communication Department facilities and to delegate editing duties rather than carry them out personally. In removing class and community members from the video-construction process, the class contradicted its primary goal of educational inclusion and artistic ownership.

Reactions and Reflections

The following are excerpts from and responses to a roundtable discussion with professors (Josef Hellebrandt, Amy Loomis), community members (Arturo Gómez, Marta Orendain),[4] and students (Silvia Quezada, Teresa Darias).[5]

Looking back at all the eight meetings with community members we've had so far, what has worked well and what has not met our expectations?

Loomis: In terms of what the community has gained, I think it is more a sense of entitlement and voice around the technology in a world that's filled with technology and whose images come to it from the outside. This is an opportunity to create them from the inside, an opportunity that perhaps other people did not think before could be a reality. So, I think what's to be gained here is not just a sense of the opportunity and the limitations but also a sense of the process. In other words, the process of learning is just as valuable as a finished product.

On the other hand, I was hoping that the majority of communication students would take a more self-sufficient role; that they would, after having experience in video production and experience in community settings from other classes, from their own upbringing . . . be motivated and excited to engage in the project in a more tenacious way. In other words, they gave up very easily if things did not go right, and I was expecting that they would have more heart, and I think that they gained that as the process was going on.

Hellebrandt: From the Spanish perspective, this collaborative class revealed the potential of participatory learning with a local community in the context of acquiring linguistic and cultural competencies as well as enhanced cooperation among instructors, students, and community members. The structure of the class with its campus-community emphasis and real-life situations showed students that purposeful language learning is aided by direct contact and meaningful contexts. Working and learning with Mexican Americans allowed students not only to enhance their language proficiency but also to challenge their cultural beliefs and to gain cultural competence and demonstrate that in various situations. Several students were able to reach this level of competence, whereas others failed to see the benefits of working outside the confines of the typical Spanish classroom.

Overall, the project allowed professors, students, and community members to experience a collaborative learning format. This proved to be beneficial and challenging — beneficial in terms of being able to recognize the process character of community video and to discuss with my colleague some of its cultural underpinnings; challenging in that collaboration was not always efficient for lack of time and a clear understanding of the others' needs.

Darias/Quezada: The advantages of this project were invaluable. For us, it gave us the opportunity to challenge ourselves and voice our critique of the project. In all, we felt we were doing it in the interests of both the university students and the community. At first, there was a sense of resentment toward the students' apathy, but after further thought, we decided that the design of the course did not give them much of an option. Despite this, there were obvious advantages — among them, personal growth, a broader definition of education, cultural exchange, and a new way to perceive the world. Some learned to understand and cope with the new circumstances, but others retreated. In light of this, the advantages far outweigh the disadvantages. The Spanish students were able to employ their language skills by interpreting and also by transforming ourselves into facilitators. The Spanish group had more of an empathetic understanding due to cultural awareness. As a result, the way the educational component of this course was viewed was much different. The Spanish students focused their efforts on trying to get the parish members empowered to take a stronger role in producing the video via . . . friendship. However, the need for control and external direction hindered the transition from theory to practice. Instead of opening up to alternative formats, they clung to their preconceived notion of learning.

Gómez/Orendain: The video, "Teatro Corazón: A Light of the Community," made us reflect about our own community and about the cultural, artistic work of educating and preaching. And thanks to SCU, it was possible to allow technology to find its way into this community. A small bridge of communication between SCU and the Sacred Heart community was built, which helped the producers of this project who represented different ethnic backgrounds share in the end the values of dignity and respect. We think that Spanish and communication classes found in this community a fountain of rich knowledge, which can only be gained through contact with life itself. We believe that the critical reflection about design and implementation highlight certain shortcomings that can easily be overcome. We really do not see any disadvantages.

How has the class altered the students' perceptions about learning in and out of the university?

Loomis: Students learned that the rules for learning within the university structure are arbitrary though they may serve a very important purpose the students can appreciate. . . . I think that it has taught them to learn more spontaneously, more from themselves and their environment, and more independently than they would have otherwise [done] within the confines of a particular class that met at the university.

Hellebrandt: I am convinced that this course helped several students make a first sincere step into Mexican-American culture. Leaving their sometimes abstract Spanish classrooms, students recognized that language can serve meaningful and concrete purposes beyond learning grammar and vocabulary. The community experience allowed them to see concrete faces and experiences behind the label of Hispanic or Mexican American and recognize the different traditions and behaviors shared by these speakers of Spanish. I know that a few students have found new friends, and I hope these learners will expect similar learning experiences from their next classes.

Darias/Quezada: This program was indeed a great experience, and to describe anything as a disadvantage would be to throw away all the learning that took place. Instead, challenges would be something more appropriate to describe those moments when the cards were against us. Some of the challenges were both academic and personal in nature. The biggest challenge was the inability to comprehend pedagogical learning beyond the text level. This complicated the ability of students to develop their leadership and team player spirit to overcome the many problems that arose about the projects' not being specific. Unfortunately, reflection about the textual material having a meaning in the project did not take place. As a result, they could not assess the situation, the new people, and the needs of the people. The parish itself was a new society for the university students. We failed to meet the challenge of understanding the background of the people we were to help. We failed to compile a profile of the people we were to help. Although we were relatively close to our project area, we were worlds apart. In the end, the trying moments, the frustration, and the openness about the confusion this project presented bonded us together.

As students we came to understand where work needed to be done for future generations to do this service. We realized that for the past 11 weeks we really did compress many elements that should have a quarter's worth of time to be mulled over. For example, the profile composition. A composition would have allowed us to gather information about the parish. In the end, this project did what knowledge does — it empowered. It empowered the parish members to look at their parish culture as having merit and value in this diverse country in which pop culture is the preferred. Further, it helped them to work with an unlikely friend, academics. As members of a migrant community who do not have much education, they came to trust us. In doing so, they came to trust in their own opinions and decisions. This project was a confidence builder for this community.

Did the Sacred Heart community gain any valuable knowledge about video production that will be useful to the community?

Gómez/Orendain: Today we have a first cultural product, the video "Teatro Corazón: A Light of the Community," in which we learned from ourselves. It also has instilled in us the desire to continue with this video workshop. We now realize the importance of multiplying our voice through technology, as well as the power of video in the education of youth and community. We know that we have to seek more and better training and obtain our own cameras to edit and copy the tapes. We hope to acquire the necessary resources. We will have to learn how to acquire them until we are self-sufficient, but in the meantime, we hope that SCU continues to assist us next year, that students continue coming to our community to nourish us with their experiences, and that our young people see in their example the importance of university education to catch up and overcome marginalization.

The Challenges of Pedagogical Redefinition

From the Student

From a student perspective the design of this project was primarily understood at a literal level: Spanish students were to interpret, and communication students were to crank out a community video. Neither student group had a healthy understanding of leadership, which required the use of other faculties such as perception, group assessment, human dynamics, etc. We agree that on many occasions students were ambivalent or even unaware that they could contribute to the direction of the course. Furthermore, the parish members themselves looked toward the university members for guidance when, unknown to them, we were looking for them to guide us. At Sacred Heart Parish this struggle over direction also occurred, and it lingered well into the last weeks of the course. As a result, we never fully developed a vision clear enough to collectively work on and appreciate the video we helped to create. Again, there was a lack of understanding about what it meant to be a leader in this class. For example, if the students lead, it would be our project and not the parish's.

As academic students, we are constantly challenged to seek answers in our work. It was frustrating and disappointing to see that we did not take the initiative to lead Sacred Heart members through an exploratory phase explaining this aspect of learning. For example, we could have walked them through a brainstorming session, the way a tutor might. Instead, we always turned to them for answers and directions, when neither were available. Leadership in our opinion also includes having an ability to critically evaluate any learning situation. Many of the students were not able to do so, and so their approach to the project became mechanical and needing constant step-by-step guidance. Failure to have a conceptual idea of the learning process severely limited them from coming out of their student mold and into a leadership role.

In the implementation phase of the course, an initial physical and emotional separation occurred between the Sacred Heart parishioners and the SCU students that impeded the course from starting smoothly. This gap was, in our opinion, caused by the difference in cultures and expectations from both parties. Although the parishioners were tremendously grateful for the commitment and resources offered to them, initially they were hesitant to participate in the class. The university students interpreted this reluctance as a sign that the course was failing. This fear gave rise to feelings of dissatisfaction, frustration, and even a sense of wasted time.

The Spanish class's experience focused more on the aspect of how to cope in the journey of immersing oneself in another culture. Class material on various theoretical models helped us understand that Sacred Heart Parish was another culture with its history, goals, and expectations. We were effectively immersing ourselves in that culture. Since Spanish students had the advantage of learning about the psychological phases that emerge, we had the advantage of going beyond learning the way our communication counterparts expected. Perhaps, it is the very nature of our study that allowed us to better cope with this new type of learning. As language majors, our assigned Tuesday readings challenged us to look at learning language in a more holistic way. To learn a language was to learn what it meant to be that language's people, to understand their notion of time, space, success, community, etc.

These insights into the differences that existed allowed a few of the communication students to look at the community video project in a different light and to act accordingly. For example, success for many Latino communities is not what has been accomplished, but rather what is getting accomplished. In retrospect, the models did not keep the Spanish group from joining the chorus of those communication students who were discontented, but the models did keep us from completely joining their ranks. This Sacred Heart community video turned out for us not just an academic exercise, but a challenge to the foundation of what it meant to be a Spanish major: our immersion competence. For us, it became a matter of relating to the people, making them feel comfortable, so that they could provide what the communication majors so desperately wanted and needed — a structure to their video production project.

From the Community

In the absence of a concrete script, taping began and we embarked on a confusing adventure. A lot of taped material was wasted, resulting in recordings of poor quality and wasted time. Even though in this project of eight weeks the SCU students had a better theoretical preparation and technical training to help with the recording and editing, their participation was minimal. We are not sure whether this was due to their lack of interest because they were told to stay on the sidelines so that the community members would do the taping and editing. If this was the case, it was simplistic and unrealistic. Upon completion of this video, only a few hours before presenting it to the community, we felt alone without SCU students and only with the support of professor Amy Loomis.

It was important to us that the video reflect how Sacred Heart's Teatro Corazón has changed the lives of certain young people in our community. Thus, we agreed that many of these young people would be interviewed. Ten SCU students arrived with two cameras but without individual microphones. The students sat down to observe as members of the theater carried out the interviews and taped. The image came out fine, but the audio was lost. Hence, from our perspective, the most valuable material that could have been used to illustrate the community theater was lost. We think that one of the cameras should have been used by the communication students to assure the quality of the filmed material throughout the whole process, and not leave us alone overwhelmed by the equipment.

From the Professors

Overall, both professors agree that the presentation of the course philosophy and goals was not sufficiently unified or clear to prepare students for the experiences they would encounter. We assumed a level of maturity and independent thinking that was only present in about 25 percent of the SCU class participants. Likewise, we assumed a more dramatic and consistent level of engagement on the part of community members present. Though both Santa Clara and community leaders thought they were clear in planning the course and course outcomes, this was not entirely true. The discrepancy between preclass expectations and visions and the actual implementation of the course was marked. Community members interpreted the students' lackluster behavior as disinterest, and so the cycle perpetuated itself. Though class content and organization were designed collaboratively, only a few people emerged from the class and the community as project leaders. This is not uncommon for community projects, nor is it an uncommon flaw in the course. It is a natural progression of small group activities, but one that is artificially denied in common classroom settings. To address student discomfort with the nature of experiential learning, we believe the course would benefit from more joint workshoplike exercises and discussions; in this case, joint class meetings to go beyond sharing information between Spanish and communication students after separate class meetings.

Suggestions for the Future

Improvements in philosophical explanation, written overview of directions, and concrete visual examples strike us as most important. In addition, with more time (perhaps over two quarters) the community component of the course could be incorporated outside of class time. We believe that greater time would allow for a more in-depth and historical explanation of critical pedagogy and the roots of community video. It would also allow more class time for video screenings. Although an open syllabus format gave flexibility to the course's direction, our failure to provide disclaimers about the alternative nature of the course and the absence of both advanced descriptions of assignments and incremental grading guidelines impeded student learning. According to students, the meaning of community video did not become clear until guest speaker Carlos Fontes came to present his research on the global development of community video. The fact that the course format and student experiences were validated primarily by an expert outsider confirmed our earlier concerns that students were unable to break away from the traditional pedagogical model of "teaching from above."

While Spanish students were relatively clear on the goal of becoming immersed in the community and practicing language skills, most communication students found the teaching process alienating because it differed so substantially from their previous field production experiences. In particular, they felt frustrated by the lack of *product orientation,* meaning that the process of teaching lacked meaning outside the purpose of completing a video. This imagined video was, for the majority of communication students, the clear measure of their success or failure in the class. To the extent that they made progress in its completion they were content with the class. The process orientation of the class itself thus radically challenged their notions of learning, teaching, and personal accomplishment. On a positive note, several communication students did value very much their experiences and enjoyed the opportunity to learn from cultural immersion. As one student noted: "I would now like to continue this [collaborative work in a culturally and linguistically authentic environment] in my career, possibly in international communication." Students who were more mature and in some cases older were able to gain more from the class as a whole.

Looking at both written and oral evaluations of the class, we noticed that student sentiment is often characterized by the passive voice (see previous section). This linguistic marker exemplifies the conceptual and pedagogical challenges of experiential learning. For the most part, foreign-language students were more comfortable assimilating into the learning process because they had less of a product orientation around the video and they could see more clearly the benefits of simply being at Sacred Heart as far as learning was concerned.

Experientially based courses do not always offer the same tidy structures as traditional campus-based classes. Increasingly, foreign-language instruction has celebrated the behaviors of a variety of cultures rather than projecting a touristlike vision of cultural identity. But students may be better assured of their progress when they are offered incremental opportunities to assess their individual and collective accomplishments. Frequently, courses taught overseas encounter similar challenges to the traditional academic format. Logistical, linguistic, and cultural problems arise when teachers attempt to apply an American educational model in a foreign context.

We strongly encourage faculty at other academic and nonacademic institutions to continue to develop community-based courses. They may be far more challenging to teach in terms of logistical difficulties and student discomfort with new approaches to learning, but the challenge is worthwhile. Only by actually implementing pedagogical theories in concrete course contexts can one move tangibly from theory to practice at an undergraduate or community level.

Notes

1. Santa Clara University offers student placements at local community agencies through its Eastside Project. See: Rose Marie Beebe and Elena M. De Costa. (1993) "The Santa Clara University Eastside Project: Community Service and the Spanish Classroom." HISPANIA 75: 884-891.

2. A process illustrated in P. Freire, (1970), Pedagogy of the Oppressed (New York, NY: Continuum).

3. The Teatro Corazón was founded in 1990. It consists of a group of young immigrants who meet regularly at the Sacred Heart Parish to rehearse and perform religious plays reenacting biblical scenes from a contemporary perspective. These plays are a great source of empowerment and community pride for both the actors and the audience.

4. The responses by the community members were translated into English by Anna M. Hellebrandt.

5. Teresa Darias was not actually present at this roundtable discussion but listened to the audiotape and responded in turn with her perspectives to fill out the view of the course from a communication student's point of view.

COMMUNITY VIDEO
COMM 138   SPRING 1997

<table>
<tr><td><u>Office Information</u></td><td><u>Class Information</u></td></tr>
<tr><td>
Professor: Amy Loomis
Office: St. Joseph 207
Office hours: T/Th 2-4 pm or by appointment
Phone: 554-4911
E-Mail address: ALOOMIS
</td><td>
Class hours: T/Th, 6-8pm
Class locations: Media Services on Tuesday
(enter via the side door if main entrance locked)
Sacred Heart Parish Thursdays
</td></tr>
</table>

I.   TEXTS

Reserve Readings (Orradre Library), Relevant Media Coverage, in-class handouts & WWW Sites

II.   COURSE DESCRIPTION & GOALS

Community Video is a team-taught upper-division course designed for both Communication and Spanish students. Working on-campus as well as off-campus, course participants will collaborate with a local community organization—the Sacred Heart Church--in order to facilitate a community-driven video project. The goals of the course are: 1) to introduce Santa Clara Students to the development of community video as a cultural practice 2) to train students in the critical examination of the mass media and 3) to immerse them in a culturally and linguistically authentic environment where they will be engaging in experiential learning and finally 4) to learn to work in new ways that are collaborative and distinct from the parameters of an ordinary classroom setting.

In the on-campus component of the course, students will examine the role of video in social and political contexts both in the U.S. and in Central and South America. We will be looking at a variety of media contexts which have precipitated the development of community video both in and out of Latino culture. Beyond understanding the historical and political development of alternative media, students will be reflecting critically on their experiences in the field--just as they would an academic text. These experiences include reviewing the processes of teaching that they are implementing, the video footage they have helped others to shoot and the planning materials used in developing community video projects.

In the off-campus component, Communication students will assist the community organization with the technical aspects of the project while Spanish students will take on the roles of mediator and translator between the collaborators. Community Video thus promotes the development of language and video skills within a "lived experience" rather than in the artificial confines of a classroom or studio setting and gives students a deeper sense of the power of cultural and visual communication. Course participants will be evaluated based on their class participation, group work and written assignments.

III.   REQUIREMENTS & EVALUATION

Your work in the following categories will determine your course grade:

Class Participation & Homework...................20%
Active participation in class discussions (not just attendance) and effective collaboration with community members and Spanish students. Including:
- Oral report on media investigation
- Discussion questions for class based on readings and experiences
- Video training exercises
- Rough cut presentation

Project......................50%
Your active involvement and contributions to the video project will be evaluated on the following criteria:
- Project Journal
- Pre-production (research, visual design, coordination of crew, etc.)
- Facilitation (working with the community crew and classmates in Spanish on the shooting of the piece including trouble shooting and instruction/suggestions).
- Editing of raw footage and re-editing according to the response of the community production team
- Design of post production evaluation and audience response.

2 Short Papers...................20%
- Critical analysis of media news coverage
- Narrative/Ethnographic analysis of film

Final Reflective Report...................10%

IV.   SELECTED BIBLIOGRAPHY

Articles on Reserve

Atwood, R. (1986). "Assessing Critical Mass Communication Scholarship in the Americas: The Relationship of Theory and Practice." In Atwood, R. and E. G. McAnany (Eds.) Communication and Latin American Society: Trends in Critical Research. Madison, WI:University of Wisconsin Press:11-27.

Blau, A. (1992). "The Promise of Public Access." THE INDEPENDENT April:22-26.

Boyle, D. (1990). "A Brief History of American Documentary Video." In Hall, D and S.J. Fifer (Eds.) Illuminating video: an essential guide to video art. New York, N.Y:Aperture in association with the Bay Area Video Coalition:51-74.

Burnett, R. (1991). "Video/Film: From Communication To Community." In: Thede, N. and A. Ambrosi (Eds.) Video and the changing world. New York, N.Y:Black Rose Books:55-60.

Costas, C. and T. Quinlan (1991). "Community Video: Power and Process." Visual Sociology 6(2):39-52.

Jain, R. (1991). "Video: For, by, and with the People." In: Thede, N. and A. Ambrosi (Eds.) Video and the changing world. New York, N.Y:Black Rose Books:41-47.

Lozano, E. (1992). "The Force of Muth on Popular Narratives: The Case of Melodramatic Serials." Communication Theory 2,3:207-220.

COMM 138   SPRING 1997

Negron-Muntaner, F. (1991). "The Ethics of Community Media." THE INDEPENDENT May:20-24.

Rodríguez, A. (1996). "Objectivity and Ethnicity in the Production of the *Noticiero Univisión*." Critical Studies in Mass Communication 13:59-81.

Stuart, S. (1989). "Access to media: placing video in the hands of the people." In MEDIA DEVELOPMENT 4:8-14.

Turner, T. (1991). "Visual Media, Cultural Politics and Anthropological Practice." THE INDEPENDENT February:34-40.

CALENDAR

DATE WEEK	PHASE	CONTENT
- 4/1 (SCU) #1		JOINT INTRO & RATIONALE FOR COMMUNITY VIDEO (CV) SPAN: History CV and (cross-) cultural awareness READINGS Explore mainstream and Spanish-language media. JOINT HW: Part I present media findings (due 4/8) Part II written/finished analysis (due 4/15)
- 4/3 (SH)	Pre-Production	CV: Rationale? Events? Purpose? Message? Cast? Getting acquainted: How do we know who we are?
- 4/8 (SCU) #2		JOINT: PREPARING FOR COMMUNITY INTERACTION / SPAN: Cult. Understanding & Mexican-Americans JOINT HW: Read Univisión article (due 4/15) Bring discussion questions to class
- 4/10 (SH)	Pre-Production	CV: BASIC INSTRUCTION: HOW TO SHOT ? (COM) WHAT/WHO? (SPAN)
- 4/15 (SCU) #3		JOINT: GUEST SPEAKER (R. HERNÁNDEZ/UNIVISIÓN) CV: Journalist stories & community issues READINGS (due 4/22)
- 4/17 (SH)	Pre-Production	CV: WHAT WILL VIDEO LOOK LIKE? Basic instruction ii (COM) Review of last week's field notes (SPAN)
- 4/22 (SCU) #4		CV: HERE AND THERE (both classes) Discussion of readings & Plan for field
- 4/24 (SH)	Pre-Production	CV: WHAT WILL VIDEO LOOK LIKE? Share readings, strategies & ideas (cultural and visual)
- 4/29 (SCU) #5		JOINT: COORDINATION OF CLASS PROJECT READINGS (due 5/6) Community Ethnography
- 5/1 (SH)	Pre-Production	CV: REVIEW PRE-PRO WITH COMMUNITY
- 5/6 (SCU) #6		CROSSING BORDERS: COMMUNITY ETHNOGRAPHY JOINT HW: Go see/Rent a Spanish language film that deals with social concerns and examine the narrative structure. Write team film reviews (due: 5/13)
- 5/8 (SH)	PRODUCTION (Taping)	CV: BEGIN VIDEO TAPING
- 5/13 (SCU) #7		JOINT: VISUAL & COMMUNITY NARRATIVES (FILMS) View raw footage and discuss film critiques HW: JOINT: Work on rough cuts (SPAN translate & COMM edit) READINGS: EMPOWERMENT/DISTRIBUTION (DUE 5/20)

- 5/15 (SH)	PRODUCTION	CV: VIDEO TAPING
		Solidify schedules/interviews, etc. SHOW ROUGH FOOTAGE
- 5/20 (SCU) #8		CV: EMPOWERMENT & DISTRIBUTION-PRODUCT/PROCESS
		SPAN/COMM: Alternative Media in USA & Latin America
		HW: JOINT: Rough cuts (SPAN translate & COMM edit)due 5/27
		READINGS: TBA
- 5/22 (SH)	PRODUCTION	CV: VIDEO TAPING - MORE TAPING taping & screening
- 5/27 (SCU) #9		**JOINT**: FINAL PLANS & COMING TOGETHER
		DISCUSSION OF READINGS
		HW: (due: 6/3) Create final scripts & distribution plan /
		Work in teams
- 5/29 (SH)	POST - PROD (Editing)	CV: REVIEW AND REVISE ROUGH SCRIPTS
- 6/3 (SCU) #10		**JOINT**: STRATEGIES & PLANNING FOR SCREENING
- 6/5 (SH)	POST - PROD	CV: CLASS ONLY SCREENING
- 6/8 (SH)	**SHOWING**	**C O M M U N I T Y V I D E O**

Abbreviations: SCU=Santa Clara University / SH=Sacred Heart

SPAN 118 COMMUNITY VIDEO

PROFESSOR: JOSEF HELLEBRANDT
OFFICE: Bannan 312
HOURS: Monday 9:30-10:30 Tuesday 10:30-11:30
PHONE: 5544-4881

SPRING 1997
T / TH 6-8 PM
T: Daly 201 (SCU)
TH: Sacred Heart
Parish

I.   TEXTS

Reserve Readings & WWW Sites (See attached bibliography)

II.   DESCRIPTION & OBJECTIVES

Community Video is a team-taught upper-division course designed for both Communication and
Spanish students. Working on-campus as well as off-campus, course participants will collaborate with a
local community organization—the Sacred Heart Church-- in order to facilitate a community-driven
video project. The goal of the course is to educate students in the development of community video
practices and to immerse them in a culturally and linguistically authentic environment. In the on-
campus component of the course, students will examine the role of video in social and political contexts
both in the U.S. and in Central and South America and develop strategies for cross-cultural interaction.
In the off-campus component, Communication students will assist the community organization with the
technical aspects of the project whereas Spanish students will take on the roles of mediator and
translator between the collaborators. Community Video thus promotes the development of language
and video skills within a "lived experience" rather than in the artificial confines of a classroom or studio
setting and gives students a deeper sense of the power of cultural and visual communication. Course
participants will be evaluated based on their class participation, group work and written assignments.

III. REQUIREMENTS & EVALUATION

Your work in the following categories will determine your course grade:

1. Class Participation & Homework: Active participation (not just attendance)   **20 %**
   in class discussions(separate and joint) and effective collaboration with COMM
   participants are essential. *Evaluation components*:
   ♦ oral report on media research
   ♦ summary presentations on readings and experiences
   ♦ cultural exercises

2. Project: Your active involvement and contributions to the video project on-campus   **50 %**
   on-campus as well as off-campus will be the most important part of the class. Thursday
   meetings with COMM group and project team members will address: pre-production, production,
   and editing. You also have to attend (with your TA and members of the COMM group)
   one Friday late afternoon workshop at Sacred Heart. *Evaluation components*:
   multiple steps, conducted by instructor and teaching assistant
   ♦ project log (in Spanish)on/off-site facilitator (translator, (cultural) interpreter)

3. Papers: 2 analytical/reflective papers (2)   **20%**

4. Final Paper: A final reflective report on the video project (process & product)   **10 %**
   Format: take-home, in Spanish, typed.

SELECTED BIBLIOGRAPHY

I. ARTICLES ON RESERVE

Conner, W. (1992). "Who are the Mexican-Americans?: A Note on Comparability? In Fiber Luce, L (Ed.) TheSpanish-Speaking World. An Anthology of Cross-Cultural Perspectives. National Textbook Company, Lincolnwood, IL:210-237.

Delgado, J. (1992). "Video Latinoamericano: Desencuentro y Concertación." VideoRed, 4, 11:2-7.

Góngora, A. (1991). "Video: ¿Crisis de identidad o de crecimiento?" VideoRed, 4, 11:14-15.

Gutiérrez, M (1989). "Video Latinoamericano: ?Reseña de un Movimiento Integrador." In Gutiérrez, M (Ed.) Video, tecnología y comunicación popular. Lima, Perú, IPAL:9-16.

Hanvey, R. (1992). "Cross-Cultural Awareness." In Fiber Luce, L (Ed.) The Spanish-Speaking World. An Anthology of Cross-Cultural Perspectives. National Textbook Company, Lincolnwood, IL.:22-33

Hopkins, J. (1979). "Estrategias Blandas: Central de Acceso al Video." In: Vidal-Beneyto, (Ed.) Video,tecnología y comunicación popular. Madrid: Centro de Investigaciones Sociológicas:355-361.

Mantle-Bromley, C. (1992). "Preparing Students for Meaningful Culture Learning." Foreign Language Annals 25, 2:117-127.

Reyes Matta, F. (1986). "La comunicación transnacional y la respuesta alternativa." In Simpson Grinberg (Ed.) Comunicación alternativa y cambio social. Tlahuapan, Puebla:105-126

Roncagliolo, R. (1989). "Distribución e intercambio: hacia la conquista del espacio audiovisual latinoamericano." In Valdeavellano, P. (Ed.) El video en la educación popular. Lima, Perú: IPAL:59-71.

Torres, R. M. (1989. "Educación popular y comunicación popular." In Valdeavellano, P. (Ed.) El video en la educación popular. Lima, Perú:13-36.

Valdeavellano, P. (1989). "América Latina está construyendo su propia imagen." In Valdeavellano, P. (Ed.) El video en la educación popular. Lima, Perú: IPAL:103-130.

II. ARTICLES/RESOURCES ON THE WEB

A. General: LatinoWeb   http://www.catalog.com/favision/latinoweb.htm
             The Azteca Web Page   http://www.azteca.net/aztec/
             CLNet Community Center   http://clnet.ucr.edu/community.html

B. Web Language: "La Telaraña Mundial" http://www.elpais.es/p/d/temas/semanal/portada.htm

C. InteRadio: Rafael Roncagliolo "Garantizando el pluralismo: Por una legislación para la radio comunitaria"
                                        http://www.web.net/amarc/globesp.htm

D. WEB Access in Costa Rica: "BUENOS DIAS Internet para todos" Armando Mayorga
                                        http://www.nacion.co.cr/ln_ee/1995/julio/18/opinion2.html#dias

E. Radio/TV-Stations/Programs:
             Univisión: http://www.univision.net/main.html
             Radioactiva: http://www.radioactiva.com/

CALENDAR

DATE WEEK	PHASE	CONTENT
- 4/1 (SCU) #1		**JOINT** INTRO & RATIONALE FOR COMMUNITY VIDEO (CV) SPAN: History CV and (cross-) cultural awareness READINGS Explore mainstream and Spanish-language media. **JOINT HW**: Part I present media findings (due 4/8) Part II written/finished analysis (due 4/15)
- 4/3 (SH)	Pre-Production	CV: Rationale? Events? Purpose? Message? Cast? Getting acquainted: How do we know who we are?
- 4/8 (SCU) #2		**JOINT**: PREPARING FOR COMMUNITY INTERACTION / SPAN: Cult. Understanding & Mexican-Americans **JOINT HW**: Read Univisión article (due 4/15) Bring discussion questions to class
- 4/10 (SH)	Pre-Production	CV: BASIC INSTRUCTION: HOW TO SHOT ? (COM) WHAT/WHO? (SPAN)
- 4/15 (SCU) #3		**JOINT**: GUEST SPEAKER (R. HERNÁNDEZ/UNIVISIÓN) CV: Journalist stories & community issues READINGS (due 4/22)

- 4/17 (SH)	Pre-Production	CV: WHAT WILL VIDEO LOOK LIKE?
		    Basic instruction ii (COM)
		    Review of last week's field notes (SPAN)

- 4/22 (SCU) #4		CV: HERE AND THERE (both classes) Discussion of readings & Plan for field
- 4/24 (SH)	Pre-Production	CV: WHAT WILL VIDEO LOOK LIKE? Share readings, strategies & ideas (cultural and visual)
- 4/29 (SCU) #5		**JOINT**: COORDINATION OF CLASS PROJECT READINGS (due 5/6) Community Ethnography
- 5/1 (SH)	Pre-Production	CV: REVIEW PRE-PRO WITH COMMUNITY
- 5/6 (SCU) #6		CROSSING BORDERS: COMMUNITY ETHNOGRAPHY **JOINT HW**: Go see/Rent a Spanish language film that deals with social concerns and examine the narrative structure. Write team film reviews (due: 5/13)
- 5/8 (SH)	PRODUCTION (Taping)	CV: BEGIN VIDEO TAPING
- 5/13 (SCU) #7		**JOINT**: VISUAL & COMMUNITY NARRATIVES (FILMS) View raw footage and discuss film critiques HW: JOINT: Work on rough cuts (SPAN translate & COMM edit) READINGS: EMPOWERMENT/DISTRIBUTION (DUE 5/20)
- 5/15 (SH)	PRODUCTION	CV: VIDEO TAPING Solidify schedules/interviews, etc. SHOW ROUGH FOOTAGE
- 5/20 (SCU) #8		CV: EMPOWERMENT & DISTRIBUTION-PRODUCT/PROCESS SPAN/COMM: Alternative Media in USA & Latin America HW: JOINT: Rough cuts (SPAN translate & COMM edit)due 5/27 READINGS: TBA

- 5/22 (SH)	PRODUCTION	CV: VIDEO TAPING - MORE TAPING taping & screening
- 5/27 (SCU) #9		**JOINT**: FINAL PLANS & COMING TOGETHER DISCUSSION OF READINGS HW: (due: 6/3) Create final scripts & distribution plan / Work in teams
- 5/29 (SH)	POST - PROD (Editing)	CV: REVIEW AND REVISE ROUGH SCRIPTS
- 6/3 (SCU) #10		**JOINT**: STRATEGIES & PLANNING FOR SCREENING
- 6/5 (SH)	POST - PROD	CV: CLASS ONLY SCREENING
- 6/8 (SH)	**SHOWING**	**C O M M U N I T Y V I D E O**

Abbreviations: SCU=Santa Clara University / SH=Sacred Heart

Expanding Our Vision of Literacy:
Learning to Read the World of Others

by Nancy Jean Smith

Boom. Boom. Boom. It was a constant dull thud, continuing at short intervals, that shook the air and shook me awake. A rooster crowed and I opened my eyes. It must be long before 6, I thought to myself groggily. A gray dusky morning light was filtering into God's room, where my sleeping accommodations had been temporarily arranged. As I became more alert I focused on a persevering rasping noise. For just a fleeting moment I was at a loss, a flutter of panic in my mind, "Where am I?" Then a flood of remembrance came and I knew what the banging and rasping were: The men were up weaving rugs on the looms, and the women were grinding on the *metates,* preparing corn for breakfast *atole* and the day's *tortillas.* I was sleepily nestled in a small Zapotec village outside of Oaxaca city, Teotitlán del Valle, where I was directing a service-learning project involving village schools and U.S. teachers.

In this article I will detail an ongoing service-learning project in Teotitlán del Valle, Oaxaca, Mexico, which connects teachers from the United States with indigenous Zapotec families and the villagers' nonindigenous Mexican teachers. A description of how this project began, changes in its structure, and various facets of the project will be presented along with a brief sharing of some of the U.S. teachers' reflections. Finally, I will remark on the current state of the project, along with plans and dreams for the future.

Learning About the Community: Listening to Their Voices

> At that time I had no idea what it meant to cross the border. I saw the border and the wire fence, but I asked myself what the difference between over there and over here could be. I looked at the people on the other side as human beings and I looked at this side and saw that we are all the same. I asked myself why we had to cross this way?
>
> — *Zapotec mother, speaking of crossing the border as a 12-year-old*

This project originally began when I was a Title VII bilingual resource teacher working with Spanish-speaking migrant students in a rural school outside of Stockton, California. As I worked with the children, teachers, and aides in the school, I became aware of an indigenous Zapotec presence, which was addressed neither in the curriculum nor in the everyday school life of the children.

The subsequent two years I spent in data collection, both in school and at home, with families in California who originate from the village of Teotitlán del Valle, Oaxaca, Mexico. My children and I were slowly included in the Zapotec community and eventually allowed to intimately experience familial relationships and activities as family members. The following are short snippets of voices that speak to some of the dominant themes collected over time and recorded in various dialogues. All of the English translations from the original Spanish were done by me, many from transcribed tapes taken from my doctoral dissertation, although some are direct translations from subsequent informal conversations. I have attempted to represent my learning developmentally by sequencing the themes presented.

As I became more inquisitive concerning both the Zapotec language and its culture, I began to find important sources of knowledge within the families that were completely invisible at school. For instance, I found that the families had a long tradition of rug weaving, which went back to pre-Colombian times. Not only did they know how to weave the rugs but they also knew how to grow the wool, and as one father told me:

If you want to have good wool to weave . . . the first thing to be concerned with is the quality of the wool. And in order to get good quality wool, well . . . that begins with what you feed the sheep.

I learned that in Oaxaca, artisans and farmers are bound together as communities through language and cultural norms, depending on the region or village. However, when Oaxacans arrive in the United States, because they speak no English and often very little Spanish, they usually find that the only avenue of work available to them is agriculture. Thus Zapotecs are found primarily in the fields, packing sheds, and canneries. Rarely do they find an opportunity to practice their art, or to share and be recognized for knowledge and wisdom handed down from generations of ancestors. As one villager living in the United States remembered:

I came when I was sixteen-years-old in order to learn some English and Spanish. I was looking for a way to sell rugs for my father and my family in Teotitlán del Valle. In my village I sold rugs, but I could not sell in Oaxaca because I didn't speak Spanish then. (Smith 1995: 194)

These families had tremendous knowledge of planting and subsistence farming. They had spent more than half their lives living a life-style very different from the one they were currently living, even though they were still working in agriculture. Ways of respecting and caring for the earth, of planting and harvesting, were much different in their indigenous world than in the large-scale, chemical and tractor farming of the San Joaquin Valley. As field workers they are often forced, out of economic necessity, into a vicious cycle of contaminating the earth and being contaminated themselves:

> [The farmers] spray a lot of pesticides when people are in the fields work-
> ing, as if we were objects. The law says they have to wait seventy-eight
> hours after spraying before the workers can go back into the field. The boss-
> es know that the pesticides are being sprayed just ahead of where the
> workers are working. Who is going to complain? Nobody is brave enough
> to complain because they know the boss will fire them. He says, "OK, if you
> don't want to work get out of here. There are more that will take this job."

> What can people do? . . . Not only do we suffer political problems, discrim-
> ination in the workplace, and manipulation but we are also made to con-
> sume chemicals that later cause health problems. (Smith 1995: 197)

Traditions and customs held in the homes that the parents grew up in
were also very different from the life the children experience in the United
States. Issues of respect, so prominent and important to Zapotec relationships and in social settings in the village, are not present in the same way in
U.S. schools, where the majority of the children spend their time, and where
much media learning takes place. Children who grow up in the village
receive very different messages:

> The first thing [the children learn] is to follow our cultural norms, that they
> treat others with respect, greet them and respect the culture of the village.
> Next that they are good workers. Create a homeplace and live tranquilly
> and happily with their family. When [the boys and I] are on the looms
> weaving we talk about it. My wife also explains how [the girls] need to act
> in life. Her obligation is to teach the girls to cook, how to be a hard worker
> so that when they are old enough they will know how to do things well in
> their homes, for their family. They must know how to cook well, and take
> care of their husbands. (Smith 1995: 218)

However, these same messages many times translate into brick walls for
girls both in the States and in Mexico. Gender issues are a major obstacle for
girls' academic and intellectual development even in California, and ultimately affect their self-determination, especially in academic decision making and control of their economic destiny. The families who live in California
can see this gender inequity and support their daughters' development,
even though they know it ultimately will alienate their daughters from village culture:

> I don't want my children to marry young, especially my daughters. I hope
> they have the opportunity to go to school and develop their mind. My sons
> too, but I'm always supporting the woman because she needs more oppor-
> tunities, sometimes she thinks that she doesn't have a brain. The boys are

favored. I don't tell my boys that they are smarter. [My husband] always gives the boys the message that they are smarter than the girls. And the children see it. Because of this I always fight for my girls, and try to help my boys see this too.

Linguistically I also found a language that was not listed on the home language surveys, in the school office cumulative folders, nor known to exist by the school authorities. It was not by chance that these indigenous roots were hidden. There seems to be a certain shame associated with indigenous identity and language that has pushed the families to hide their heritage:

When I was asked where I was from, I would say that I was from Puebla. I would never say that I was from Oaxaca. I was ashamed. I wanted to for- get where I was from. . . . Upon hearing that you are from Oaxaca, they despise you and they don't even know a single indigenous word. They think of Indian and an image of a stupid Indian that doesn't know anything comes to their mind. They laugh at you because you can't speak Spanish and they call you a damn illiterate. They say things just to make you feel inferior. Our brown skin is the first thing they see. They describe us as being totally brainless, and make us into objects that are unable to think. (Smith 1995: 171)

I began to understand why people stay silent about themselves (Skutnabb-Kangas 1992), denigrating their identity in the process (Seda 1980), and how in self-defense they gradually stop speaking Zapoteco. In California, they continue to internalize the well-taught message from the village schools that they should stop being Zapotec and adopt Mexican ways:

Many times I would try not to speak it [Zapoteco]. This is what has always been the case with the youth of Teotitlán. They pull away from their lan- guage. Principally it came from the schools. When I was in school, the teachers told us not to speak our language, they would punish us. It's still the same today. (Smith 1995: 205)

The same linguistic oppression is experienced in the United States when Zapotec people are among other Latinos. The self-imposed strategy of silence is often employed to avoid conflict and further isolation:

If they [other Latinos] heard me speak Zapoteco they would turn around. Many times I would have very serious problems. A couple times they almost killed me. And speaking Zapoteco was the cause of it all. My friends from Oaxaca usually don't defend themselves, but I do. But even if I won, I still lost, there was no way to win. They thought we were talking about them. It's a serious problem, don't think it's simple. (Smith 1995: 196)

Slowly I came to realize the depth of exploitation (Murphy and Stepick 1991) within which life is framed for these people:

> None of this vast knowledge has been validated economically. Rather, the Zapotec people have suffered incessant economic exploitation. A constant barrage of tourism has created a market that demands goods at prices which keep indigenous artisans in poverty. An international market likewise exists for Zapotec produced goods, and many national and international art dealers live well off these artisans' labor. . . . Today art dealers keep the how of selling to the world at large non-negotiable knowledge, protecting their marketing of goods and ensuring that the artisans will not be able to market their own products. (Smith 1995: 9)

The issue of wresting economic control from a U.S. capitalist system whose suffocating fingers reach far and wide resounded loudly in the dialogues. Even though the Zapotec rug business is extremely lucrative, the financial gains do not go into the pockets of the Zapotec weavers:

> Those who make the rugs are paid half of what is earned selling in the United States. [The United States vendors] are taking advantage of the people. There are some Americans who go to Teotitlán and pay people just a little bit and then resell the rugs for a high price. They also give the people the wool to make special order rugs, because most people don't have the money to even buy the wool to weave. And those who do the work stay poor. (Smith 1995: 223)

This economic situation results in dangerous and frightening illegal border crossings for people of all ages:

> We were all in Tijuana waiting at the border. There were seven children. The boy came to take the three youngest across, I was twelve-years-old and he was younger than I. It was time to cross because the immigration changed and went to eat, it was a short time when there was no one watching. He took them across as if they were his brothers and sisters . . . [telling] immigration that they were lost. My father took a while and the boy, now on the other side, didn't know what to do with the children so he took them in the bathroom. We crossed and waited but they didn't come. They took about three hours. My mother was desperate and crying. We heard rumors that at the border people steal children and sell them. (Smith 1995: 193)

A few thousand dollars earned in the United States can build a house, create self-sufficiency in one's ability to buy wool, and pay for village customs that cannot feasibly be financed through daily weaving in the village.

The more time I spent with the Zapotec families in Stockton, the more respect for them I developed, and the more intrigued I became with their social context. It became evident to me that the pre-Columbian systems of governing, known as the *tequio*, and social organizing structures, known as the *guelaguetza*, were imported into the fusion of cultures taking place. The collective struggle, strength, and daily efforts on the part of all family members to better their economic situation was remarkable:

> *A person is forced to accept conditions because they are so far from home. If you don't accept the orders you won't have a job. A person comes to earn money, for themselves and for their family. Most people borrow money from other family members to make the trip, which puts them in debt even before they get here. You have to do the work even if you don't want to. (Smith 1995: 196)*

I also found that parents' hopes and dreams for coming north to seek work and better their economic situation are often frustrated with the reality they encounter:

> *Before I thought that the United States was a palace, where you could go to work in luxury. But when I got here it was worse than I had imagined. The workers were a closed group and to go to the bathroom there were only rows of toilets. In my village we are private about how we go to the bathroom. Everything was fast, there was never enough time to eat slowly, and nourish oneself well. Here people run out the door to work with a tortilla still in their hand. There is nothing tranquil about this place. (Smith 1995: 168)*

The more I learned, the clearer it became to me that there was a process of linguistic genocide taking place, that few children were learning the Zapotec language of their parents, and that when they did have the opportunity to visit their extended family in Oaxaca, the lines of communication between family members were linguistically limited:

> *When we went to Oaxaca for two and a half months with the whole family, you could count three hours that they [the children] talked with their grandfather. With their grandmother there was no communication. All communication was completely cut off. (Smith 1995: 185)*

Most frightening to me was the realization that many of the children have little sense of who they are and where they come from. Many of them have been raised speaking Spanish, but because Spanish is not taught in school, they now are caught not only between cultures but also between languages. They can maintain a conversation neither in English nor in Spanish.

This has resulted in a situation of semi-lingualism, in which the media also plays a major role:

> When they were small they spoke only Spanish. Now they speak English between themselves. The serenity in the house is not the same anymore. They have begun to act like what they see on the television. When they were small they saw the television, but they did not understand it. Now they see it and imitate what they see, they want to become what they see there. (Smith 1995: 169)

Not only are they cut off from family knowledge because they cannot converse with grandparents and relatives, but they are denied a potential parental safety when they have problems, need advice, or someone to talk to. They suffer this identity crisis on a deep level, knowing nothing of the peace and harmony that form the order of the day in Zapoteco.

This confusion that they feel manifests itself in a variety of ways. Sometimes they react by withdrawing, by alternating between feeling alienated from school and making an effort. They fill themselves with material wishes:

> They think that being American is better. That it is the most happening, and coolest culture at the moment. They think that by wearing a jacket from the United States, you are now part of that culture. But you are being manipulated if you are not aware of how it works. (Smith 1995: 201)

The same effect also takes place in the village among youth who come in contact with northern material goods brought back by others:

> What happens is that young men come back to the village who were working in the fields in the United States. They buy clothing there. When they get to Teotitlán and the other kids see the clothing that they have they want it too. They go to the United States with this idea of at least buying United States clothing, and thinking that they will get it easily. They don't know how hard the other kids had to work to buy the clothing. The youth think that they can go and earn a lot of money easily. We can't make them understand because they only look at what others have and what they think they need. (Smith 1995: 200)

As material possessions and the U.S. media-hype life-style become the major focus on which youth model their lives, linguistic relationships become negatively complicated (Wong-Fillmore 1991). As a familial language shift (Fishman 1991) occurs, home conversations become superficial:

> Everything that [their father] has seen, everything that he has learned in his village, all of his experiences from his childhood, like when he went to

cut wood with his brothers, means a great deal to him. But when he speaks to his children, it's as if the memories no longer have the same meaning, he feels separated from them. Spanish is very different than Zapoteco. He is drifting apart from his children and they from him. They don't know each other well. There does exist some communication, but it's not good quality communication. (Smith 1995: 187)

As I explored these many areas of frustration and oppression, a pattern emerged that clearly indicated and explained the situation of linguistic and cultural imperialism institutionalized in the U.S. and Mexican schools, and in the social and home lives of the families. Cultural norms of respect and community building constructed over many, many thousands of years have traditionally found little acceptance or understanding in mainstream educational institutions. This phenomenon became the focus of my doctoral thesis. I was most interested in identifying the conditions that Zapotec people living in California experience that keep them from speaking their language, and in turn sever the line of linguistic and cultural connection that should be their children's heritage.

The name of the study I conducted is "The Struggle for Cultural and Linguistic Survival: A Participatory Research Study With a Zapotec Community in California" (Smith 1995). I finished it thanks to the wisdom and guidance of my friend and sister, my advisor and chair, Dr. Alma Flor Ada at the University of San Francisco in San Francisco, California. By now, Dr. Ada has guided more than 100 participatory research studies, many of which connect with and support this specific service-learning project (Andriola-Balderas 1993; Gomez-Valdez 1993; Igoa 1995; Laughlin 1996, and Silva 1993).

Work in the area of educational and social liberation and participatory research has also expanded through Dr. Ada's many students now working in classrooms and institutions throughout California. The growing volume of international work being done using a participatory research methodology creates a generalizable voice and lends strength to the methodology, even though the importance of the research lies principally in highlighting those voices not often listened to, those whose stories and experiences have historically been marginalized from traditional forms of data collection. Ultimately, the goal of this research is social justice through a process of dialogue, reflection, and action that points us toward daily acts of compassion, personal transformation, and human dignity.

Participatory Research as Service-Learning

As noted above, the methodology employed for this research is known as participatory research. It is based on the work of the Brazilian educator, Dr. Paolo Freire (1970, 1973, and 1994), Dr. Alma Flor Ada (1993), and Ada and Beutel (1993), and emphasizes an emancipatory feminist stance toward research, proposing personal and societal liberation as the purpose of the research. It both challenges and offers an alternative to dominant, quantitative research that has traditionally been viewed in the West as the only legitimate and valid source of knowledge (Maguire 1987). Grounded in the belief that scientific neutrality does not exist, it seeks to illuminate oppression, validate alternate ways of knowing, and establish a way to struggle for personal and social emancipation (Smith 1995).

Participatory research is part of a larger qualitative movement that has sought to reconceptualize the social sciences in the pursuit of social justice (Park 1992). By connecting research with action, it seeks to create an opportunity to dialogue critically, to rethink and recreate what is known while demystifying systematic exclusion and confusion. Additionally, it strives for clarity in understanding structures of oppression through solidarity and a fundamental conviction that we all know something and have something important to add to the dialogue and base of knowledge under investigation (Freire and Faundez 1992; Freire and Horton 1990; Freire and Macedo 1987).

Thus, the tenets of participatory research work closely with the ideals and goals of service-learning. Both are looking at service to another community, learning from another community, regarding that community not as an object to modify or take knowledge from but as the other member of a partnership in which both parties can learn from each other, listen in love to each other, and amplify the necessity of understanding human needs better. Through this process, we hope to equalize relationships, and in reaching out to one another, become more fully human in our actions and reflections.

From Dissertation to Service-Learning Project

True to the emancipatory framework of participatory research, this project did not end with the completion of my dissertation — in fact, just the opposite has ensued. Near completion of the dissertation, the participants requested that the dialogic nature of the research we had been engaged in California be extended to their village of Teotitlán del Valle. They wished to expand the dialogue to the Zapotec villagers and Mexican educators who worked in the village but lived elsewhere. Thus, the community issued an invitation to begin a linguistic and cultural interchange project, inviting further dialogue on the issues of emancipatory education and the linguistic and cultural reality community members faced in their daily and institutional school lives.

This invitation came at a time when I had had the privilege of spending the two previous summers in Puerto Rico observing a fellow doctoral candidate's participatory research project. At that time Dr. Kristin Brown was collecting data on the educational effects of Puerto Rican circular migration. Her study involved bringing Puerto Rican and New York teachers together to investigate the issues that Puerto Rican children and youth face when they migrate either to New York or back to the island (Brown 1995). Through a partnership between New York's Brooklyn College, the University of Puerto Rico at Piedras Negras, and Project Orillas, an international telecommunications project, funding and arrangements were established.

As I watched Dr. Brown's project develop, it became clear to me that considering the masses of Mexican and Mexican-American children and youth in California, a like-minded exchange project was needed between Mexican and Californian educators with the goal of investigating and bettering the education of Mexican children, and ultimately all children.

Therefore, when the participants in my research came to me requesting a continuation, I was eager to comply. With the idea of creating an eventual two-way teacher exchange, I made a trip to the village with the intention of finding out if it was truly possible to set up a project of this type. I was interested in finding out if support was present in the village for such a project, and how I could begin planning for lodging, food, and daily activities. I found support and enthusiasm both among the villagers and in the schools, and it was decided to move ahead with planning a seminar.

It was at this time that the Seminar on Transformative Literacy, as the initial California teachers to Oaxaca project is called, became a reality. With the guidance and support of Dr. Ada, a team of instructors was put together: Dr. Isabel Campoy, Dr. Marcos Guerrero, Sylvia Dorta-Duque de Reyes, and myself. Fifteen teachers — from California, Oregon, Texas, and Arizona — signed up for the seminar, along with nine doctoral students of Dr. Ada's from the University of San Francisco. The seminar was also open to partners, children, extended family, and friends who wanted to stay in the village, but did not want to participate in all aspects of the seminar. All together the group was composed of 35 members.

As the project coordinator, I went to the village before the seminar to finalize preparations. It took more than a week to locate adequate housing, organize three meals a day, and manage the appropriate social protocol to legitimize the seminar with village and school authorities.

The First Annual Seminar on Transformative Literacy

The group officially arrived in the village on a hot afternoon the last Sunday of June 1995, meeting first at the airport in Oaxaca. After loading everyone and all the baggage into a big second-class bus, we headed out to the village. There is an enormously huge tree on the way from Oaxaca City to Teotitlán, on the Pan American Highway, well-known as El Tule. It offered us a cool place to rest and discuss where we were going, what we would be doing for that day and the next, and review the basic knowledge the teachers would need to initially feel comfortable. Because the teachers had come from so many different places, it had been impossible for us to meet previously as a group. I had, however, written several group letters with the purpose of keeping everyone informed of developing plans.

We rolled into town in the midafternoon, and slowly went through the process of settling everyone in with her or his family. Some streets in the village are nicely paved with big stones, but other homes are up on the hillsides and difficult to access by car, so the process took several hours, as much of the luggage had to be hand carried to the homes. Those who own cars in the village are still few, and walking is the most usual means of transportation.

After a short afternoon siesta, the group came back together in a local restaurant for a late afternoon dinner. Various villagers were invited, and this was the beginning of some deeply held friendships. As we finished our meal, the *Banda Cecilia* arrived at the restaurant and announced that they were accompanying us to the main civic plaza where a village reception was awaiting us. As we walked along, children joined us and many people gathered to see what we were about, what we looked like, and what the president of the village and the leaders of the project might have to say.

The reception that ensued is something that has marked the memory of all who were present. It was a tenderness of cultures coming together and a hope for the future. The village has a group of children dancers who performed to the accompaniment of their peers who are members of a music group. It was thrilling to see the love and care given to these children, despite limited resources on the part of the families.

A village speaker hosted the event, and the village president welcomed us, officially calling for the opening of the seminar. While we were warmly received, we were also given sound advice and asked some difficult questions publicly. We were reminded to view all that we saw and felt as part of a long and ancient tradition and that, as we watched the children dance and perform musically, we saw them not as artifacts to be observed, rather we felt their dance as it came from the seed of their ancestors.

In an effort to publicly clarify our presence in the village right from the start, we were asked why we had come to Teotitlán del Valle. We responded that we were glad this question had been posed. It reflected the position that all Teotitecos have the right and responsibility to question those who come into their village. It also opened a dialogue on a highly significant issue, one we had come in the hope of gaining greater insight into; namely, the extreme exploitation of indigenous Mexicans (Burgos-Debray 1984). Our reason for being in the village was directly tied to this question. In searching for better ways to educate Latino children in the United States, a deep understanding of oppression is needed (Cummins and Skutnabb-Kangas 1988). We welcomed and honored the question for the integrity it demonstrated, and spent much time afterward discussing it within the group, with the villagers, and in our families. This had been the perfect opening for the dialogue in which we wished to engage.

Teotitlán del Valle has no motel or place for tourists to stay. Twenty years ago one of the villagers decided to open a small market next to the civic plaza to sell rugs directly to the tourists. Shortly thereafter a new road was built giving direct access to the village from the Pan American Highway. The idea caught on and various families now have a stall in the little market, and visitors often come for an afternoon. This has changed the village in subtle ways. There are now two restaurants, and all along the main road, storefront shops sell rugs, their prosperity evident in the quality of the storefront presentations.

However, despite the tourism now present in the village, there had never been any kind of permanent presence of outsiders, except for the rug exporters who would come to drop off wool and pick up rugs for resale. So our presence in the village was unique and offered special challenges. We had entered the village not as tourists, acutely aware of the special privilege we held, knowing the importance of respect within the culture, yet wanting to learn from the people. We had come with a thirst to understand how inequity is structured (hooks 1990) in an effort to unstructure it in the schools. This situation created tension on many levels — for the villagers, the Mexican teachers, and the seminar participants.

The seminar would never have been possible if it had not been for the support of Salvador Hipolito, a local weaver whom I had met in California, and who understood clearly the seminar's goals from the beginning. Because Mr. Hipolito was not only willing to take the risk of supporting the idea in the village but also able to actively recruit additional support from villagers, we were able to build, through him, a strong base of understanding. The success of this project would lie in the access to the community that he facilitated and continues to facilitate.

That first year the seminar was held at the local junior high school. We balanced our time between building relationships with the families who so warmly hosted us and getting to know and working alongside the teachers, students, and authorities in the village schools. (A syllabus created for the first seminar, and subsequently updated, can be found at the end of this paper. It reflects the goals and purpose of the seminar.)

Besides spending time with local teachers, the U.S. teachers also prepared investigations of various village customs to report back to the group. Participatory research methods were employed as a base for the teachers' investigations, and much class time was devoted to the subtleties of doing such research. Many hours were also spent in dialogue clarifying the nature of critical pedagogy and its implementation in classroom practice (Wink 1996).

Through the work of the participants, much information was amassed and presented back to the group as a whole. This made it possible for each person to acquire a much richer understanding of the cultural traditions of the village than he or she would have been able to acquire through personal experience in the two weeks spent in the village. Ultimately, this allowed the teachers greater insight into and more baseline information concerning the customs and ways of many of the families they work with on a daily basis in the United States. A chronicle of events was also kept to record the history of the seminar.

Another phase of the seminar called for each participant to create a book. The nature of these books was entirely left to the imagination of the participants. They were, however, shared in the classes with the Mexican teachers and students. As many of the U.S. teachers brought materials with which to make books in the schools, this activity became a major focus in many classes.

Apple Computer generously donated an LC520 computer to the junior high school. No one at the school knew how to turn it on, let alone operate it, so we gave daily instruction in its operation. The schools have no phone lines, but it is our hope that in the near future we will be able to connect the school to U.S. schools by adding a modem.

In gratitude for an incredibly rich experience, the seminar hosted a good-bye party on the eve of our departure, in the same civic plaza where we had been so warmly received. It was a time to publicly give back to the community — in material donations to the schools and in words of appreciation.

Reflections of U.S. Teachers

The teachers from the United States wrote reflections at the end of their stay. They were asked to consider what they had learned, how they had grown personally, and how the praxis of their teaching had been enriched. All of the teachers wrote about, and verbalized in discussion circles, transformative aspects of the seminar that had — personally and professionally

— touched them deeply. The following statements articulate the service-learning aspect of the time spent in the village and the effect of working alongside the Mexican teachers:

> I've learned how much I can learn from others. I have had an incredible opportunity to work with and interact with some extremely talented and knowledgeable people, from our group and the Mexican community at large. I've been reminded again how enrichingly human and fulfilling it is to share thoughts, feelings and work with others.

The possibilities of relationships were newly discovered within this context, and relationships were built on new understandings of dignity and humanity:

> Although I may not be as experienced as others in working with the Latino population, I still have something to offer in a seminar like this one. I think that by being open, flexible and trusting in others, that which is good in one surfaces and comes out. This experience will enrich my daily life. It is important that we put into action things that we claim to profess as our "philosophy." Too often this philosophy ends up to be quite shallow in terms of how we practice it on a daily basis.

There were other similar reflections on the same topic:

> I have learned from my interactions with the people, and feel an incredible bond with some of the members of the community. I have developed friendships with a few people who will always be a part of me. These friendships developed despite cultural, political, or economic differences. I am more conscious of what constitutes the feeling of being rich. The embodiment of this idea exists within the richness of the friendships with children of the family with which I lived.

Within the conceptual framework of this project lay the belief that all change must include a component for personal transformation. In our case we were looking to make changes in the sociocultural infrastructure of educational institutions with regard to curriculum choices and pedagogical implementation. Personal experiences were the base on which visions were formed, and that made it possible to critically step out on the balcony and survey our human interactions on a larger, broader scale of knowledge production:

> The experience here has been unforgettable, the sights, sounds, and personal exchanges between people have given me not only a perspective on this unique community but has also given me a deeper understanding of myself. I see the strength in community — a community made of imperfect

individuals and the need to accept some of the imperfections within ourselves and within others. Cultures have many strengths to share with one
another.

For another teacher, her willingness to move beyond her social and personal knowledge base caused her to expand her world view and make it
more inclusive:

> I have never even stayed on a farm before. My life has been spent in the
> suburbs of a large city. I was born and raised in a white, middle class sub-
> urb of Los Angeles. Now I have learned to value and treasure a culture and
> people very different from me. Learning about a culture in context is
> extremely effective and I feel that I truly lived what I was learning at a
> multitude of levels.

In the following statement we are able to witness the depth of personal
transformation created in another of the participants:

> I have learned to trust my inner voice more. I am more empowered by the
> manner in which I was confronted and sometimes threatened by my own
> cultural background as a Latino. I now feel more honored at my being a
> Mexican ancestral person. I have gained an immense perspective into the
> lives my parents have lived. Throughout this journey I was in the compa-
> ny of my father and my mother in spirit. Sometimes I was moved to tears
> at the recognition of some detail — like the sight of a goat skin drying in
> the heat, which echoed something in my unconsciousness. I felt love to and
> from my parents. In many respects, this journey has taught me that I am
> not so alone as I once thought. I have the company of a spiritual entity that
> I recognize as my heritage and God.

This project sought to effect a more human and inclusive pedagogy
within the infrastructure of both U.S. and Mexican schools, one that would
ultimately lead to healthier schooling for all children. One of the most
important sources of this lofty goal lies in the small transformative seeds
planted through personal interactions. These personal experiences translate
into new understandings that, in turn, transform one's personal pedagogy:

> I will now be more open to people different from me. I will appreciate what
> I have more and be less wasteful. I will continue my commitment to love
> and serve children. I am proud to be a teacher. There is a common bond
> among us which transcends language, culture and nationality.

Sometimes the act of leaving our familiar reality can propel us into new
areas of clarity and precipitate important insights in a short period of time:

I have seen a lot that has opened up my eyes in appreciating things back home. Seeing what kind of background my students may come from and being able to relate to them has also given me a new awareness. People may have different ways of living, beliefs, etc., but in the end we are all the same with dreams and worries of our own, and a heart.

Life in the United States is often hectic, and the leisurely hours spent in discussions during the seminar were a treat for those whose busy lives left little time for reflection. One participant felt that the expansion of time and peace he experienced during the seminar would directly transfer into his teaching practice:

Because I feel a little more at peace with myself I sense that I will be a more effective educator. My very life is an educational tool, I can teach, I can learn from others, most of all, I am a keeper of knowledge as much as anyone else.
- *I want to listen more. I have learned this here.*
- *I want to listen more to my own voice.*
- *I want to trust my own voice.*
- *I want to be more open to others.*

All who participated in this project felt some initial trepidation at the prospect of the seminar. We often worried that our cultural antennae will not extend deep enough or be sufficiently sensitive and respectful, that we may be misunderstood, and that unknowingly we may offend in some way. We were concerned lest our large numbers make the villagers feel uncomfortable. We hoped that "being members of a large group in a small *pueblo* [would not be] perceived as an 'invasion.'"

Second Annual Seminar on Transformative Literacy

I also helped organize the second year of the project with the help of a team of instructors: Dr. Marcos Guerrero, who attended the first year; Dr. Frank Espinoza; Dr. Helena Janes; and a well-known children's musician Jose Luis Orozco. The many lessons we learned from the first seminar led us to make slight modifications in the second-year format, but did not affect in any way our basic goals. Because participants were hungry on rising, we decided to eat breakfast first thing in the morning at a local restaurant, instead of, as we had done the first year, eating at the local breakfast time. We also spent much more time with the Mexican teachers, in their classrooms and after school, discussing our teaching strategies and education in general. Our first-year experience taught us that we needed to invest much more time building bridges with the Mexican teachers, and we realized that this would be a priority of the seminar.

The addition of music by Jose Luis Orozco made an incredible difference in building community among seminar participants, in the schools and in the community at large. As music is an important point of cultural life in the village, it brought people together and facilitated relationship building that would not have been possible without it.

This second year we solidified the practice of cultural book exchanges between classes in the United States and those in Teotitlán del Valle, paving the way for future telecommunications projects and publications in the village children's native language, Zapoteco. We also expanded our base of friendships and support in the village. One of the side satisfactions of the project has been that the money we pay in lodging has bought many a bed in the village for others who had in the past slept on the floor, or has allowed families to buy more wool and build some momentum toward economic self-determination.

For the teaching team, there were two themes that announced themselves loud and clear to be incorporated in new ways into the second-year seminar. The first was that the mainstream culture of the United States is one of anonymity when juxtaposed to the village culture. Here everyone is known, and everyone is recognized. There is no invisibleness allowed or socially accepted. Second, we had to make our collective experience metacognitively understood by participants on a deeper level. We felt that some of the richness that was experienced passed as mere experience and needed to expand metacognitively to higher levels of processing, levels that eventually influence interactions and understandings of those same interactions.

Finally, we felt that ongoing community building was needed if we were to continue to strengthen our relationship with the Mexican teachers and administrators in the various village schools. We had made tremendous inroads, but further work was needed to solidify and extend that beginning. This extension, we realized, would take time and patience and much more contact.

The Third Annual Seminar Expands

As we spent time with the teachers in the schools, it became highly apparent that this project could not sustain itself by merely bringing teachers from the United States to the village. The first thing the Mexican teachers wanted to know from the very beginning of the project, and continued asking through subsequent years, was when they would be able to visit schools and teachers in California.

As the third annual seminar was being organized, the opportunity presented itself to arrange for the Mexican teachers to travel to California. This was the important piece that completed the exchange process. With the support of the Mexican Ministry of Education, the Mexican Department of Foreign Relations, and California State University, Stanislaus, Mexican teachers were invited to Stockton, California, where they could work with children in area schools for two weeks, exchange pedagogical strategies and build relationships with local bilingual teachers, and participate for one week in the Great Valley Writing Project.

This teacher exchange program was supported through funds saved from the Seminar on Transformative Literacy; local businesses that helped with food costs; host families that offered bed and breakfast; the Mexican Ministry of Education that paid plane flights and arranged passports and visas; California State University, Stanislaus, that offered organizational support; and the Office of Extended Education within that institution that provided funds for in-state travel.

The original seminar in Oaxaca had also expanded to include a second two-week seminar, codirected by Dr. Peggy Laughlin and me. That seminar was based on the work of Luis Moll (1990) and Lev Vygotsky (1978). The infusion of new ideas by Dr. Laughlin changed slightly the focus of the seminar.

Where We Go From Here: Reflections and Dreams

Even with the support of village members, there are many roadblocks to creating a project such as the one described in this article. The motivation to continue, however, comes from the service objective itself. It comes from the heartfelt thanks and encouragement of villagers who participated and the anxious requests of those who wished to participate. Most profound, it comes from the emerging close-knit network of teachers on both sides of the border working in solidarity to create better learning conditions for all children.

Many times I have returned to this quotation by Patricia Maguire (1994) for inspiration and strength:

> . . . the redistribution of power, among and between the world's women and men, is a long-haul, collective struggle in which there is work for each of us. Participatory research is but one tool in that struggle. However, transformation, social and personal, is not an event. It is a process that we are living through, creating as we go. It is dangerous to compare our modest beginnings and exhausting middles to the successful, documented endings of others' work. For we never know when we begin where the work will take us and those involved. (176)

The first time I saw the children from the village dance, a seed was planted in my heart to one day see the *Niños Danzantes* dance for the children in schools throughout California. And not only dance from a cassette, but dance as they did that first evening in the civic plaza to the music played by their classmates, relatives, and friends, the children's music group in the village. What a powerful role model children can provide for one another, creating ethnic pride and positive identity development for other children, who have all too often witnessed their rich, diverse Mexican culture patronized, simplified, and monoculturalized! I look forward to the day when the seminar can facilitate workshops, dialogues, and assemblies to share knowledge currently denied to the vast majority of children in institutions of education throughout the United States. As I wrote in my dissertation:

> There was a great deal of work and trepidation involved in organizing a trip of this kind, but the richness of the interchanges and the lifetime friendships formed will continue to transform not only the people of Teotitlán, but also the consciousness of those United States teachers who saw first hand the beauty of the Zapotec people and the ugly results of generations of domination.

Those teachers know the true value of a Zapotec rug, in sweat, and in terms of human sacrifice. They can value the intelligence, strength, and knowledge passed down since ancient times, and pass that respect on to their students. They will be allies for the Zapotec people out in the world, and listen more loudly to all students' voices (Smith 1995: 256).

References

Ada, A.F. (1993). "Mother Tongue Literacy as a Bridge Between Home and School Cultures." In *The Power of Two Languages*. Edited by J. Tinajero and A.F. Ada, pp. 158-164. New York, NY: Macmillan/McGraw-Hill.

Andriola-Balderas, V. (1993). "Writing Lived Histories as Curriculum: A Participatory Research Project." Ph.D. dissertation, University of San Francisco.

Brown, K. (1995). "Circular Migration of Puerto Rican and Neorican: Listening to Students' Voices." Ph.D. dissertation, University of San Francisco.

Burgos-Debray, E. (1984). *I, Rigoberta Menchú: An Indian Woman in Guatemala*. London: Verso.

Cummins, J., and T. Skutnabb-Kangas, eds. (1988). *Minority Education: Shame to Struggle*. Clevedon, England: Multilingual Matters Ltd.

Fishman, J. (1991). *Reversing Language Shift*. Philadelphia, PA: Multilingual Matters Ltd.

Freire, P. (1994). *Pedagogy of Hope*. New York, NY: Continuum.

——— . (1973). *Education for Critical Consciousness*. New York, NY: Continuum.

——— . (1970). *Pedagogy of the Oppressed*. New York, NY: Continuum.

Freire, P., and A. Faundez. (1992). *Learning to Question*. New York, NY: Continuum.

Freire, P., and M. Horton. (1990). *We Make the Road by Walking*. Philadelphia, PA: Temple University Press.

Freire, P., and D. Macedo. (1987). *Literacy: Reading the Word and the World*. New York, NY: Continuum.

Gómez-Valdez, C. (1993). "The Silent Majority Raise Their Voices. Reflections of Mexican Parents on Learning and Schooling: A Participatory Research Study." Ph.D. dissertation, University of San Francisco.

hooks, b. (1990). *Yearning: Race, Class and Gender*. Boston, MA: South End Press.

Igoa, C. (1995). *The Inner World of the Immigrant Child*. New York, NY: St. Martin's Press.

Laughlin, P. (1996). "Euro-American Educators Teaching in a Bilingual Context: A Participatory Research Study." Ph.D. dissertation, the University of San Francisco, San Francisco.

Maguire, P. (1987). *Doing Participatory Research: A Feminist Approach*. Amherst, MA: The Center for International Education, University of Massachusetts.

——— . (1994). "Challenges, Contradictions, and Celebrations: Attempting Participatory Research as a Doctoral Student." In *Voices of Change*. Edited by P. Park, M. Brydon-Miller, B. Hall, and T. Jackson, pp. 157-176. Westport, CT: Bergin & Garvey.

Moll, L.C. (1990). *Vygotsky and Education: Instructional Implications and Applications of Sociolinguistic Psychology*. Cambridge, NY: Cambridge University Press.

Murphy, A., and A. Stepick. (1991). *Social Inequality in Oaxaca: A History of Resistance and Change*. Philadelphia: Temple University Press.

Park, P. (1992). "The Discovery of Participatory Research as a New Scientific Paradigm: Personal and Intellectual Accounts." *The American Sociologist* 23(4): 29-42.

Seda, E. (1980). *Requiem para una cultura*. Rio Piedras, PR: Ediciones Bayoan.

Skutnabb-Kangas, T. (1992). "Linguistic Genocide." Paper presented at the Language Policy in the Baltic States Conference, Mahwah, NJ.

Smith, N. (1995). "The Struggle for Cultural and Linguistic Survival: A Participatory Research Study With a Zapotec Community in California." Ph.D. dissertation, University of San Francisco, San Francisco.

Vygotsky, L.S. (1978). *Mind in Society*. Cambridge, MA: Harvard University Press.

Wink, J. (1996). *Critical Pedagogy: Notes From the Real World*. White Plains, NY: Longman.

Wong-Fillmore, L. (1991). "When Learning a Second Language Means Losing the First." *Early Childhood Research Quarterly* 6: 323-346.

California State University, Stanislaus
Teacher Education Department

Seminar on Transformative Literacy: EDUC 4600
Teotitlán del Valle, Oaxaca, Mexico

Instructors:

Dr. Nancy Jean Smith
Dr. Peggy Laughlin
Dr. Gilbert Valadez

Summer Session 1999
June 26th - July 10th 1999

COURSE DESCRIPTION

Through this course students will have the opportunity to learn about, reflect on, and act upon transformative education and its potential for a vibrant classroom response to social justice both in Mexico and the United States. Through joint efforts of eductors in the United States and Mexico this course offers a cross-cultural collaborative teaching/learning experience that will engage students in rich cultural encounters within a Zapotec community that can lead to greater understanding of education as a social practice.

The profoundness of Zapotec culture provides a rich context to understand and develop a pedagogy of literacy, which requires an eye on reading the world as well as the word. Students will generate three copies of a personal book, which is meant to foster positive family relationships and bridge academics with the home in both a Mexican and United States context. These books may be expressions of student's reality or be inspired by their Oaxacan experience. Participating in a new environment is an excellent opportunity to reflect upon previous knowledge with new eyes. Students will also be expected to keep a reflective journal.

The seminar will physically be held in the local elementary school, but teachers may also spend as much time as they like in the village pre-school, and junior high classrooms. A chronicle of the seminar will document our journey, collaboratively written by instructors and participants.

COURSE OBJECTIVES

The focus of this course is on curriculum development as connected by culture and language, from both a theoretical and practical viewpoint. By the end of the seminar students will be able to:
- Explain how the traditions and practices of the Zapotec families they met provided knowledge that is transferrable to curriculum and educational practices in their school and classroom in the United States.
- Describe the Mexican educational system and how their new knowledge of that system will impact their own teaching in the United States.

- Articulate why the personal book they created is an important piece of a transformative pedagogy for their own classroom.
- Identify instructional models and strategies for appropriate teaching of linguistically and culturally diverse students.
- Bridge the gap between multicultural concepts, theories and practices in United States schools.

COURSE CONTENT

Personal Books

We all have stories to tell, people to recognize, ideas to explore. Each student will create one original and two copies of a book. Any literary genre may be used, including but not limited to: picture books, fiction, legends, fables, folklore, poetry and plays. The books need not be extensive, but certainly should be personal and original. These books should be sturdy enough to hold up after extensive use by young and older readers. They are intended to accompany core curriculum (math, science, social studies, language arts, reading, etc.), as well as be creative expressions of one's own uniqueness. Examples of past books will be shared. At the end of the seminar a closing workshop will be held, and all personal books will be presented to the local community and Mexican teachers. One copy of each book will be donated to the local library.

Teacher Interchanges

Students will spend part of their day in village classrooms, exchanging teaching ideas and strategies with Mexican teachers. They will work directly with children, sharing good teaching practices with Kindergarteners to 9th graders. United States teachers will chose the grade level with which they prefer to work.

Seminar Workshops

The seminar teaching team will present different constructivist workshops on core curriculum, with emphasis on math, science and social studies, and other subjects solicited by the Mexican and United States teachers. The expertise of the university faculty teaching team will be intermixed with the extensive knowledge represented by the Mexican and United States teachers. All efforts will be made to facilitate time for related instructional practices to be shared.

Reflective Journal

Keeping a journal for constant reflection is an essential part of the learning process. Students are asked to keep a daily journal, writing thoughts, as well as feelings, emotions, concerns and insights, related to themselves as learners, their emancipatory role in society, and research as a tool for social transformation, along with thoughts on the attainment of social justice within the realm of education. It is meant to keep students focused on their role as practitioners of education and the learning process as a part of the human experience. At least one day will be chronicled by each participant in lieu/as part of their journal assignment.

Journal entries need not be extensive, they can be brief statements, poetry, letters, essay, narrative, etc. but should contain pertinent and accurate information. The purpose is for students to document their experience and growth, as well as learn from their own thinking. Journal entries will be turned in every other morning during the seminar.

Chronicle

Every collective action is an historical event. This seminar is no exception. As we meet together to reflect on possible actions to transform society through our teaching and learning, we are creating history. When history is chronicled and the events are written down at the time that they are taking place, a new possibility for reflection is opened which can lead to more effective action. Chronicling is done in a reflective manner, tape recorders, abundant notes, photographs, personal journals and the immediate environment all offer ample material for the chronicle. We analyze not only the content but also the process of the seminar, making the chronicle another tool for understanding and making meaning of our work.

Technology Component

The seminar will conduct beginning computer orientation for Mexican teachers and students. This is a strand of the seminar that will happen congruent to daily activities. Computers in the village are Apples, and there are no school telephones lines as yet for modems. Any expertise participants bring to the training is greatly appreciated.

COURSE READINGS

Each student will receive a reader. One month prior to the course, all registered students will receive a reader that they will be expected to have read by the time they arrive at Teotitlán del Valle. While in the village students will be expected to be actively involved with local Mexican educators and families in discussions and information gathering. There will be little time for reading during the seminar.

SUGGESTED READINGS: REFERENCES

Fredrickson, J. (Eds.), (1995). Reclaiming our voices: Bilingual education, critical pedagogy and praxis. Ontario: California Association for Bilingual Education.

Freire, P. and Macedo, D. (1987). Literacy: Reading the word and the world. South Hadley, MA: Bergin and Garvey Publishers.

Laughlin, P. (1996). Crossing borders: Transformative experiences of Euro-American bilingual teachers in a Spanish speaking context, a participatory study. Doctoral dissertation, University of San Francisco.

Moll, L., Gonzales, N., Floyd-Tenery, M., Rivera, A., Rendon, P., Gonzalez, R., and Amanti, C. (1993). Teacher research on funds of knowledge: Learning from households. No. 6. National Center for Research on Cultural Diversity and Second Language Learning.

Skuttnab-Kangas, T. and Cummins, J. (1988). From shame to struggle: Minority Education. Multilingual Matters, Philadelphia.

Smith, N.J. (1995). Linguistic genocide and the struggle for cultural and linguistic survival: A participatory research study with a Zapotec community in California. Doctoral dissertation, University of San Francisco.

COURSE REQUIREMENTS
1. Punctual and active attendance at school and seminar functions.
2. Course packet read before arrival in Teotitlán del Valle.
3. Maintenance of a reflective journal integrating class discussions, readings and village experiences.
4. Interactive collaboration with local Mexican educators and students.
5. Investigation integrated into the creation of a personal book with two copies.

GRADE EVALUATION

Grades will be calculated on a 100% scale and earned according to the following point structure:
   A=90%, B=80%, C=70%, D=60%, F=below 60%

- Reflective Journal (25%)
- Seminar Workshop (25%)
- Personal Book and two copies (25%)
- Teacher Interchange (25%)

COURSE SCHEDULE

Week 1: June 26th - July 4th, 1998

Saturday: June 26th
- Students arrive and are met at Oaxaca City Airport
- Stop at El Tule rest area for lunch and days course of events
- Introductions of host families and United States teachers
- Dinner - Tour of village, time with host families

Sunday: June 27th
- Breakfast, Orientation, visit to Tlacolula Outdoor Market, lunch,
- Afternoon free with host family

Monday: June 28th
- Welcome by school principal and Mexican teachers:
- Investigation of personal goals and framework of seminar work
- Historical overview of the Zapotec community
- Perspectives on transformative education

Tuesday: June 29th
- Literacy within a transformative framework: Personal Books
- Perspectives on the MesoAmerican/Mexican Experience
- Organization of Seminar core curriculum workshops
- Afternoon dialogue session

Wednesday: June 30th
- Seminar Workshop with Mexican Teachers

	• Hike to the top of Picacho
Thursday: July 1st	• Mexican Classroom Exchanges
Friday: July 2nd	• Visit to Primary School in Santiaguito • Lunch in Oaxaca City and visit to Zocalo • Evening free in Oaxaca City or Teotitlán
Saturday, July 3rd	• Excursion to archeological/cultural sites, Mezcal factory.
Sunday, July 4th	• Free day to visit Oaxaca City or other places

Week 2: July 5th - July 10th

The Fiesta de Julio begins Monday and ends Sunday. Festivities in the village continue all week celebrating La Santa Patrona de la Preciosa Sangre.

Monday: July 5th	• Seminar Workshop and Book Production • Calenda and Music at the Church
Tuesday: July 6th	• Seminar Workshop and Book Production
Wednesday: July 7th	• Indigenous presence in the Americas: Danza de la Pluma • Main day of the village fiesta • Danza de la Pluma all day at Church
Thursday: July 8th	• Seminar Workshop Book Production • Primary School Closing Ceremonies (Clausuras)
Friday: July 9th	• Closing ceremonies with schools • Presentations and donations of books Seminar Ceremony

During the seminar there will be spontaneous activities with local artisans and residents. Flexibility is an important quality that makes the seminar successful. Local dancers, children's groups and adults will also talk with students about the significance of Zapotec traditions and culture, we will also gather with the children's village dance group and children's band who perform the Danza de la Pluma.

A typical day will go something like this, however please allow for alterations:

7:00	Breakfast at the Descanso Restaurant
8:00	Morning in schools / seminar workshops / or excursion visits
2:00	Lunch
3:00	Afternoon Dialogue Sessions / Free afternoon for research
7:00	Evening Meal

The Chongón-Colonche Hills in Western Ecuador: Preservation Through Community Empowerment

by Clarice R. Strang

Western Ecuador is one of the planet's conservation hot spots, and one of 18 geographic areas declared worldwide as being in the greatest danger of biological extinction from human intervention. More than 90 percent of the forests here have been cleared in the last generation and this has had a critical impact on a part of the globe that has high endemism and is rich in plant and animal species. Ranging from the coast up through the transition zones to 800 meters, the Chongón-Colonche Hills are centrally located within this geographic area. Clouds driven in from the Pacific Ocean come up against the ridges, creating a variety of unique microclimates. This ecological importance, coupled with the needs of the inhabitants to pursue alternative economic development, triggered the interest of several groups in offering support.

In this article, I will describe the efforts of the Pro-Pueblo Foundation that involve the inhabitants in a rescue plan to reverse destructive trends. First, I will summarize the history of the Chongón-Colonche Hills, the people who settled there, and briefly list key environmental challenges this part of Ecuador faces. Second, I will highlight the collaborative ecological and social framework that has emerged in light of these challenges and then describe in more detail the work of Pro-Pueblo and various participatory projects with the local people as well as the work of international students. In the last portion of this section, I will offer informal strategies for assessing various community projects. Finally, I will conclude with a look ahead at the remaining challenges.

The Chongón-Colonche Hills

Chongón-Colonche has a very rich heritage. Its inhabitants and ancestors belong to several of the earliest civilizations in the Americas (5,000-10,000 years ago). Their history is closely entwined with the natural wealth of the region, and today most of the major settlements are situated along watersheds, as were those of their ancestors.

I would like to acknowledge the participation of my friend and colleague Victoria Longland in an earlier draft of this paper.

The ancient people settled in the river basins, fishing and developing an agricultural system adapted to the seasons: planting on high flatlands in the rainy season and in the wetter valley bottoms in the dry season. They were some of the earliest farmers on the continent, planting maize and squash and collecting wild cotton. The early societies developed a complex system of land allocation for production and settlement. It was a cooperative land ownership limited to extended family and kinship ties that prevented the land from being shared out too thinly. Populations flourished, and even with the arrival of the Spaniards, the people managed to stay independent, maintaining their traditional social systems. Evidence suggests that populations were greater than those at present but did not destroy the natural balance. Forest exploitation did not mean irreversible destruction and the communities lived compatibly within their environment.

Even as the fine hardwoods from the Chongón-Colonche forests became increasingly known for a variety and quality not found in other areas, the impact of logging was still negligible. The diverse properties of these woods made them ideal for furniture, house construction, and ship building. Guayacan (*Tabebuia chrysantha*, and other *Tabebuia* species), Cascol (*Caesalpinia paipai*), and Guasmo (*Guazuma ulmifolia*) have been used from the 16th century on, when the first shipyards opened in Guayaquíl; homes in Lima, Peru, were built with timber from this region.

Deforestation took on serious proportions with the turn of the present century. Two major fires in Guayaquíl sharply increased demand for building materials, and the new railroad to Quito used sleepers cut from wood in the area. Oil was exploited commercially in the 1920s by Anglo-Ecuadorian Oilfields Limited, and although its extraction helped to sustain the national economy, it also brought serious ecological and social consequences to the region. The people who had for centuries supported themselves with a sustainable farming economy were enticed into a new cash-based form of work. When the company's 50-year domination of the area came to an end, there were massive layoffs, and many were forced to head for the cities in search of work. To offset this crisis, the company helped train exworkers as furniture makers. Ironically, even though this measure eased some hardship in the short term, it ultimately intensified the destruction of the forest by causing such a depletion of local wood that nowadays the raw material has to be brought in from as far as Esmeraldas to the north and the Amazon Basin, just to keep the approximately 800 furniture shops in business.

The oil industry also introduced charcoal as a safer fuel than firewood in the camps. Its production alone has become the single greatest cause for massive deforestation and desertification in extensive areas around the well heads. Salt refineries also did their damage. One refinery in the 1960s, for example, required 20 truckloads of wood daily for its refining process. The use of wood today as a domestic fuel for both the coast and the cities is still widespread. From recent surveys, we estimate that only 1 percent forest cover remains in the Chongón-Colonche range. A side effect of the aforementioned activities has been the construction of a penetrating network of roads that made access to the forests even easier. This, plus one of the \fastest growing population rates in Latin America, has put an unbearable strain on the natural resources of the whole country.

Prolonged droughts are a legacy of this century's misguided drive for development at all costs. The rains fail and crops are meager. Loss of soil fertility through erosion forces remaining farmers to rely more and more on expensive irrigation systems and damaging chemicals to improve yields. The desert creeps up from the south, a warning sign that looms over the communities farther north. Many people can no longer support themselves. Slowly they are leaving to try their luck in the cities and the congested crime-ridden slums of Guayaquíl.

The Ecological-Social Alliance for Reform

The Framework of Collaboration

Realizing the urgent needs of Chongón-Colonche, Fundación Pro-Pueblo (FPP), Fundacion Natura's Reforestation Project (FN), Public Health International (PHI), People Allied for Nature (PAN), Programa Manejo Recursos Costeros (PMRC), Plan Internacional, have become an ongoing presence in the area for five years now. Their common objective has been to develop projects that involve the inhabitants in the search for economic alternatives and the improvement of the standard of living while incorporating in this process the protection of natural resources.

The larger foundations (FPP, FN, PHI, and PMRC) have thus created a climate in which all aspects of livelihood are being attended to, to a higher or lesser degree, depending on the participatory levels of the inhabitants. Smaller organizations and individuals (PAN, Peace Corps, APROFE – Planned Parenthood) are taking on specific villages or working with smaller groups of individuals. Moreover, the integration of all these programs has made it easier and more attractive for other organizations to come in and consider involvement (Plan International, Armed Forces, CARE — Cooperativas Americanas de Remesas al Exterior, FECD or Fondo Ecuatoriano Canadiense de Desarrollo, REIPA or Recicladores y Protectores Ambientales).

The Pro-Pueblo Foundation

The Pro-Pueblo Foundation (FPP) was founded in 1992 by the National Cement Co. (La Cemento Nacional C.A.) with the primary objective of supporting a sustainable and participatory program of integrated economic development in villages along the western slopes of the Chongón-Colonche Hills. To achieve this goal, the foundation identified the following five main fields of action: (1) cultural and educational programs, (2) environmental health, (3) agricultural programs, (4) handicrafts, and (5) ecotourism. I will describe concrete projects from each field in the section on examples of collaboration.

Central to this program is the improvement of the standard of living of local inhabitants — a process that incorporates a conservation educational program for the protection of natural resources. Pro-Pueblo's initial community projects began in 1992 in the town of La Entrada, a village on the border between the provinces of Guayas and Manabí. In June of 1994, the foundation established permanent headquarters in Manglaralto and has since taken the lead in the development process.

The *Comuna* System

The fundamental approach of Pro-Pueblo is to reach and work with the people who live in the area. Throughout the history of the region, a constant has been the traditional comuna system of social organization. One outcome of the labor and social crisis following the oil company's decline was the official recognition and legalization of comuna lands throughout the area. This recognition greatly consolidated the people's identity and provided them with legal control over their ancestral lands. Pro-Pueblo reaches 38 such comunas, which altogether include 54 villages at the northern part of the Chongón-Colonche range. All are descendants of the original indigenous settlements. The comunas, with their historical kinship ties and an internal democratic process for decision making, are ideally constituted to be the main protagonists in the process of protecting valuable forest remnants, increasing forest cover and taking charge of the future to improve the quality of life.

Collaboration: Pro-Pueblo and Comunas

FPP's main goal is to work toward comuna empowerment. We believe that if commitment can be achieved through the comuna structure, it may be possible to safeguard a rich heritage. Workshops with individual communities have led to proposals that are put to practice and begun only after a formal request has been presented by a comuna. The structure is participatory, consisting of training, action, and evaluation.

The most important link with the comuna is the "extensionists" — inhabitants from the comunas who have been trained by volunteers or technicians hired by the foundation. Extensionists and democratically elected health, ecological, forestry, and home garden committees have been instrumental in providing communities with new options and proposals. The FPP acts as a facilitator by identifying needed resources and reinforcing the know-how to improve standard of living while still caring for the environment. This care starts inside each person's house and extends into the hills surrounding the villages. The extensionists are in tune with day-to-day and door-to-door activities, and are the first to alert the foundation about any unforeseen problems as well as advances or failures. They become the "resident professionals" who drive the assimilating process and its multiplying effect. Thus, comuneros themselves provide the know-how to associations, communities, and youth groups, offering an opportunity for specialization in what most applies to life-styles and natural inclinations. Extensionists are very important in the periodic evaluations that take place for every program or project. Fundación Pro-Pueblo has put the most emphasis on workshops aimed to equip individuals with practical knowledge in different areas. This way, they progressively acquire experience in what could result in an economic alternative. The family unit is very important and is considered to be a key factor in the process of change. Wherever possible, the workshops draw on the experiences of the comuneros themselves — always sharing information and experiences.

Children are vital components in any learning process. They represent the future, and the more knowledge they assimilate when young, about the environment and the devastation caused by human abuse, the better equipped they will be to deal with that abuse. Whatever their age, children are able to contribute by weeding in the vegetable gardens; helping with handicrafts such as palm ivory, recycled paper, wax candles, toquilla straw hats, and ceramics; planting trees; recycling garbage; and presenting "ecological theater."

Keeping communication lines open is vital and comuneros are encouraged to participate in the monthly newsletter El Comunerito and in the weekly radio interviews of the program La Voz del Comunero to express their thoughts, suggestions, and anxieties. These outlets provide a key opportunity to give updates on various programs and to further consolidate community spirit.

Examples of Collaboration

Pro-Pueblo works primarily with communities that respond to participatory involvement. Programs are considered successful if they are assimilated by the inhabitants in their daily lives. Since 1992, Pro-Pueblo has supported a variety of projects in all five areas of action.

Culture and Education. The construction of the Amantes de Sumpa Museum is one initiative that illustrates the foundation's first area of concern. It features a collection of archaeological pieces representing the traditional Las Vegas culture of the Santa Elena peninsula, including the skeletal remains of the *Amantes de Sumpa*. On this site, which was discovered by the archaeologist Karen Stothert, 200 skeletons were found, two of which lay in an embraced position, giving the site its name. Following the donation of the land by the municipality of Santa Elena, Pro-Pueblo was able to build the Amantes de Sumpa Museum on this 10,000-year-old site, the oldest human cemetery in the Americas.

The Salango Museum and Center of Investigations is another example of honoring and preserving the region's archaeological treasures. The museum exhibits coastal archaeology, combining photographs, display cases, and maps, and maintains an archaeology lab, a bone lab, and meeting facilities in its Centre House. Shortly after the death of the museum's founder, Presley Norton, in 1996, Pro-Pueblo assumed the administration, maintenance, and financing of all new infrastructure.

The radio program *El Comunerito* and the monthly newsletter *La Voz del Comunero* are efforts aimed at encouraging community participation in all of Pro-Pueblo's programs. Both media keep communication lines open for sharing experiences, successes, and failures across the Chongón hills.

Environmental education is yet another goal in this category. Such education goes beyond mere classroom teaching and involves many elementary school children in outdoor projects, walks, ecological theater, and story writing. Up to now, this effort has resulted in the planting of 1,200 trees in several villages.

The curriculum of Manglaralto High School, with its animal husbandry and agricultural programs, allows Pro-Pueblo to offer an integral farm model. Students learn about vermiculture, pigs, guinea pigs, goats, poultry, fowl as well as horticultural and citrus plantations.

Environmental Health. With regard to the foundation's second field of action, two programs that aim at improving the villages' sanitary situation stand out. The first involves water distribution systems that have been set up in three years. Twenty-three villages have been attended to and each system consists of a well, a cistern, and an underground polyethelene hose for distribution to taps. Better access to water has improved sanitation and these systems have helped curb health problems. The foundation also offers workshops on water use and rationing.

The second program is a comprehensive recycling effort that involves the participation of 54 villages and 73 health educators. Trained in door-to-door consciousness raising on waste management, these educators have contributed to the construction of 48 recycling patios that can collect plastic, paper, carton, glass, and aluminum for reutilization. As a result, 10 of these recycling patios have been able to generate sufficient income — and hence incentive — to work effectively.

Agricultural Programs. In this area, Pro-Pueblo supports two programs, one in organic gardening and the other in honey production. In the third year of the first program, 420 women work organic family plots combining vegetables, fruits, ornamental plants, medicinal plants, and herbs. This has made a substantial improvement to family economy, nutrition, and health. Some women have also taken to making jams and marmalades.

In the area of agiculture, comuneros have formed 12 bee associations involving approximately 150 beekeepers. Their goal is to produce 3,000 litres of honey per year to get into the competitive markets of Guayaquíl and Quito. These associations also produce beeswax candles, pollen, and royal jelly.

Handicrafts. This fourth program area comprises efforts that include a variety of products and skills. Women's groups in nine villages are currently active in producing cards, stationery, certificates, folders, paper maché boxes, dolls, and trophies made of recycled papers. This program involves approximately 70 women between 12 and 50 years of age. It is interesting to note that recycled paper products have found more acceptance in the international than in local markets.

The nut of a native palm from the Chongón hills has become another important raw material. It is a source of inspiration for seven groups (male and female) producing buttons, necklaces, bracelets, and earrings. This program, which is built around palm ivory products, is resulting in a very realistic economic alternative for over 100 artisans who are gaining experience in improving quality and design.

Ecotourism. Pro-Pueblo's various program areas and community efforts are ideally suited to promoting the richness of the Chongón hills of western Ecuador. This advantage is being developed slowly along with the cultural and educational programs. Five routes have been established that combine various elements from scenery, biological diversity, and trekking to sites rich in archaeological finds and ethnic traditions. Community members are being trained to function as the future managers of visits to their villages, developing sensitivity to the values of their protected environments and caution so as not to overexploit tourism. Ecotourism represents another viable strategy for inhabitants anxious to become more productive and efficient in their homeland.

The projects and programs I have described in this section have been established to promote the investigation and preservation of the region's various archaeological and cultural treasures, to reestablish an equilibrium in the ecosystem, and to encourage new agricultural programs, environmental awareness, and reforestation.

Furthermore, besides promoting community development and conservation projects, Pro-Pueblo serves as an informal clearinghouse for international education. In the past three years, it has facilitated a variety of experiential learning projects involving students from the United States, three of which I would like to briefly identify.

Cameron Penn (1997) has examined how artisans have begun to benefit from the use of the tagua nut for handicrafts as well as its general artistic and ecological implications for the Chongón-Colonche Hills. A study by Meghan Fallon (1997) focuses on the production of coffee and cacao sacks from cabuya fibers. She has analyzed how working with cabuya has affected the small town of El Chorrillo. Crystal Henle (1995) compared organic gardening in Salango and Dos Mangas, two coastal towns. She documented how both projects helped the communities protect local resources.

Challenges to Collaboration

Of course, the collaborative projects between Pro-Pueblo and the comunas are not immune to many social and political ills. An invasion of comuna land is one of the most socially insidious problems to challenge the projects, but it is one that has received official support for many years. The ecologically disastrous Agrarian Reform Law of the 1960s assumed that forests were unproductive land and promoted their destruction by either forcing landowners to convert that land into agricultural production or confiscating woodland tracts and handing them over to colonists from already deforested provinces. Illegal settlers, or *invasores,* now encroach on legally owned comuna lands, wiping out the forest for timber. These tracts may later be converted to croplands that become progressively more unproductive. The invasores have no respect for the ancient and legal rights of the comunas and no interest in the comuneros' efforts to save their ethnic traditions. They also have no loyalties to the land. Encouraged by land traffickers and protected by bogus settlement agreements, they hide behind gunfire and mark their stolen territory with fire.

The armed forces and their local military bases are proving to be enthusiastic supporters of many programs. Not only have they provided protective backup for newly replanted areas against machete attacks by illegal settlers, but they have also laid aside their own weapons to work alongside the comuneros in reforestation, garbage collection, and emergency health assistance. There are plans to involve the armed forces in forest patrols at key locations where timber continues to be extracted.

Assessment and Recommendations

Looking back, we can see that the community acceptance of Pro-Pueblo took about a year — a year in which workshops involving community leaders gave us all a chance to get to know each other and to begin working together. Workshops were also coordinated with women, youth groups, and health committees. This first year of workshops helped us identify priorities and develop together a work program. As we began putting ideas into practice, credibility, acceptance, and participation improved.

I know our work is successful through its visible results (e.g., the amount of garbage on the road or in the villages). The dynamics of the various associations has helped determine the program's relative success. Levels of motivation and participation are clear factors. Some objectives take much longer to achieve (e.g., levels of environmental consciousness, self-esteem, community spirit). Indeed, in some areas substantive improvements may take a few years. However, as long as some short-term results appear and our relationship with the community remains healthy, it is worth working toward long-term benefits that may not be immediately visible. After all, many of the problems being addressed in Chongón-Colonche need to be faced all over the world.

When the foundation's collaborative efforts are not successful, meetings with community members are arranged, and we collectively decide whether to keep trying or to drop our efforts and resume them at a later date when community members may be more willing and ready to assimilate changes. Some efforts prove to be premature, and it is best to give them more time.

From my experience, I can only emphasize that effective outreach and collaboration require that communication be clear, transparent, and honest. If this is the case, comuneros respond to foundation initiatives. The communities have had enough white elephants or projects left unfinished by other organizations (generally government projects). This has made them very cautious. They demand serious, sustained commitment, and that works both ways because Fundación Pro-Pueblo also demands such commitment when agreements are made.

Conclusion and Outlook

The environmental and social crisis of Chongón-Colonche and other global hot spots is in part a consequence of economic development aid sent to Third World countries by wealthier but resource-hungry nations. What seemed to be a life-giving injection of foreign help actually encouraged a devastating exploitation of the environment and its natural resources. Mere short-term gain for impoverished countries created long-term destitution because no one bothered to count the real cost of the exploitation. Ultimately, with uncontrolled environmental exploitation, jobs are not created, the economy is not benefited — neither the invasor nor the comunero can have a future in a desert wasteland.

It is neither just nor possible to convince the communities involved in the projects described here of the need to save forests and replant if there is no alternative by which they can live. These are hard times, marked by rampant inflation and economic insecurity.

Furthermore, habits do not change overnight. Still, the comuneros are beginning to see that they can in fact do something. Their new understanding of the real effect that the environment plays in their lives complements the tradition of their ancestors. They can fully appreciate the crucial importance of protecting and building on what remains of their forests.

References

Fallon, M. (1997). "The *Cabuya* Wove El Chorrillo's History: The Social, Economic and Cultural Intertwinement of Cabuya Sack Weaving and a Small Town." Unpublished independent study, Manglaralto, Ecuador.

Henle, C. (1995). "Organic Gardens: A Comparative Study in Salango and Dos Mangas." Unpublished independent study, Manglaralto, Ecuador.

Penn, C. (1997). "La tagua artesanal como "desarrollo" y "cultura" en la Cordillera Chongón-Colonche." Unpublished independent study, School for International Training, Ecuador.

Appendix

Annotated Bibliography

by Aileen Hale

Ada, A., and C. Beutel. (1993). "Participatory Research as a Dialogue for Social Action." Unpublished transcript.
> Discusses how participatory research can be used as a tool to promote social action in a given community.

———— , and C. Peterson. (April 1990). "The Educator as Researcher: Participatory Research as an Educational Act Within a Community." Workshop conducted at the National Association of Bilingual Educators Conference, Tucson, Arizona.
> Provides a detailed example and explanation of how to do participatory research in a community setting.

Allen, E. (1968). *Modern Foreign Languages*. Washington, DC: Association for Supervision and Curriculum Development.
> Addresses a broad range of problems related to language learning and teaching facing administrators and teachers. Included in these problems are methodology, materials, equipment, evaluations, and future trends in curriculum development.

Applegate, R.B. (1975). "The Language Teacher and the Rules of Speaking." *TESOL Quarterly* 9(4): 271-281.
> Acknowledges that effective communication of a language requires more than mastery of grammar. Includes social and cultural aspects of language use, such as intonation, conventions of politeness, and set social formulas.

Bartlett, T. (1988). *Educating for Global Competence*. Report of the Advisory Council for International Educational Exchange. New York, NY: CIEE.
> Argues for the imminent need of internationalization at the highest educational levels to address the world perspective. Recommends increasing the overall number of college students abroad; identifying and encouraging students with leadership abilities to study abroad; and encouraging study abroad in developing countries.

Bourque, J. (1974). "Study Abroad and Intercultural Communication." In *The Challenge of Communication*. Edited by Gilbert A. Jarvis, pp. 329-351. The ACTFL Foreign Language Education Series, Vol. 6. Lincolnwood, IL: National Textbook Co.

> Discusses the paramount importance of incorporating study-abroad programs into the university curriculum. Purports this as the most effective means for linguistic and cultural preparation.

Brown, H.D. (1994). *Teaching by Principles: An Interactive Approach to Language Pedagogy*. Englewood Cliffs, NJ: Prentice Hall Regents.

> Offers an interactive approach to language pedagogy and a user-friendly teaching methodology for beginning and practicing ESL/EFL teachers.

——— . (1991). *Breaking the Language Barrier*. Yarmouth, ME: Intercultural Press.

> Designed as a guide for second-language learners, the book combines an analysis of the language-learning process with creative steps the individual learner can take to succeed in his or her learning process.

Burn, B., and R. Smuckler, eds. (1990). *A National Mandate for Education Abroad: Getting on With the Task*. Washington, DC: National Task Force of Undergraduate Education Abroad.

> This report advocates for more international content in higher education throughout the United States. Five major recommendations for internationalizing the curriculum are presented and discussed.

Dewey, J. (1938). *Experience and Education*. New York, NY: Collier Books.

> Provides a theoretical and philosophical rationale for experience-based learning. Endorses experiential education as a means for students to develop their curiosity, strengthen their initiative, and develop their intellectual and moral capacities.

Dunnett, S., F. Dubin, and A. Lezberg. (1986). "English Language Teaching From an Intercultural Perspective." In *Culture Bound: Bridging the Cultural Gap in Language Teaching*. Edited by J. Valdes, pp. 148-161. Cambridge, NY: Cambridge University Press.

> Suggests techniques, materials, issues, and implications for EFL teachers wanting to bring culture learning to the EFL classroom.

Freire, P. (1970). *Pedagogy of the Oppressed*. New York, NY: Continuum.
Provides a theoretical basis for educating illiterate people, especially adults, based on the conviction that every human being is capable of looking critically at the world.

Frye, R., and Thomas Garza. (1979). "Authentic Contact With Native Speech and Culture at Home and Abroad." In *Teaching Languages in College: Curriculum and Content*. Edited by Wilga Rivers, pp. 225-241. Lincolnwood, IL: National Textbook Co.
Incorporates the role of the native speaker and necessary materials for authentic contact with language in domestic programs; discusses the immersion concept at home through language houses, immigrant communities, and others.

Harrison, Roger, and Richard L. Hopkins. (1966). *The Design of Cross-Cultural Training, With Examples From the Peace Corps*. (EDRS: ED 011 103).
Describes portraits of Americans abroad. Designed to reduce ethnocentrism and provide insight into the nature of cross-cultural communication.

Jay, C. (1968). "Study of Culture: Relevance of Foreign Languages in World Affairs Education." In *Toward Excellence in Foreign Language Education*. Edited by Pat Castle and Charles Jay, pp. 84-92. Springfield, IL: Office of Public Instruction.
Argues that an indispensable asset to bilingualism or the learning of a second language is sensitivity education: knowledge of the social, religious, and economic attitudes of a people.

Kendall, J., and Associates, eds. (1990). *Combining Service and Learning: A Resource Book for Community and Public Service*. Vol. 1. Raleigh, NC: National Society for Experiential Education.
The first volume of a three-volume resource book covering policies, issues, and programs in colleges and universities, K-12 schools, community-based organizations, and others. It is intended for those seeking to start, strengthen, or support a program or course that combines community or public service with academic learning.

Kolb, D. (1981). "Learning Styles and Disciplinary Differences." In *The Modern American College: Responding to the New Realities of Diverse Students and a Changing Society*. Edited by A. Chickering and Associates, pp. 232-255. San Francisco, CA: Jossey-Bass-Hall.

> Discusses an approach to learning that seeks to integrate cognitive and socioemotional factors: the experiential learning theory. Investigates how individual learning styles affect academic performance.

Lambert, R.D. (1987). "Durable Academic Linkages Overseas: A National Agenda." In *The Fulbright Experience and Academic Exchanges*. Edited by Nathan Glazer, pp. 140-153. The Annals of the American Academy of Political and Social Science, Vol. 491. Newbury Park, CA: Sage.

> Argues for a national overseas agenda aimed at the critical need of raising second-language competency for the American public, in order to avoid parochialism and isolation.

Littlewood, W. (1984). *Foreign and Second Language Learning*. New York, NY: Cambridge University Press.

> Describes the influence of first-language acquisition studies on second-language acquisition. Suggests ways in which recent ideas about learning may influence our approach toward teaching.

McLaren, P. (1989). *Life in Schools: An Introduction to Critical Pedagogy in the Foundations of Education*. New York, NY: Longman.

> Documents the current crisis in American schooling. Presents the day-to-day struggle of teachers and students in a ghetto school and provides a theoretical context for analyzing their struggles.

McLuhan, M., and Q. Fiore. (1967). *The Medium Is the Massage*. New York, NY: Bantam.

> Discusses how best to educate our students to prepare them for the global village of today.

Newell, B. (1987). "Education With a World Perspective." In *The Fulbright Experience and Academic Exchanges*. Edited by Nathan Glazer, pp. 134-139. The Annals of the American Academy of Political and Social Science, Vol. 491. Newbury Park, CA: Sage.

> Notes critical deficiencies of international expertise existent in American businesses and the military. Argues that business competitiveness depends on the speed of American educational institutions to incorporate an international perspective.

Nostrand, H. (1966). "Describing and Teaching the Socio-Cultural Context of a Foreign Language and Literature." In *Trends in Language Teaching*. Edited by Albert Valdman, pp. 1-25. New York, NY: McGraw-Hill.
  Argues for the critical necessity of teaching the cultural context of a second language so that individuals may learn in greater depth the life-style of peoples whose language they are learning.

Politzer, R. (1965). *Foreign Language Learning: A Linguistic Introduction.* Englewood Cliffs, NJ: Prentice-Hall.
  Discusses three fundamental questions of language and language learning: (1) What is language? (2) What are the problems involved in language learning? (3) What are ways of dealing with these problems? Focuses on how students learn a second language.

Seelye, N. (1974). *Teaching Culture: Strategies for Foreign Language Educators.* Lincolnwood, IL: National Textbook Co.
  Teaching strategies and activities are presented that combine specific teaching techniques and ideas with other human and cultural resources in and out of the classroom.

Simon, P. (1980). *The Tongue-Tied American: Confronting the Foreign Language Crisis.* New York, NY: Continuum.
  Discusses concerns with the monolingualism of the United States. Considers the less traditional approaches to language learning and how they serve to meet a national need that traditional academia is failing to meet.

Valdes, J.M. (1986). *Culture Bound: Bridging the Cultural Gap in Language Teaching.* New York, NY: Cambridge University Press.
  A compilation of both theoretical and practical essays designed to give teachers a basis for introducing a cultural component into their teaching.

Contributors to This Volume

Volume Editors

JOSEF HELLEBRANDT is an assistant professor of Spanish at Santa Clara University where he coordinates the first-year Spanish program and the department's multimedia instruction. His research focuses on using technology for cross-cultural learning and communication.

LUCÍA T. VARONA is a Spanish lecturer at Santa Clara University. She also has worked for many years with community-based programs in Guatemala and San José, California.

Authors

JONATHAN F. ARRIES has a Ph.D. from the University of Wisconsin-Madison. He is an assistant professor of Spanish at the College of William and Mary where he teaches Spanish and preservice teacher-education courses. His research in curriculum and instruction focuses on the design of inclusive second-language courses for students with and without disabilities and also strategies for teaching culture.

MARK BALDWIN has an Ed.D. in educational leadership from Northern Arizona State University/Pt. Loma. He is an assistant professor of education and Single Subject Credential Program co-coordinator at California State University San Marcos. He works closely with a variety of multicultural/multilingual groups regarding career to school projects, community relations with high schools, and the school change process, all of which have ultimate connections to service-learning.

J. PATRICK BOYLE, Ed.D., is the associate director/director of staffing and programs of the Placement and Career Services Office at the University of Pittsburgh. He earned his doctorate in higher education administration with a specialization in college student personnel from the University of Pittsburgh.

TERESA DARIAS studies economics and communications at Santa Clara University (expected graduation June 2000). She is an active member of the Multicultural Center, where she helps in raising awareness of multicultural issues and assists in promoting diversity among the university community.

ROSARIO DÍAZ-GREENBERG has an Ed.D. in international multicultural education from the University of San Francisco and is an assistant professor of bilingual/multicultural education at California State University San Marcos. Her present interest in multicultural/bilingual service-learning stems from both her personal involvement as a volunteer in El Salvador, New York, and Florida and her integration of service-learning projects with students during her secondary teaching career.

ARTURO GÓMEZ directs the Teatro Corazón, a community theater group in San José, California. His strong commitment to working with Mexican Americans dates back to his involvement in the Teatro Campesino in the early 1970s.

AILEEN HALE, a professor of languages and cultures, is dedicated to facilitating greater cross-cultural understanding among peoples. Her implementation of service-learning in the fields of language and culture has proven to be an effective means to this end.

ESTELLE IRIZARRY is professor of Spanish at Georgetown University and editor of *Hispania,* the journal of the American Association of Teachers of Spanish and Portuguese. She is the author of 25 books, the most recent of which are *Informática y literatura* (Barcelona: Proyecto A Ediciones, 1997) and *Altruismo y literatura: Odón Betanzos Palacios* (Rociana del Condado, Huelva: Fundación O. Betanzos, 1998). She is a member of the North American Academy of the Spanish Language, corresponding member of the Royal Spanish Academy, and recipient of the Alfonso X el Sabio Cross and Instituto de Puerto Rico NY Service Award in Literature.

JOSEPH KEATING has a Ph.D. in multicultural science education from the University of New Mexico. He is an assistant professor of science education and Single Subject Credential Program co-coordinator at California State University San Marcos. His present interest in multicultural/
bilingual service-learning stems from both his personal involvement as a volunteer teacher for the Jesuit Volunteer Corps on the Colville Reservation in the state of Washington and his integration of service-learning projects with his American Indian students during his secondary teaching career.

CARMEN LIZARDI-RIVERA received her B.A. in French literature from the University of Puerto Rico in 1988. She received her M.A. and Ph.D. in Romance linguistics from Cornell University in 1991 and 1993, respectively. In 1995 she joined the Foreign Languages Department at San Jose State University as assistant professor of Spanish.

AMY LOOMIS has a B.A. in international communications from Lewis and Clark College and a doctorate in communication from the University of Massachusetts, Amherst. She has developed workshops in community video and a community studies minor at Santa Clara University.

JEANNE MULLANEY is an assistant professor in the Department of Foreign Languages and Cultures at the Community College of Rhode Island. She has presented workshops at regional and national conferences on the applications of language-acquisition theory to classroom practice.

DENISE OVERFIELD received her Ph.D. in Hispanic applied linguistics and methodology from the University of Pittsburgh. She is an assistant professor of Spanish at the State University of West Georgia, where she teaches Spanish and teacher-education courses.

MARTA ORENDAIN is finishing a teaching credential in mathematics and Spanish at San Jose State University. She has been actively involved in community affairs and has been working with youth groups at Sacred Heart Church, in San José, California.

SILVIA QUEZADA graduated from Santa Clara University in 1997 with a B.S. in political science and a second major in Spanish. She resides in Virginia, where she pursues a career in international law.

NANCY JEAN SMITH is an assistant professor at California State University, Stanislaus, where she works in the Teacher Education Department. She is a former Title VII scholar whose research interests lie in the area of transformative education and social change.

CLARICE R. STRANG, director of the Pro-Pueblo Foundation in Manglaralto, works with villages along coastal Ecuador promoting community development. Previous experience includes work as a naturalist guide and research projects with the World Life Fund in Brazil, the Chilean Forestry Service, and as a penaid-larval biologist in the shrimp industry in Ecuador.

PATRICIA VARAS is an associate professor of Spanish in the Department of Foreign Languages and Literatures at Willamette University. She teaches Latin American literature, with a special emphasis on women writers.

Series Editor

EDWARD ZLOTKOWSKI is professor of English and founding director of the Service-Learning Project at Bentley College. He also is senior associate at the American Association for Higher Education.

About AAHE

AAHE's Vision AAHE envisions a higher education enterprise that helps all Americans achieve the deep, lifelong learning they need to grow as individuals, participate in the democratic process, and succeed in a global economy.

AAHE's Mission AAHE is the individual membership organization that promotes the changes higher education must make to ensure its effectiveness in a complex, interconnected world. The association equips individuals and institutions committed to such changes with the knowledge they need to bring them about.

About AAHE's Series on Service-Learning in the Disciplines

The Series goes beyond simple "how to" to provide a rigorous intellectual forum. *Theoretical essays* illuminate issues of general importance to educators interested in using a service-learning pedagogy. *Pedagogical essays* discuss the design, implementation, conceptual content, outcomes, advantages, and disadvantages of specific service-learning programs, courses, and projects. All essays are authored by teacher-scholars in the discipline.

Representative of a wide range of individual interests and approaches, the Series provides substantive discussions supported by research, course models in a rich conceptual context, annotated bibliographies, and program descriptions.

Visit AAHE's website (www.aahe.org) for the list of disciplines covered in the Series, pricing, and ordering information.